Explorations in Theology 2

Explorations in Theology 2

C. F. EVANS

SCM PRESS LTD

334 01972 9

First published 1977
by SCM Press Ltd
58 Bloomsbury Street, London

Phototypeset by Western Printing Services Ltd, Bristol
and printed in Great Britain by Billing & Sons Ltd,
Guildford, London and Worcester

Contents

Preface

These lectures are of various times and origins.

Those on 'The Passion of Christ' have been delivered more than once and in more than one form. In their present form they were given at Bryn Mawr College, Philadelphia, in March 1975 as the open lectures (hence the restriction of reference to literature on the subject to that which is available in English) required of the Roian Fleck Resident in Religion. I would like to take this opportunity of thanking the authorities of the College and Mrs Isobel Fleck both for the honour conferred on me by their invitation to hold that office, and also for all that they did to make my stay in that College such a remarkable experience.

'Hermeneutics' is a paper read to The London Society for the Study of Religion in 1974, and subsequently printed in the *Epworth Review*, Vol. 2, no. 1, 1975, pp. 81–93. It is reproduced here by permission of the editors.

'Queen or Cinderella' was an Inaugural Lecture to the Lightfoot Chair of Divinity in Durham, delivered in February 1960.

'Christology and Theology' is (with a revised introduction) the Albrecht Stumpff Memorial Lecture delivered at Queen's College, Birmingham, in May 1959.

'Parable and Dogma' was given as the Ethel M. Wood Lecture for 1976 before the University of London, and is reproduced here by permission of the Athlone Press.

Finally, the three lectures on 'The Christian' were the Theological Lectures for 1972 in the annual series established by the Church of Ireland to be given in The Queen's University of Belfast. Since publication of these lectures is requested, I would like both to thank the University authorities, and the Chaplain who acts as sponsor, for their invitation and hospitality, and also to apologize for their belated appearance here.

Introduction

As indicated in the Preface, these papers have had various origins, and some were delivered much less recently than others. Whether they are, or ever were, substantial enough to merit publication together, especially in a series with the general title of *Explorations in Theology*, fortunately does not depend on the judgment of their author. Certainly I have never thought of myself as an explorer. The subjects of the papers were those which seemed important in the study of Christian theology, and especially of the New Testament, at various times within a period which began for me as an undergraduate who had the great good fortune to find himself a pupil of Sir Edwyn Hoskyns when that remarkable New Testament theologian and teacher was coming to the height of his powers. With hindsight they seem to me now to reflect three things in particular which, amongst a host of others, I learnt from him.

The first was the importance of the critical method in the study of the New Testament. The concern for the theology of the New Testament which was so evident in his lectures and writings has led some to suppose that he sat light to the critical method. His pupils knew otherwise, for they had their noses rubbed in it, and were not allowed to talk theology apart from it. His own confidence in the method as answering to the nature of the material to which it was being applied and as serving to uncover where the principal theological issues were, breathed through the book *The Riddle of the New Testament* which he wrote in conjunction with his most distinguished pupil F. N. Davey. This immensely influential book – it was translated into eighteen languages – in the judgment of the publisher of the German version described 'the situation of New Testament research after a century of historical and critical study in a more complete and impressive fashion than any other book'. W. G. Kümmel, who chose to end his

magisterial survey of the problems of the investigation of the New
Testament since the Enlightenment with this book, also found it
'extremely impressive', though he went on to observe that many
of its theses were vulnerable, and to indicate that in its search for
a unified theology in the New Testament its exercise of the critical
method had not been rigorous enough. The Inaugural Lecture,
'Queen or Cinderella', was based upon an observation in the
opening pages of *The Riddle of the New Testament*, and aimed to
spell out in more detail how the method had emerged as part of
the scholarly heritage along with the modern study of history
itself by a long and sometimes painful development in the university faculties, especially in Germany, and it ended by hinting
that the method was likely to be open to further development in
the future by contact with other disciplines than the historical.
This has in fact come to pass, most recently in relation to disciplines of a more literary-critical kind, and with the upthrust of
hermeneutics, or the principles of interpretation as such, into the
forefront of theological debate. That the method, however modified, is still essential as a basis of New Testament study is
suggested by the fact that it can happen that its employment is
the only thing agreed in common by a representative group of
exegetes, whose methods of interpretation begin to diverge
markedly from this point.

The second thing from which I learnt was Hoskyns' concern
with christology. This concern was in part due to the fact that
much of his theological work was being done in conscious or
unconscious reaction to a prevailing climate of thought, called at
the time and later 'liberal', according to which the words and
message of Jesus were of primary, and the person of the one who
uttered these words of secondary, importance. Both at the more
popular level of *The Riddle of the New Testament* and in more
specialized studies he sought to uncover at the base of the tradition of the words of Jesus in the synoptic gospels what he called a
christological penetration, which in the Fourth Gospel is explicit
and unavoidable. Nevertheless, christology was never for him,
as it became for some others, a subject in itself and on its own. It
remained always an aspect of theology and of the doctrine of
God. And despite appearances to the contrary I doubt whether
he would have been happy with the so-called 'biblical theology'
which came to predominate, and which claimed to establish a
theological unity of the Bible as a christological unity by inter-

preting the Bible always in terms provided by the Bible itself. For he was innately suspicious of systems, and was conscious of the Bible as a book of rough edges, and so like life itself. Some aspects of this question were treated in my paper 'Christology and Theology', and again and from a rather different angle in 'Parable and Dogma'. Recent publications have shown that it is still a burning question.

The third thing I learnt was that however much it was pursued, and very properly pursued, as an academic discipline in the universities, theology was in the last resort a function of the church, and that sooner or later the theologian must show himself responsible to the man and woman in the pew, and if possible to the man and woman in the street. He may not dictate their faith to them, but he must attempt to say how things look to him in central matters of faith which he may share with them and to show the relevance to human life of the language, sometimes inevitably a kind of jargon, which biblical and theological study is using. Hoskyns regularly applied himself to this in notable courses of sermons which he preached, admittedly to a rather special type of audience, in the College chapel. As a student, and later a member of the staff of the Theological College at Lincoln, I inherited a tradition whereby annual lectures were given by visiting lecturers on the Passion of Christ as an academic preparation for the devotional use of Holy Week. This again was in some ways a specialist audience of men who were to be ordained, but the lecturer had in mind that they were men who would later be committed to speaking to others on what is on any showing a central matter of Christian faith, and that they could only speak with conviction if they had critically mastered the material on which it was based and had themselves been mastered by it. The lectures on the Passion of Christ are direct descendants of this tradition. Those on The Christian belonged in a wider context of a request for some sort of 'apologetic' for Christian faith in the modern world. The fragmentation of knowledge in that world raises the question acutely whether apologetic is a possible even if it is a proper exercise. It certainly cannot be done by renouncing for the time being a critical method, but only in the conviction that the material to be studied critically answers at some point, which cannot be determined in advance, to the questions raised in the minds of ordinary people (whoever they may be) by their experience of living, itself also critically analysed.

PART I

The Passion of Christ

1

✐

The Tradition of the Passion

If there may be said to be any single focus common to the diverse writings that make up the New Testament it is the death of Christ apprehended through his resurrection. The gospels proceed from a variety of subject matter towards this as their conclusion and climax; the Pauline letters proceed from this as their starting point to confront a variety of subject matter. Acts rehearses it in a series of speeches; Hebrews contains an extended exposition of it as that which spans heaven and earth; Revelation places it in the centre of heaven; I Peter applies it to the earthly situation of its readers. Celebrated as the Christian Passover it provided at the first the sole Christian festival, while later it controlled the liturgical tradition in its development, so that the Christian year came to move up to and away from Holy Week and Easter. In this way it has continued to be a kind of nerve centre of Christian faith and piety.

This has not, however, secured it against inadequate treatment or even perversity. As every student of the subject knows, the area of doctrine concerned with stating the significance of the death of Christ for faith is one that is peculiarly strewn with wreckage. When Anselm attempted his statement of it he had first to offload an interpretation close on a thousand years old, according to which on the basis of a literal and simplistic understanding of certain New Testament passages the death of Christ operated as a trick outwitting the devil. And while Anselm's own statement, and those which were to follow, served their own times, they proved to be too heavily conditioned by sociological factors of those times to become permanent. Further, it would surely be one of the more comic moments of church history, did it not reflect one of the most appalling of the church's tragedies, when the Second Vatican Council solemnly acquitted the Jewish people of the charge of deicide in respect of the death of Christ. For in this charge there had been down the ages two fearful naïvetés of popular thought and piety rolled into one. The first was that the divinity of Christ was a matter of plain observation, which is ridiculous by the standards of the New Testament itself, where it is consistently represented as veiled and as discerned by faith arising from the resurrection; and the second was that the responsibility of a whole people – if indeed there can ever be such a thing – was transmissible across the generations, which is lunatic by any standards.

As central, then, to the Christian faith and as subject to grave distortion it calls for constant scrutiny, and this scrutiny has been given a particularly searching character by certain features peculiar to our own times. The chief of these is the emergence of what we now understand by the study of history. The ancient world before Christ had already known the conspicuous death of a historical figure, Socrates, but while this had continued to haunt men as a paradigm, it was not native to Greek thinking to invest it with saving significance. The Jewish faith had had its first experience of martyrs in the Maccabaean crisis of the second century BC, and had sometimes come to ascribe a measure of expiatory value to their deaths, but these deaths had been many and varied, and such value had not become attached to any of the principal figures of Jewish history and faith. Contemporary mystery cults had a common pattern of salvation via death to immortality, but these were also many and in competition, and their cult figures were mythological and devoid of historical reality. The tradition of the death of Christ came to combine elements strongly resembling all these. It was single and paradigmatic; it was a death issuing in life; it had saving significance. In addition, however, it was all these things in being historical. For that reason it has not merely to endure the kind of historical investigation that is now held proper, but actually invites it.

It follows almost by definition that such an investigation will be at its most difficult and delicate in the case of the passion of Christ. This is not only because modern historical investigation proceeds by putting its sources on the rack and subjecting them to the severest possible cross-examination, whereas in the Christian tradition the gospels have been highly privileged documents to which the attitude has been to the greatest possible degree receptive. It is also because in the nature of the case the problem of the interrelation of event and interpretation is most acute here, and it may not be sidetracked by the somewhat facile observation that all history writing involves interpretation both in the historian's selection of what he deems significant and in the context and manner in which he presents it. For there is a certain shape and actuality of event as event which persists as part of its capacity to carry a meaning and to speak, and which for the historian is not to be dissolved into a general truth or idea. When in his speech at Pentecost Peter says of Jesus 'that man, given up to you by the determinate will and foreknowledge of God, you by the instrumentality of heathen men crucified and slew' (Acts 2.23), the two sides, the human and the divine, the event and its ultimate context, are simply juxtaposed without further connection. Exploration of this connection is the work of the theologian, which work he cannot now perform without also adhering to the methods of the historian.

Of even greater consequence than the historical method itself is that to which in the course of time it has given rise, namely historical consciousness. For this may well turn out to have brought about as profound a change in human thinking as did the evolutionary view of nature. Historical consciousness, it has been said, emerges with the apperception that the past is really different from the present, and it is of comparatively recent emergence. The Christian religion, like some other religions, lives out of a strong sense of continuity between present and past, so that, for example, I am able to say with conviction and not simply as a religious cliché that Abraham is my father, and to recognize myself immediately as belonging within the biblical world. The more historical consciousness operates, however, the more aware I become of the extent to which Abraham and I are foreigners to each other, and the harder I have to work to see the biblical world as my world. In a study significantly called *The Eclipse of Biblical Narrative*, Hans Frei argues that up to the eighteenth century those sections of the Bible that are narrative or history-like in character – that is, the gospels and considerable sections of the Old Testament – conveyed their truth through their narrative or story form. They were united into a single cumulative story through figuration or typology, which related occurrences or persons to one another in a providential design. This single story pictured the real world within which the reader was to see himself embraced. Frei then traces how this complex was gradually broken up with a consequent loss of the power of narrative to establish its own world of discourse, so that the unity of the biblical story had now to be argued on other grounds.[1] This could have a special bearing on the story of the passion of Christ, where the connection between spiritual truth and history-like narrative is closer perhaps than anywhere else in the Bible.

A third feature of modern scrutiny, and one which is not wholly unrelated to historical investigation and historical consciousness, is a preoccupation with language. What are words to be supposed to mean, and what in this connection is to be meant by meaning? Much of the language of the gospels, including language about the death of Christ, is metaphor, parable or symbol. As such what is it good for? How far are words like 'ransom' or 'sacrifice' to be pressed? In so far as the language intends to be more than metaphor and is inseparable from a first-century world view which it expresses, then the problem arises of its adequate translation, of addressing to it the question proposed by Leonard Hodgson, 'What must the truth have been [and be] if it appeared like this to men who thought and spoke like that?'[2]

Before such a question can be put to the tradition which is to be translated the tradition itself has first to be sufficiently understood, appreciated and absorbed in its own terms. Where is this understanding to begin? In what may well be the earliest piece of written tradition in the New Testament (I Cor. 15.1–5) Paul reminds his Corinthian readers what the core of the gospel had been both as to form and content which he had handed on to them, he himself having first received it from others. It had taken the form of the statement that 'Christ died for our sins according to the scriptures; and that he was buried; and that he was raised the third day according to the scriptures; and that he appeared . . .' If the first part of this statement is isolated – 'Christ died for our sins according to the scriptures' – it is apparent that already there was no immediate and direct access in the tradition to a bare historical event, but only to that event as apprehended and absorbed through the medium of the Old Testament. How far is this apprehension reflected in the gospel passion narratives themselves?

'According to the scriptures' is in itself unspecific, and is indicative of a general underlying conviction and expectation. Its equivalent is found occasionally in the gospels, as when Luke expands the last of the three predictions of the passion he takes over from Mark with 'all the things written through the prophets will be accomplished' (Luke 18.31; cf. Mark 10.32ff.); or where in Luke the risen Christ 'beginning from Moses and all the prophets expounded in all the scriptures the things concerning himself' (Luke 23.27); or where later he affirms that all the things written in the law of Moses and the prophets and the psalms concerning himself had to be fulfilled, and is said to have opened his hearers' minds to understand the scriptures to the effect that the passion and resurrection of the Messiah were their substance (Luke 24.44–46).[3] Such an equivalent appears once in Mark in the curious form of an aposiopesis, when at his arrest Jesus asks 'Did you come out as against a brigand with swords and staves to take me?', and then proceeds with 'I was daily with you teaching in the temple and you did not lay hold of me. But in order that the scriptures might be fulfilled . . .', and the story breaks off without indication of how scripture throws light on the arrest or the manner of it (Mark 14.48f.).[4]

Generally the use of scripture is more specific, and it can be made in more than one way and at more than one level. At the surface level a sentence may be expressly quoted as a proof text. Or, without any express quotation a narrative may contain a sufficient collocation of words to indicate that they have been taken from a particular Old Testament passage – though there can be cases when this is in debate. Or, more indirectly and without containing any such tell-tale phrases a story may be told in such a way as to suggest that a particular Old Testament passage has contributed to its telling. What kind of passages are used? In view of the fact that 'according to the scriptures' meant basically 'in fulfilment of scripture', and since it is prophecy that most often speaks in the future tense, one might have expected the use of prophecy to predominate. In fact this is not so. It is the psalms which predominate. This may be illustrated.

At the head stands Ps. 22, which Tertullian with his customary exaggeration described as 'totam Christi continens passionem'.[5] Since its opening words, 'My God, my God, why hast thou forsaken me?' are according to Mark and Matthew (though not according to Luke and John) the last words of Jesus, and since it is unlikely that they have been put into his mouth, it is possible that his use of them already directed the attention of Christians to this psalm. Clearly a great deal was found there.[6]

> Ps. 22.7: All who see me mock at me, they make mouths at me, they wag their heads (cf. Ps. 109.25).

This has influenced all three synoptic accounts of the mocking by the rulers at the scene of crucifixion, the first two with a reference to the wagging of the head (Mark 15.29; Matt. 27.39), and the third with the actual word for mocking in the LXX version (*exemukterizon*, Luke 23.25).

> Ps. 22.8: He committed his cause to the Lord . . . let him rescue him, for he delights in him.

This is added by Matthew to the words of mockery which he otherwise takes over from Mark (Matt. 27.43).

> Ps. 22.15: My strength is dried up like a potsherd, and my tongue cleaves to my jaws.

This is possibly the scripture for whose express fulfilment Jesus in John's account says 'I thirst' (John 19.28).

> Ps.22. 18: They divide my garments among them, and for my raiment they cast lots.

This affords an example of usage at more than one level. In all three synoptic accounts some of its language in various forms serves to describe the action of the soldiers at the scene of crucifixion (Mark 15.24; Matt. 27.35; Luke 23.34). In John the action is first narrated without such language and is then said to fulfil scripture, which is then expressly cited. Further in defiance of the rules of Hebrew parallelism whereby the same thing is said twice in variant form, the verse is taken to refer to two things and not one – to a partition of garments (plural) and to casting lots for raiment (singular) – so that in John there is a double action of sharing the garments and of casting lots for a robe that cannot be divided. Here evidently the scripture has moulded if indeed it has not created the incident.

Other psalms are employed, some of them with a similar ethos to Ps. 22.

> Ps. 31.5: Into thy hands I commend my spirit.

This becomes in Luke the last words of Jesus, replacing the opening words of Ps. 22 which Luke does not take over from Mark.

Ps. 31.13: They scheme together against me, as they plot to take away my life.

This probably lies behind the transition from the trial before the Sanhedrin to the examination before Pilate that Matthew supplies with the words 'They took counsel against Jesus to put him to death' (Matt. 27.1).

Ps. 34.20: He keeps all his bones; not one of them is broken.

This, rather than the regulation that the legs of the Passover lamb were not to be broken (Ex. 12.46), may be the scripture which in John is said to be fulfilled expressly when the soldiers refrain from breaking the legs of Jesus (John 19.36).

Ps. 35.11: Malicious witnesses rise up; they ask of me things I know not.

This probably lies behind the narrative of the first charge brought against Jesus at his trial, a charge said to be brought by false witnesses alleging some form of statement that he would destroy the temple and in three days erect another, to which charge Jesus makes no reply (Mark 14.56–60; Matt. 26.59–62).

Ps. 38.11: My friends and companions stand aloof from my plague, and my kinsmen stand afar off.

This may lie behind the statement with which Mark and Matthew conclude the story of the crucifixion that there were women watching from afar, while some of its language appears in Luke when, in addition to the watching women he has 'all those known to him (*hoi gnostoi*) stood afar off' (Mark 15.40f.; Matt. 27.55f.; Luke 23.49).

Ps. 41.9: Even my bosom friend in whom I trusted, who ate of my bread, has lifted his heel against me.

This has a deliberate echo in the awkward form in which Mark gives Jesus' prediction that he will be handed over, 'one from among you shall hand me over, he who eats with me' (Mark 14.18), while in John the whole verse is first cited and then the actual prediction made (John 13.18).

Ps. 42.5: Why are you cast down, O my soul, and why are you disquieted within me?

This verse probably supplies in its first half the wording of Jesus' introductory statement in Gethsemane according to Mark and

Matthew, 'My soul is cast down to death' (Mark 14.34; Matt. 26.38), and in its second half the wording in what is a kind of equivalent scene in John where, in reply to the approach of certain Greeks, Jesus says 'Now is my soul disquieted' (John 12.27).

Psalm 69, which particularly resembles Ps. 22, has at v. 4 'More in number than the hairs of my head are those who hate me without a cause', the last words of which (if is not an identical phrase in Ps. 35.19) are probably referred to in what is nevertheless a curious statement in John 15.25 that the hatred by the world of the Father and the Son was for the fulfilment of 'the word that is written in their *law*, "They hated me without a cause"'. Further, in v. 21 the sufferer, looking for comfort amongst the insults, complains that 'they gave me gall for food, and for my thirst they gave me vinegar to drink'. This verse has affected the account in Mark and Matthew of a bystander offering to Jesus on a reed a sponge filled with vinegar (Mark 15.36; Matt. 27.48), and more specifically, perhaps, Luke's account, where it is an action of mockery on the part of a soldier (Luke 23.36). And since in the psalm the giving of vinegar is preceded by a reference to thirst it may be this verse rather than Ps. 22.15 that is said to be fulfilled by Jesus' utterance 'I thirst' in John 19.28. Moreover, a prior offering in Mark's narrative of wine mingled with myrrh (Mark 15.23) becomes in Matthew's version wine mingled with gall (Matt. 27.34).[7]

Finally, amongst the psalms is one of a different type, Ps. 110. This is one of the few psalms with an explicitly doctrinal content. Its opening words, 'The Lord says to my lord, "Sit at my right hand, till I make your enemies your footstool"', has been judged the most influential single verse on early Christian thought, lying behind any statement that Jesus is at the right hand of God. In the passion story it occupies an important place in contributing to the reply Jesus makes to the high priest's question 'You shall see the Son of man sitting at the right hand of power' (Mark 14.62; Matt. 26.64; cf. Luke 22.69).

So it is the psalms that predominate in comment upon, or in explication of, or in moulding of the narrative. Prophetic passages are also used, though not altogether in the manner which might have been expected. The reply to the high priest adds to the statement that the Son of man will be seated at the right hand of power that he will be seen 'coming with (upon) the clouds of heaven' (Mark 14.62; Matt. 26.64 – not in Luke), and this echoes words from the vision in Daniel 7.9–14 of one like a son of man who comes 'with the clouds' to the Ancient of Days to receive an eternal kingdom, to which the enigmatic and semi-technical term 'the Son of man', and whatever doctrine came to accrue to it, are ultimately to be traced.

The greatest number of prophetic passages come from Zechariah 9–14, which modern scholarship ascribes to a different author from 1–8, and which are more than usually obscure, consisting of a succession of highly coloured oracles of final judgment upon Jerusalem and upon the nations, and of salvation. In the course of these it is said to Jerusalem as a promise of deliverance, 'Lo, your king comes to you; triumphant and victorious is he, humble and riding on an ass, on a colt the foal of an ass' (Zech. 9.9), and this clearly lies behind the story of the carefully contrived entry of Jesus into Jerusalem, and is expressly quoted in Matthew's and John's versions of it (Matt. 21.4f.; John 12.14f.).[8] This same prophecy continues with the words, 'Because of the blood of my covenant with you, I will set your captives free from the waterless pit' (Zech. 9.11), and these may be the origin of the somewhat awkward form of words spoken with respect to the cup, 'This is my blood of the covenant' in Mark's and Matthew's (though not in Luke's or Paul's) accounts of the Last Supper, rather than the words of Moses at Sinai, 'Behold the blood of the covenant which the Lord has made with you' (Ex. 24.8), upon which, however, the statement in Zechariah may itself be resting. In Zech. 12.10, in the course of a prophecy of victory for Jerusalem it is said, though without any explanation, of the inhabitants that through a spirit of compassion given them by God 'when they look on him whom they have pierced, they shall mourn for him', and this is quoted by John in connection with the lance thrust which is a feature peculiar to his account of the crucifixion (John 19.37). In Zech. 13.7, in the course of a pronouncement of judgment on the land, God says to one described as the man who stands next to him, 'Strike the shepherd, that the sheep may be scattered'. This, in a slightly variant form, is quoted by Jesus in Mark and Matthew in support of his own prediction that all the disciples will take offence (whatever is meant by that), and this is the only express citation made in the whole of Mark's passion narrative (Mark 14.27; Matt. 26.31). In Zech. 11.4–14 there is a passage of the greatest obscurity, in which a shepherd appointed by God over a flock that is doomed to oppression at the hands of false shepherds agrees with these to renounce his position with the words 'If it seems right to you, give me my wages; but if not keep them'; and it continues, 'And they weighed out as my wages thirty shekels of silver. Then the Lord said to me, "Cast it into the treasury" – the lordly price at which I was paid off by them! So I took the thirty shekels of silver, and cast them into the treasury in the house of the Lord'. A version of this, but corresponding to no known translation of the Hebrew text, and incorrectly ascribed to Jeremiah (perhaps because Jeremiah had arranged for the purchase of a field, Jer. 32.6–9), is applied to, and is probably largely responsible for, a feature peculiar to Matthew's gospel, the repentance and suicide of Judas, which is one of the apocryphal supplements that is all Matthew has by way of addition to the Markan narrative he transcribes (Matt. 27.9f.).

Finally, with respect to the prophets, there is the vexed question of Isaiah 53. The question is vexed because this chapter has tended to be treated as an isolated unit in a manner foreign to the first century, and to be regarded as the principal clue to the whole matter, with almost any reference to suffering in the gospels being traced to it. Hence the simpliste equation has been produced that Jesus took the figure of the Son of man and combined it with the figure of the Suffering Servant of Isaiah 53, and that is the end of the matter.[9] But while there is evidence for the use of this chapter elsewhere in the New Testament in order to make a number of different points,[10] it has in fact left very little trace on the passion story itself. It is explicitly quoted only once and probably for a limited purpose when the obscure command to the disciples to possess themselves of purses and swords that Luke places at the end of a discourse at the Last Supper is followed by, 'For I say to you, this that is written must be accomplished in me, "And he was counted among the lawless" ' (Luke 22.37; cf. Isa. 53.12). Whether the recurrence of the word 'many' in the interpretative section of this chapter of Isaiah (Isa. 53.11f.) is the reason why in the words over the cup at the Last Supper the blood of the covenant is said to be poured out for many (Mark 14.24; Matt. 26.28), and why the mission of the Son of man is defined as giving his life a ransom for many (Mark 10.45; Matt. 20.28), is more open to question than is sometimes assumed.[11] There is, however, an instance in which a single word does seem to establish a connection, for when in both the Markan and the Johannine accounts of the buffeting of Jesus he receives 'blows' (Mark 14.65; John 19.3; cf. John 18.22) the word here used (*rapismata*) is a rare and unusual one which is found elsewhere in the Greek Bible only at Isa. 50.6: 'I gave my cheeks to blows'.

This analysis is by no means exhaustive,[12] but any analysis has to be sufficiently detailed if an adequate impression is to be gained of how early Christians gave effect to their general conviction that what they were concerned with was according to the scriptures. What for us is a laborious matter of hunting in concordances, lexicons and dictionaries was for them more immediate. It was in their heads and hearts. To be able to detect them at work in this way is, to use the language of one who has made an exhaustive analysis, to be peering in at the windows of the early Christian workshop, and to observe the beginnings of Christian theology.[13] For to speak of something theologically as distinct from historically, politically, psychologically or sociologically is to dare to speak of it in its relation to what is believed to be the ultimate purpose of God. And that for the early Christians was already to be found largely in the Old Testament.

The result of their work in general is clear. Almost all the main constituents of the passion story – entry into Jerusalem, cleansing of the temple, the opposition, betrayal, desertion, denial, Last Supper, Gethsemane, arrest, trial before the Sanhedrin, and the attendant circumstances of the crucifixion – either have attached to them explicit Old Testament citations or have Old Testament vocabulary woven into the narrative. In this way it was precluded that the events, and hence the total event which they made up, were either haphazard or accidental. They were removed from the sphere of the contingent, which is what we particularly associate with the historical. They were removed also from the sphere of fate, which for the Greeks brooded over the life of man, and in the last analysis operated even behind the lives of the gods. When, therefore, it is said repeatedly that the Son of man *must* suffer, or in Luke's wording that he goes his way in accordance with what has been decreed (Luke 22.22), this is the 'must' and decree not of fate but of the divine will. They were also removed from the sphere of tragedy, perhaps the highest of the Greek categories of thought, in which the poet through the medium of the noble figure condemned to defeat wrestled with the enigmatic and intractable elements of human existence. This

result was achieved all the more forcibly when the chief protagonist in the story, Jesus himself, not only is made to use
scripture to express the character of the events and the participation of his own will in what is decreed, but also to use it
alongside and in support of what he independently initiates and
predicts.

What is new, however, is that by literary-critical analysis we
can detect this work being done. In consequence the celebrated
argument from prophecy, which along with its twin the argument from miracle, has operated from the second century to the
nineteenth as the chief pillar of Christian apologetic, collapses,
and can hardly be re-erected at least in its traditional form. Just as
the argument from design was stood on its head by the theory of
evolution, since the interlocking order of nature which had previously been taken as evidence for the hand of a Creator could
now be accounted for otherwise as what would be the inevitable
result of survival by natural selection, so the coincidence of
prophecy and event, which phenomenologically has appeared as
such an impressive, indeed unique feature of Christianity
amongst the religions of the world, now appears at least in
considerable measure to be the inevitable product of the interpretative faculties of the first Christians.

While the result of their work in general is clear, what it is good
for in particular is not so clear. How far is their use of Old
Testament language to be pressed? This is not an easy question to
answer and there are two views on the matter which have been
called the maximizing and the minimizing views. On the maximizing view when an early Christian behaved in this way he did
not mean to stop at the words actually quoted or used, but
intended these as indicators to the whole passage and context
from which they were taken, as if to say 'Look up the passage and
draw from it all that is to be found there'. Thus, when 'He was
counted among the lawless' from Isa. 53.12 is quoted by Jesus
with reference to his imminent arrest, this carries with it that the
speaker was conscious of himself as playing the whole role of the
Servant as it is depicted in that chapter and anything that that role
may be held to imply. Or when Zech. 13.7 is quoted with reference to the coming desertion of disciples it is intended thereby to
interpret that moment in accordance with the original context of
the saying as being part of a final judgment on Jerusalem. Or
when certain psalms are selected for use, this is because they

betoken and rest upon an already formulated doctrine in Judaism of the righteous sufferer.[14] Or even, and this is something of a *tour de force*, when the opening words of Ps. 22 are uttered this is not to be taken for what it appears, a cry of dereliction by God, but rather as the opposite, since the sufferer who there utters it has come by the time he reaches the end of the psalm to proclaim confidently his own deliverance by God with the words (in the Greek version) 'My soul lives to him' (Ps. 22.29). Along this line the particular selection of passages that came to be made and the use to which they were put can be regarded as highly distinctive and theologically creative. Passages that had already been interpreted of the Messiah in Judaism, passages that had not been so interpreted but were eschatological in character and spoke of an ultimate judgment and deliverance, and passages about one who suffers innocently for his faithfulness to the divine purpose, were synthesized in their application to Jesus or in his own application of them to himself and his movement. In this way a picture emerges of him as acting as the representative of the destiny of Israel, of drawing together previously contradictory strands of experience, and so of bringing to birth a new form of existence and a new people.

The difficulty of this maximizing view is to know whether it was in fact the case or is being read into the text, and to establish criteria for recognizing whether it was the case. The minimizing view takes its start from the known fact that in much Jewish exegesis of the time words and phrases from the Old Testament were employed without consideration of their original or wider contexts and to perform a limited task of making connections which were largely verbal. It could be so here. Since the passion as a whole and some of the events within it – desertion, betrayal, denial, dishonour – were such as to occasion bewilderment or offence, the use of the Old Testament with respect to them could have been restricted to the largely negative and apologetic role of asserting verbally that despite appearances they belonged within the purpose of God without at the same time intending to indicate positively what that purpose might be. If that were the case the events may well have occurred more nearly as they are described, since the influence of the Old Testament language will have been more on the surface. Or it could be that along the line of oral tradition one teacher had been a maximizer and another a minimizer, or even that the same person had moved from one position to another. It is difficult to judge.[15]

The question at issue may, therefore, be posed in a more general form. Does this original matrix of Christian interpretative thought mean that that thought is permanently bound to the Old Testament and to the view of things found there, and if so in what sense? The answer could be a qualified affirmative in the sense that it could be claimed that nowhere else were the basic constituents present in combination for that understanding of human life which the Christian story presupposes, and which it claims to illuminate and reinforce. Religion may, perhaps, be said to consist basically in a sense of awe before a power that is other and holy, Rudolf Otto's *mysterium tremendum et fascinans*, and cannot exist apart from this. As such, however, it is not necessarily either moral or rational. In the course of the development represented in the Old Testament it can be seen to become both. It became moral as the other and the holy are identified with the righteous will of God. It became rational as this righteous will is the will of the one God who is universal Creator in his wisdom. Men come to know, especially through the agency of the prophets and of prophecy mediated through law, that they stand as human beings under a divine, creative, moral imperative. But to the extent that this is so there breaks out in human life its greatest tribulation, which is that this righteous and creative purpose is frustrated, and that the human will is deeply faulted. This is particularly the witness of the psalms, which do not, however, at this point, take refuge in some kind of cynicism, but rather, while exposing the frustration to the full, look confidently in hope to the overcoming of the frustration in some way by God himself.

Parts of this complex existed elsewhere, and existed in combination. Thus, other religions, especially the mystery religions of the first century AD to which some versions of Christianity, including the Pauline, bore more than a passing resemblance, witnessed to a strong religious hope of deliverance from frustration and of salvation at a time when, in Bury's words, the ancient world showed signs of losing its nerve. Since, however, these had not emerged on the basis of monotheism they did not lead to rationality and were in competition with one another, each of the divinities, Mithras, Isis, etc., being ends in themselves and falling short of being the Creator of the world. In some cases the world was seen not as divine creation but as an initial mistake.

Philosophy of various kinds kept rationality and justice in the forefront but tended to be divorced from religious aspiration. In the circumstances of the first century AD and of previous centuries in the Graeco-Roman world it could only advance by undermining religion. Only Judaism held all these elements together albeit with considerable tensions, and in that sense it was necessary for the apprehension of the Christian gospel. There is, however, a qualification. The Christian gospel became the Christian religion and as a separate entity moved out of Judaism to speak to Gentiles who were without such presuppositions. Granted that early Christians, including such thoroughly Gentile Christians as those at Corinth were, or were expected to be, soaked in the Old Testament, it was not necessarily so, nor was it always to be so. The time would come when the Christian gospel was embraced because its statement of the case seemed to be pre-eminently human. But then the initial question rebounds upon itself. For has it not been a consistent claim of Judaism that it exposes more fully than elsewhere what it is to be human?

2

The Event of the Passion

So far the early Christian formulation 'Christ died for our sins according to the scriptures' has been taken as a starting point, and some attempt has been made to give more precise content to the general interpretative phrase in it 'according to the scriptures' by reference to the actual use made of the Old Testament in the passion narratives of the gospels. How far is it possible by reference to these narratives to do the same for the historical element in this formulation 'Christ died', or the theologico-historical element if 'Christ' here, despite the absence of the definite article, still retains anything of its original force of 'the Messiah'? What was the history that had provided the basis for such scriptural defence or interpretation, and that had been felt to demand it? the question is posed by the interpretation itself. For a narrative so soaked in significant Old Testament language and accompanied by predictions arising from the foreknowledge of the chief protagonist is bound to leave the overall impression of actions that proceed according to some solemn pre-arranged liturgy, with God as their secondary as well as their primary cause. Where here is the facticity of event? It is also posed, so far as the New Testament as a whole is concerned, by the place of Paul in it. For while on the one hand Paul is the theologian of the cross *par excellence* and is prepared to see almost anything in the light of it, on the other hand he hardly refers to it as an external historical event at all, and he is content to denote even its inner meaning so far as Christ himself is concerned largely by the single and general word 'obedience'.[1]

If such questions prove difficult to answer – and perhaps cannot be answered at all in a manner satisfactory to a dogmatic theologian in search of a historical basis for doctrine – this lies chiefly in the nature of the gospels as documents when they are subjected to critical analysis. How many events would be required, of what kind would they have to be, and what measure of connected sequence and causal nexus would they need to have, in order to qualify here as history? As E. Käsemann has observed, the work of the historian 'presupposes the categories of time and space. A world without shadows and historical contours cannot be investigated. He must be able to localize an historical object in order to recognize it.'[2]

Source criticism or literary criticism, which was the method of analysis in the earlier decades of this century, tended to claim this localizable character for Mark's gospel, which it had only fairly recently established as the first gospel to be written. To quote one of its most distinguished representatives, F. C. Burkitt, 'It is the only one of the gospels, canonical or uncanonical, which does give an intelligible account of the process by which Jesus Christ broke with the Synagogue, that is the official embodiment of Jewish religion, or rather the process by which the Synagogue broke with Jesus Christ and forced him to withdraw from their system'.[3] However, the method of analysis that was to follow, form criticism, went far to dissolve the basis for such a claim. By means of a type of dissection which, so far from doing violence to the synoptic gospels and their material or the material of any of their supposed sources, actually answered to its character, form criticism succeeded in breaking this material down into what bear the marks of having been at one time separate and autonomous units of tradition. Each of these units had at some time circulated on its own during the thirty or so years of oral transmission. Each had stood on its own feet and had had its own story to tell. In the process of telling it had become so shaped as to make its point in itself as a self-contained story irrespective of anything coming before it or following after it. Here, indeed were sharp contours to be seen, but they are religious and theological rather than historical contours. When any of these generally very succinct units was brought into focus, what stood out in sharp relief was the authoritative utterance it enshrined or the powerful action it depicted. Questions could then be asked of it as to why it had come down in this form, and what particular religious needs it had been told to satisfy. But as to where, when, to whom, in what precise circumstances and with what consequences the utterance had been made or the action performed, this did not stand out in

sharp relief but was blurred in the background, if it was there at
all. Furthermore, the links which each evangelist has supplied in
his task of converting these separate units into a sequence that
would tell a continuous story were often minimal and vague, and
they seldom if ever amount to establishing connections of such a
kind that a historical process could be detected through them. His
arrangement of the units would seem to have been under the
headings of topics and subject matter, or in accordance with some
pattern that was theologically significant; and this goes for Mark
as well as for the others.

It is true that form critics have commonly tended to make an
exception to all this precisely in the case of the narratives of the
passion. They have claimed to be able to trace here a more solid
block of tradition with the marks upon it of having been told from
the first as an historical sequence of events. Their reasons for this
conclusion have been that the material here changes somewhat in
character, being less episodic and more compact. There are more
precise notes of place – Jerusalem, the Mount of Olives,
Gethsemane, Golgotha. There are more notes of time – the Passover, the first day of unleavened bread, in the evening, early in
the morning, the third, sixth and ninth hours of the day, the
sabbath. These tie the events together so that one leads into
another. To be sure, this original compactness has not been
claimed for any of the passion narratives as they now stand. For
these would appear to have incorporated into them, and to have
been filled out by, stories that could once have stood on their own
feet and have been told for their own sake, and some of which
even now can be lifted out of the narrative without much difficulty and without unduly disturbing its sequence. Such stories
could be the anointing at Bethany, the Last Supper, the prophecy
of desertion, Gethsemane perhaps, and the denial of Peter. The
claim was made rather for a hypothetical briefer version than any
we now have, which has been expanded by these additions. This
earlier version would presumably have been made up of those
constituent elements without which the narrative could not have
been a narrative of this particular historical event at all – the
arrest, an examination before the Jewish authorities, an examination before Pilate, and crucifixion told with greater or less
detail. This briefer version is then likely to have been the oldest
piece of tradition to have taken shape and to have circulated in
the churches.[4] Two reasons are advanced for its early existence in

this form. The first is that the death of Christ had been, on the evidence of some parts of the New Testament, the core of the Christian message from the start in a way that neither his teaching nor his acts had been. The second is that this message would soon have needed to be proclaimed not simply as a bare statement, 'Christ died for our sins according to the scriptures', but in the form of a narrative that would provide some explanation of how it came about that Jesus the Christ had met this particular end.

This may be a correct assessment of the matter, but there are some considerations that may stand against it. Thus, if it is to be supposed that a number of such passion narratives gained early currency in the churches, it is somewhat surprising that apparently Matthew's church, whichever it was, seems not to have had one of its own, and that Matthew was reduced to slavishly reproducing Mark's story with one or two clearly late and legendary additions. It would be even more surprising if it were the case that Luke and John also did not have available independent passion narratives of their own, but were dependent on Mark's which they supplement and edit – though whether this is in fact the case remains a highly debatable and much debated matter. Moreover, if the purpose of such an original passion story had been to give a causal explanation of the cross in historical terms in the course of proclaiming it as a message, then it is curious that the result in our present passion narratives should be that they are weak precisely at the point of historical nexus and causation and strong rather in explanation in terms of divine decree by the use of the Old Testament. Nor do the notes of place and time add up to very much. The possibility, therefore, has at least to be left open that there was no previously formulated passion story to hand when Mark wrote, and that here as in the writing of a gospel at all he was a pioneer, and that here as elsewhere in his gospel he composed by placing in a sequence independent stories which had had a previous circulation on their own to make their point, though here he would have been guided, as he would not have been elsewhere, by a certain necessary and inevitable course of events.

This is not, however, all that comes up for consideration under the head of the character of the sources. To the extent that the passion story has a self-contained character, the question arises of its connection with what precedes it, that is, its connection with what is generally called the 'ministry' of Jesus, which in the synoptic gospels, though not in John, is located entirely in Galilee. Does this ministry merely precede the passion in time and is simply for some reason or other overtaken by it, or does it in any way lead up to it? Did the death of Jesus have any organic relation to his 'life'? And if so, to what in that life? There is a statement made by Martin Kähler, which once gained considerable currency, to the effect that the gospels were in a sense written backwards, and were basically passion narratives to which introductions of different kinds had been prefixed by the evangelists. This statement is certainly unbalanced, and possibly quite erroneous, but it serves to draw attention to a genuine problem. This problem is the hiatus between the two parts into which the gospels may be said to fall, and which are connected, in the case of the synoptic gospels, by a journey to Jerusalem from Galilee for which no reason is given except divine decree. Thus, the death of Christ in the second part is represented as being the result of a judicial verdict; but is it a verdict on anything that makes its appearance in the first part? The material in the first part is often cast in the form of conflict, even bitter conflict which might lead to the death; but the conflict is generally with Pharisees, or with scribes and Pharisees, who for the evangelists – though in this they have probably exaggerated – are the stock opponents. In the second part the Pharisees do not appear, and the opponents are high priests, scribes and elders. No doubt this may be accounted for in part by the change of scene. It might be presumed that Pharisees will be around in Galilee (though on two occasions in Mark when accompanied by scribes they have to be brought down from Jerusalem to engage in the conflict; Mark 3.22; 7.1), whereas it is in Jerusalem that the official representatives of Israel, the chief priests and elders, are to be found (though in fact the Sanhedrin was largely composed of Pharisees). But this is only a partial explanation, for the controversies in the first part are represented as being over such matters as the profanation of the sabbath, the gratuitous association of Jesus with those beyond the pale, his exorcistic activity which is deemed to be of satanic origin, certain pronouncements abolishing the distinction between clean and unclean, and a claim to forgive sins that is held to be blasphemy (Mark 2.23ff.; 2.15ff.; 3.20ff.; 7.1ff.; 2.1ff., and the parallels in Matthew and Luke). None of this, however, reappears as the ground or substance of the charges brought in Jerusalem. There it is a matter of a statement by Jesus that he would destroy the temple and build another, which is incoherently presented and in any case is not proceeded with, and of a reply to a question whether he is the Messiah, which is taken as blasphemy (Mark 14.53ff. and parallels). Here there are often sharp contours in individual units of tradition taken by themselves, but they do not join together to yield an overall picture that is clear.

The point may be illustrated from F. C. Burkitt's successor, C. H. Dodd, who in his final reflections on the subject wrote as follows:

> There is something about the antagonism, as it is reflected in the gospels, which seems to draw from an even deeper spring than apprehension of a threat to the national heritage. Jesus was charged with 'blasphemy'. The term is a heavily loaded one, and the charge suggests an affront to powerful sentiments of religious reverence and awe, evoking both hatred and fear. The charge of blasphemy expresses not so much a rational judgment as a passionate, almost instinctive, revulsion of feeling against what seems to be a violation of sanctities. There must have been something about the way in which Jesus spoke and acted which provoked this kind of revulsion in minds conditioned by background, training and habit. It was this, over and above reasoned objections to certain features of his teaching, that drove the Pharisees into an unnatural (and strictly temporary) alliance with the worldly hierarchy, whose motives for pursuing Jesus to death were quite other.[5]

In this sensitive and carefully worded judgment three things may here be noted. The first is that the coherence of the gospel account here is grounded on something very different from Burkitt's confident reliance on the historical character of Mark's gospel. The second is the tentative form of the statement 'There must have been something about the way in which Jesus spoke and acted which provoked this kind of revulsion.' And the third is the necessity, in establishing this coherence and in identifying this 'something', of giving to the word 'blasphemy' a more general meaning than it would normally bear, or than it has any right to bear, in a community whose life was governed and whose religion was protected by the judgments of a religious court of law.

As already observed Paul, who is our earliest witness in writing, is not likely to be of much help in historical as opposed to theological matters. There is, however, one piece of highly compressed theological argument from which it has been deduced that we catch glimpses of how Paul saw the cross not only theologically but also historically.[6] In Galatians 3 Paul is arguing for the necessity of faith over against works of the law in view of the inability of men to keep the law. He first quotes Deut. 27.26, 'Cursed is everyone who does not remain in all the things written in the book of the law to do them.' Then by way of word association he goes on to say, 'Christ redeemed us from the curse of the law, having become a curse for us, for it is written [here he quotes Deut. 21.23] "Cursed is everyone who hangs on a tree"' (Gal. 3.10–13). What is the argument here? Christ becoming a curse clearly refers to his death, but why is it glossed by this particular passage in Deuteronomy, since a cross is not a tree? Moreover, the hanging on a tree referred to in Deuteronomy is not a mode of execution, but what is to happen to the corpse after death by way of public execration and disavowal by the community. 'When a man is convicted of a capital offence and is put to death [i.e. by one of recognized Jewish methods of execution] you shall [i.e. after he is dead] hang him on a tree, but his body shall not remain on the tree overnight; you shall bury it the same day, for a hanged man is offensive (accursed) in the sight of God' (Deut. 21.22f.). What constituted a capital offence was of course debated, but one such offence would seem to have been false prophecy which led God's people into fundamental religious error. If something more than verbal association is in Paul's mind here, his application of this passage of Deuteronomy to the crucifixion of Jesus indicates that he saw it as being, however and by whomsoever carried out, a fundamentally Jewish affair. For all that the cross was for him theologically and spiritually that which now defined human existence and penetrated to the marrow of that existence, it had taken place as an event upon the public stage, which was an Israelite stage. What in these circumstances it had amounted to was an official judgment by Israel on Jesus as guilty of a capital offence and his excommunication from the people of God through the operation of the law of God. This had come to involve for Paul a schism at the heart of things than which no greater was conceivable, for in the light of his subsequent Christian belief in the resurrection of Jesus at the hand of God and in the lordship of Jesus which was deduced from that resurrection, God on the one hand and God's people and law on the other were now shown to have been on opposing sides on the most crucial issue possible within Israel. It is probably this view of the matter, rather than any supposed psychological revolution in Paul on the Damascus road, that was the source of that radically dialectical character of Paul's thinking about all things, whereby the affirmation of the divine possibilities of life can be made only by way of a negation of human capacities of however exalted an origin.

Was Paul right in so seeing the death of Christ as an event in which fundamental issues for Israel's life had come to a head? In another highly compressed passage he asserts, in face of the pretensions of Jew and Greek alike, 'We preach Christ crucified' (I Cor. 1.23). The mere juxtaposition of the words 'Christ' and 'crucified' points to a more complex historical situation, though Paul himself nowhere develops it in his letters, and perhaps has no reason to do so. For 'Christ' or 'the Christ' is only intelligible on the background of a culture such as the Jewish in which kings and priests were appointed to their office by anointing with oil (which is what the word literally means), and so could become a designation of the hoped for king in the divine kingdom. Likewise, though there is some slight evidence for the practice of crucifixion in Palestine before the Roman occupation, and even of its theoretical contemplation by Jewish courts as a possible method of punishment, there can be little doubt that in Palestine at the time 'crucify' must have denoted what was exclusively Roman, as 'guillotine' was to denote what was exclusively French. Thus the very conjunction of the words 'Christ crucified' betokens a situation of a particular kind, a Jewish-Roman situation which had been brought about by the occupation of Judaea by the Roman imperial power, and so to an event which of necessity had two sides to it. The question then is of the relation of these two sides to each other, and here the gospels themselves show a wide disparity. In Mark the passion is a predominantly Jewish affair, with a comparatively protracted examination by the Sanhedrin, compared with which the Roman side is perfunctory in the extreme, the examination before Pilate being covered in five verses. In Luke the balance is more even, with the Jewish side shorter and the Roman side expanded to include official charges brought before Pilate and Pilate's threefold attestation of Jesus' innocence. In John the story has come down heavily on the other side; any formal Jewish examination has as good as disappeared, and the whole is concentrated on the confrontation of Pilate with Jesus and the Jews.

It is not, however, only the gospels themselves which present difficulties here. History, by which is meant in this connection the literature and documents that have happened to survive, together with any archaeological data available, has a habit of leaving lacunae. This may not be of great importance when the matter in question lies on the circumference of the story. Thus, for example, we do not have any evidence apart from a possible but disputed implication of a statement made in the Mishna, for any custom, improbable in itself, of releasing a prisoner at Passover time, according to which Barabbas is asked for and obtained in exchange for Jesus[7] – and it may be noted that on those reconstructions of the passion story which see it as almost entirely a Roman affair this exchange of prisoners would move from the circumference of the story to its centre. It is otherwise with the question whether the Jewish authorities were permitted any powers of capital punishment under Roman rule or not. This is not a peripheral matter, for the story can be made to hinge on it, as when at John 18.31f. Pilate attempts to pass responsibility back to the Jews with the demand 'Take him and judge him according to your law', and, somewhat surprisingly, has to be reminded of the fact that 'It is not permissible for us to put any man to death'.

That this is such a vexed question is itself evidence of a certain historical complexity. One would have supposed both on grounds of general probability and of what is known of Roman imperial practice that the occupying power would reserve the right of executing the death penalty entirely to itself. This is in most circumstances almost a definition of what being an occupying power is. The Romans, however, had become well aware that occupation of Judaea was never straightforward, and that they were engaged with a people for whom the customary demarcations between the political and the religious spheres did not obtain. It is possible that by special arrangement the Jewish authorities had power on what were adjudged religious issues up to and including the death penalty. Unfortunately, the available evidence for either view happens to be of such a kind that, in the words of a recent writer, 'the problem has been treated with wearying frequency and disappointing inconclusiveness'.[8] Nevertheless, on the view taken can depend an assessment of the events as a whole. Thus Paul Winter and others, starting from the position that the Jewish authorities did possess the power of capital punishment in religious matters, with the corollary that they must have carried out any such sentence themselves in their own manner even if it required ratification by the Romans, have reached the conclusion that since the condemnation 'the King of the Jews' was framed in political terms and the execution carried out in the Roman manner it must have been a Roman affair in the first place, and that the present form of the story in the gospels is the product of an increasing anti-Jewish bias in the tradition born of subsequent hostility between Christians and Jews.[9] And even the supposed anti-Jewish bias is here capable of a rather different explanation, as in the following:

> What we do find in the Gospels, I suggest, is often the attempt to resolve what must have been a profoundly disturbing and exquisitely delicate dilemma. Most of the early Christian communities perforce had to grow – indeed, survive – for three centuries (the crucial period for the texts) within the Roman Empire. They proclaimed and maintained and had to explain a religion intimately centering on a figure who had been officially tried for and convicted of the highest crime in Roman law; treason. And he had been executed in a manner reserved for the worst criminals; crucifixion. For three centuries this must have been as dead a weight as any group has had to carry – in fact, it is unique. . . . The Christian communities had constantly to avoid (or, failing that, to talk down) this untoward political (worldly) beginning. The very historicity of Jesus must have almost at once been a stumbling block in this respect.[10]

Or is the mediating position of Solomon Zeitlin nearer the facts when he contends that there had been as institutions in Judaism two forms of Sanhedrin, the religious Sanhedrin for deciding the central issues of the nation's faith and life, with its procedure for that reason very carefully laid down, and a political Sanhedrin for dealing with contraventions of the law of the state *qua* state, *ad hoc* in its character and rough and ready in its methods? Although the latter had ceased to exist as an institution under Roman rule, its activities and methods in Zeitlin's view continued in the circle of the high priests, who were thus not the spokesmen of the nation on its deepest issues, but agents of the procurator in political cases. This may be so, though it may be noted that Zeitlin, like others, has to resort to hypothesis at a crucial point in his reconstruction of the story from the gospel sources when he states, 'Apparently the high priest so presented the case to his Sanhedrin that Jesus, who claimed to be the messiah, should be delivered up to the Romans.'[11] In that case the core of the passion as historical event, so far from being a confrontation between Jesus

and the leaders of the spiritual life of the nation over the ultimate
issues of God's dealings with his people (as is suggested by Paul),
could have been that in visiting Jerusalem for some purpose
undisclosed he happened to fall foul of a high placed gang of
collaborationist thugs.[12]

It therefore comes about from the character of the sources and
from the lacunae in our historical information with respect to
what in any case was a complex historical situation that almost all
the main factors in the story have become problematical. What
was in fact the so-called triumphal entry that was conceived or
interpreted in terms of Zech. 9.9? What was the so-called cleansing of the temple so that it should be, in accordance with Isa. 56.7,
a house of prayer for all the nations? What was the character of
the arrest of Jesus, a small scale or a large scale operation? And
who were its primary agents? The night session of the Sanhedrin
in Mark, the single morning session in Luke, the location of these
in the high priest's house, the manner of the Sanhedrin's conduct
of its business, the occurrence of these transactions on a feast day
and its eve – do these contravene, or do they not contravene,
regulations to be found in later Jewish sources, and are those
regulations to be accepted, or are they not to be accepted, as
having been in force at the time? How is blasphemy to be defined
and did acknowledgment of messiahship constitute blasphemy?
These are all in the nature of the case matters of acute debate, and
while it may be hoped that some of these problems may yet be
solved by patient research, it is unlikely that this will be so to the
extent of making the contours sufficiently sharp and the nexus of
action and reaction, of cause and effect, evident.[13]

A particular instance of uncertainty as to historical action and
the motives lying behind it is Judas. And this could be important
rather than peripheral, since he is represented as the link between the private circle of disciples around Jesus and the
authorities, and as having in some way set the wheels of public
machinery in motion. But what it was that he did, and why he did
it, have been the subject of constant speculation. This has already
begun in the New Testament, where over and above the prediction of Jesus, scripture and Satan, plain avarice is suggested as
a reason. This has continued down the ages in terms of what any
particular age has considered to be treachery, of which he has
become the archetype. Two recent assessments of reputable
scholars on the matter stand in direct contradiction. On the one

hand O. Cullmann sees the action of Judas as stemming from disillusionment, coming to a head at the Last Supper, at Jesus' refusal to pursue the course of political Messiah.[14] On the other hand S. Zeitlin sees it as stemming from Judas' belief as an apocalyptist that Jesus was the Son of God, and his fear that the other disciples would make the disastrous mistake of declaring him to be political Messiah.[15]

In these circumstances it is not simply a tempting desire to be trendy at a time when there is much talk of revolution and of philosophies and theologies of revolution that has led to the publication – or rather the re-publication – of the Zealot hypothesis, according to which Jesus and his movement were far more politically orientated than the gospel traditions and the gospels as wholes now allow them to appear.[16] Attention can be drawn to odd features still to be found, as it were, lying around in the gospels, and nuances of language that tend to escape in the difficult task of translation.

There is first the hard core which is hardly disputed by anyone that Jesus died as 'the king of the Jews'. This is to be distinguished from 'the king of Israel' (Mark. 15.32; Matt. 27.42; John 1.50), which could be an equivalent of the Messiah, Israel being a religious conception. It is framed in external, political terms belonging to the vocabulary of the Romans, who did not mind how many religions there were provided that none of them was treasonable, and for whom the Greek word 'basileus' had a sinister sound not conveyed by the word 'king'. It was a word increasingly denied by them to anyone other than the emperor at Rome. Then there is the word 'lēstēs'. This is what Barabbas is called, with (in Mark and Luke) the addition that his imprisonment had some connection with 'stasis', which is the regular Greek word for revolt. At his arrest Jesus expresses surprise that they have come out as if against a lēstēs, and he is crucified between two who are called such (Mark 14.48; 15.6–8; 15.27 and parallels). It is impossible to find a single adequate English equivalent for this word. Like 'guerrilla' its nuance depends on who is using it of whom. It can denote 'robber' but never simply in the sense of 'thief', the robbery always implying violence of some kind, generally of those who chose, or were compelled, to live off the land. It is a semi-technical term with Josephus for those whom he would doubtless have designated differently so long as he was a general in the Jewish army in Galilee, but whom, once he had changed sides and was writing propaganda under the aegis of the Romans, he regarded as irresponsible revolutionaries at whose door he placed the disaster of the Jewish war. It was a word expressing the government point of view, and in Roman law the *lēstēs* was one for whom the cross was specified as the punishment. There is also a word going along with it, *machaira*, incorrectly translated 'sword'. It is rather a butcher's knife or dagger, like the Latin *sica*, and the *sicarii* occur in Josephus as one branch of the guerrillas in the Jewish war. Again, Jesus expresses surprise that they have come out against him with clubs and daggers, and one of the disciples draws a dagger and cuts off the ear of a servant of the high priest, and (in John) is told to return his dagger to its sheath (Mark 14.43–49 and parallels; John 18.11).

There are also certain sayings of Jesus that are difficult to interpret. At the close of the brief table conversation which Luke alone of the synoptic evangelists supplies at the Last Supper the disciples are told that from now on their mode of life is to change, and that whereas previously they had lacked nothing, he who did not possess a purse was to sell his cloak and buy a dagger, since the prophecy is about to be fulfilled with respect to Jesus, 'He was reckoned with the outlaws'. When the disciples draw attention to two daggers Jesus replies either 'That is enough' or 'Enough of that' (Luke 22.36–38). This is so obscure that commentators are baffled and generally have to fall back on irony as an explanation, which is always something difficult to establish when the tone of voice of the speaker can no longer be heard. Or there is the scarcely less obscure saying in its Matthaean form 'From the days of John the Baptist until now the kingdom of God suffers violent treatment (or, makes its violent way), and violent men are seizing it' (Matt. 11.12). Does this say something different from the more innocuous sounding Lukan equivalent 'The kingdom of God is preached, and everyone is forcefully entering into it' (Luke 16.16)? Who are these violent men, and is the statement expressing approval or disapproval? Finally, there is the presence among the disciples of a certain Simon who is called by Mark and Matthew 'the Cananaean', and by Luke with a Greek equivalent for the Aramaic '*ho zēlōtēs*'. The designation could be of a general kind and mean 'the man of zeal', but certainly later in Josephus it is a semi-technical term 'zealot' which he used for one group in the liberation front, and which could have been intended to cover most of them. In the opinion of some experts 'Cananaean' is an Aramaic equivalent for 'zealot' in this sense, and some have seen zealot associations in the names of the disciples – 'Iscariot' in the case of Judas, 'bar-Jona' in the case of Peter, and 'Boanerges' in the case of the sons of Zebedee.[17]

On the principle of no smoke without fire, a principle to which the historian has on occasions perforce to resort, such features and others along with them have been made the basis for a reconstruction of the aims and activity of Jesus which, if it does not turn them into a zealot movement, approximates them to it to a greater or less extent. The gospels are then seen as palimpsests, in which the writing still dimly to be descried here and there underneath tells a significantly different story from what is written on top. This thesis cannot be examined here in detail. It has been so examined and has generally been found wanting.[18] It creates far more problems for the understanding of the tradition than it solves. It has to suppose a somewhat ridiculous mini-movement with apparently an unarmed entry into Jerusalem and with remarkably few daggers in evidence. It is incompatible at too many points with sayings and actions of Jesus, whose authenticity there is no good ground for doubting, which point in a different, sometimes indeed in an opposite direction, and it fails to explain why at the critical juncture Jesus alone was arrested, and why when his followers came to be arrested later it was, so far as our information goes, for significantly different reasons of a religious rather than of a political kind.

The hypothesis is not, however, simply to be dismissed out of hand in order to make a return to an interpretation of the matter that shall be purely religious and spiritual, at least as those terms are often understood. For the hypothesis, even if false, draws attention in its own way to an acute question of a more general kind concerning the language of religion and spirituality. To state it somewhat crudely, in those historical circumstances could an itinerant Galilean preacher (to put it no higher than that), unless he was a simpleton, be unaware that much talk of the kingdom of God and its associated language was bound to strike upon the ears of his audience with a wide variety of meaning and to elicit an equivocal range of response? Indeed, is there in any circumstances a religious language as such which is both adequate to its subject-matter and also immune from serious misunderstanding, unless it be a language that as far as possible has abandoned the visible world – in which case is it any longer adequate to its subject-matter? This was a question with which the Christian church was to become involved up to the hilt once it moved out of Judaism into the Graeco-Roman world. For there it encountered forms of thought and language which for want of a better word may be called 'gnostic', and which appeared to offer that immunity from misunderstanding and to be more adequate to the spiritual subject-matter of religion – but only at the price of abandoning the world. It was a mythological language, though of a rarefied kind; a philosophico-religious language with words like 'light', 'spirit', 'mind' and 'fullness' which now owed as little as possible to material origins.

But this question may be said to have been posed already within Judaism itself. The standing charge of Jews against Gentiles had been the charge of idolatry, of fatally mixing up the creation with the Creator. The critique exercised upon natural religion by the prophets and the law had brought it about that a necessary wedge was driven between God and the world so as to bar the road to this identification. The circle of nature – sun and rain, seedtime and harvest – were not themselves the manifestation of divine life; nor was sexuality and reproductive power. God was not an extension of the nation, dependent for his existence on its existence. The king was not divine, nor were his rulings as such divine law. The language thrown up by human life, once freed from this fatal identification, could, however, provide the words in which to express the hope of a future action of God in the completion of his creation, when he who was the father of his household, the ruler of his people and the shepherd of his flock would veritably exercise truth and righteousness. But then the question arises whether such language would take one step further and float entirely free of its earthly origins, so as either with the apocalyptists to turn into increasingly bizarre fantasies of the future that had no chance of being realized historically, or with such as the Jewish philosopher Philo to go further in the direction of Platonism and end up as symbols only, shadows of the realities laid up in heaven? Could they be brought down to earth again into the historical as a proper expression of the subject matter without reverting to the old idolatry?

There is a concrete illustration of this at the very heart of the passion story, at least in its Markan version. This is the occurrence of the term 'the Son of man'. But to pass to this is to jump out of the frying pan into the fire, for as every student knows this is the most hotly and inconclusively debated term in New Testament study. What was the current meaning of this term with which the synoptic gospels are studded, and which is not absent from the Fourth Gospel but which would seem to have dropped out of the Christian vocabulary, presumably because it was no longer intelligible or serviceable, only to be picked up later to serve up to the present day as an expression of the humanity of Christ in contrast to his divinity? What had been the process by which Daniel's vision of 'one like a son of man' had taken on the precision of 'the Son of man'? Was there a theology attached to this figure, and if so to whom was it intelligible and what did it convey? How far did Jesus use it in all or any one of the ways represented in the synoptic gospels, as the personal vindicator of men before God, as the judge of men on God's behalf, as the one who effectively gathers God's elect, as already operating with a more than human authority in the sphere of human life, and as destined to be rejected by men themselves? All these and other connected questions are matters of debate, upon which the literature already mounts to high heaven. But here, if anywhere, was an image which, however it might be blown up to outsize proportions and float away on the clouds into heaven, demanded to be brought to earth again, since it could not escape the fact that it had had an earthy origin and referred to man. Its occurrence at a crucial point in the passion narrative is puzzling, and the commentators do not quite know what to do with it. When the high priest asks his question 'Are you the Christ, the son of the Blessed?' the reply in the Markan version is 'I am, and you shall see the Son of man sitting at the right hand of God and coming with the clouds of heaven' (Mark 14.61). What is the force of 'and' here? Since 'I am' is sufficient answer to the question as asked, is the further statement about the Son of man simply an added piece of gratuitous information? Or is this in the last resort the connecting link between the issues that had been at stake in Galilee and the issues now at stake in Jerusalem? And was it precisely here that Jesus was judged fatally to have overstepped the boundaries which it was Israel's divine vocation to preserve, and to have mixed up the categories of the earthly and heavenly? The fact that one is forced to put these as questions only is a further indication of the character of the sources.

3

The Passion of Mark and the Passion of Luke

The death of Christ was given a particular shape by the specific circumstances in which it took place, even if those circumstances can only on occasion be glimpsed. It was given significance perhaps from the first by being proclaimed with reference to, and in the vocabulary of, the Old Testament. Eventually, there emerged four written forms of this narrative proclamation, three of which, while not being identical, were sufficiently similar to be called 'synoptic'. Of these Matthew's may be set aside as being for the most part a transcription of Mark's with a few additions of a legendary and dispensable kind.[1] The other two, those of Mark and Luke, may legitimately be considered in juxtaposition as being at one and the same time both similar and dissimilar.

To juxtapose the passion narratives of Mark and Luke in this way is to raise in a form peculiar to the New Testament the general problem of the composite in religion. The religious mind is by nature unificatory and synthetic. When the author of the Epistle to the Ephesians exclaims 'One Lord, one faith, one baptism, one God and Father of all' (Eph. 4.5) he is making a recognizably religious statement. For religion anything that is of primary rank is one. This has often been so also for philosophy, which Plato defined as the search for the one in the many. Analysis, on the other hand, whether scientific, historical or linguistic, stands at the opposite pole. Its aim is to break down into components so that each individual thing may be seen in its own distinctiveness, and may be allowed to speak as far as possible for itself. Any unity there may be has to take account of this distinctiveness and to be inclusive of pluriformity.

Christianity experienced a form of the tension between synthesis and analysis from the first. For it emerged, at least in its Pauline form, with what was called 'the gospel', and this gospel was by definition one. Others might use the word 'gospel' in the plural to denote a succession of benefits from a variety of sources, but as Christians used it it was a singular noun that did not admit of a plural; it denoted the gospel of the one and only God intended for the whole world and for all time. Nevertheless, it came about by a process we can only guess at that the churches of the second century found themselves in possession of four books, each of which in its own way gave expression to this gospel. This was evidently unacceptable to some, and we know of one attempt to undo it, the *Diatessaron* of Tatian, in which the four were scrambled to produce a single story.[2] Such attempts failed presumably (though this is also guesswork) because each of the four had so established itself somewhere that it could not be dropped, and in a well-known passage Irenaeus appealed to evidence of fourfoldness within nature and outside it to justify the now established fact that the one gospel was quadriform.[3] The decision to have four gospels rather than one was without doubt of great and lasting benefit. It secured that the church's tradition should be diverse and rich rather than minimal and uniform. However, the problem it posed did not thereby go away, but only shifted to the sphere of exegesis. How were the four to be interpreted so that they told essentially a single story? The answer was by harmonization. To a considerable measure each was interpreted in the light of the others and in such a way as to arrive at a synthesis. So from the third century until comparatively recently Christians have lived by a harmony of the gospels, and therefore by reference to what may be called a composite Christ. Analytical criticism has in its turn made this unacceptable in the sense that truth conveyed in this way ceases to carry conviction. Each gospel has now to be seen first in its distinctiveness and to be allowed to speak sufficiently for itself, and any unity there may be of the gospels as a whole is to follow from that.

In attempting to delineate this distinctiveness we are no longer engaged in the search of form criticism for originally independent and self-contained units of tradition, but with redaction criticism. This attempts to look at a gospel as a whole, but as a whole made up of those types of material that form criticism has already

established as having been in existence, and it seeks to deduce
from the particular selection each evangelist has made from this
material, the sequence he has given it, and the editorial links he
has himself supplied, what it is that he intended to write, and for
what purpose and for whose sake he wrote it. Redaction criticism
will also find itself returning to the older literary or source criticism if and when it appears that the work of an evangelist as
editor included his use and adaptation of earlier written documents.[4] Whether Mark had already to hand a passion narrative in
written form or was the first to·put one together from isolated
units of tradition is uncertain. Where, so far as we can see, he was
a pioneer was in combining a passion narrative with what has
come to be called a 'ministry' in Galilee. That in doing so he
produced a remarkable, not to say puzzling document would
appear from the fact that after a century or more of concentrated
study of it there should be so little consensus of opinion amongst
scholars as to what exactly it is that he wrote and why it is what
it is.

One cannot here enter into detail. Suffice it to say in broad
terms that, to an extent we might find surprising were we not so
familiar with it, it is built up as far as chapter 10 of a series of
accounts of the type misleadingly called 'miracle', interspersed at
chapters 2, 4 and 7 with sections of teaching, the first and last of
which take the form of conflict and controversy. This first part
would seem to have been constructed around the ideas conveyed
by two Greek words which occur not infrequently in it, *dunamis*
and *exousia*. *Dunamis* is one of the Greek words for power, and at
one point (5.30) is said to be what Jesus perceives to go out from
himself when he performs one of these actions. In the plural the
word is used to designate such actions as works of power (6.2, 5,
14; 9.39). *Exousia* is a synonym for *dunamis*, and is the word used
for this power when transmitted to disciples (6.7), but since it has
the additional nuance of authoritative power it can also be
applied to teaching. How closely the two are associated in Mark's
mind appears from the story with which he chooses to open his
account of the Galilean ministry. Jesus is in a synagogue and his
teaching there evokes astonishment as being with *exousia* in contrast to that of the official teachers, the scribes. One would expect
a specimen of this teaching to follow. What in fact follows is a
scene of exorcism of considerable violence, to which the reaction
of the audience is 'A new teaching; with authority he commands

the unclean spirits and they obey him' (1.27). From this beginning there follows in chapters 1–9 a succession of such actions of
power with respect to fever, leprosy, total paralysis, partial paralysis, storm, demon possession, haemorrhage, death, food,
water, demon possession, deafness and dumbness, blindness,
demon possession, blindness. From time to time editorial notes
are added to the effect that this kind of thing is constantly happening (1.32–34, 38–39; 3.7–12; 6.53–56). At one point such activity is connected with the unexplained term 'the Son of man' when
the healing of the paralytic is said to be evidence that the Son of
man has *exousia* to forgive sins (2.10), and in a dispute with
Pharisees over the disciples' contravention of sabbath regulations
their conduct is defended on the ground that the Son of man is
lord of, or has power over, the sabbath.

From chapter 8 onwards the narrative begins to change in
direction and tone, and in this the Son of man again figures. At
three points Jesus predicts in greater or less detail that the Son of
man is destined to be rejected (8.31; 9.30–32; 10.32–34). I take
these to be editorial constructions of the evangelist. With the
possible exception of the first they are isolated and self-contained
units, and it can hardly have been the case that three of them so
similar came down in the oral tradition sufficiently labelled as to
be recognized as distinct utterances or with indications as to
where they were to go in a connected narrative. They are, rather,
devices by which Mark in his redaction links what has gone
before with what is to come. Their language as such deserves
careful attention. Apart from those details which make the predictions correspond with what was actually to take place later,
three things are said of the Son of man – that he will suffer
(much), that he will be rejected by men, and that he will be set at
naught. What do these expressions intend to say?

We have long been accustomed to speak of the 'passion' or
'suffering' of Christ, and to our sensibilities – partly as a result of
traditional Christian piety of the cross – suffering tends to denote
primarily physical or mental pain. The gospels would appear,
however, to show little or no concern with this, if indeed they are
even aware of it. In the Greek language the verb 'to do' (*poiein*)
does not possess a passive with the sense 'to be done to'. What
did service for this was another verb *paschein* (from the Latin
equivalent of which the English word 'passion' is derived), and
the first meaning given in the dictionary for this word is 'to have

something done to one; the opposite of "to do" '. To suffer in this primary and original sense of the word is to be the object of the actions of others, the patient as opposed to the agent, as in T. S. Eliot's lines:

> They know and do not know, what it is to act or suffer.
> They know and do not know, that acting is suffering
> And suffering action. Neither does the actor suffer
> Nor the patient act. But both are fixed
> In an eternal action, an eternal patience.[5]

Since the force of a sentence lies in the conjunction of subject and verb, what it means that the Son of man suffers depends on our having a sufficiently clear picture of who the Son of man is supposed to be, and this unfortunately we do not have.[6] If, however, on the basis of statements in the gospels themselves, and perhaps of those in our only other source where the term is found frequently, the much debated book I Enoch, we may say that the Son of man expressed for some circles at least the agent of God *par excellence* and of his ultimate purposes for mankind in judgment and deliverance, then to say that the Son of man suffers, and that this particular agent becomes patient, is to state in these terms the extreme to which theological paradox can go. Similarly, with the second word to be so used, 'to be rejected'. This is from the Greek word *dokimazein*, which means to assay or scrutinize. It is used of wine, or of the coinage to test whether it rings true or is counterfeit, or of men to examine whether they are qualified for an office. In the gospels (as also in I Enoch) it is one of the functions of the Son of man that he is to scrutinize all men, and on his recommendation and verdict depends their standing with God (cf. Mark 8.38; Matt. 19.28; Luke 12.8). When, therefore, the scrutineer of all men is himself the object of the scrutiny of men and of their adverse verdict, it is in these terms again the height of paradox. The third verb, *exoudenothenai*, is almost confined to the biblical literature. It is constructed from the Greek word for 'nothing', and means in its reduplicated form 'to reduce absolutely to nothing'. The one who by his office and function is supremely someone is to become a non-entity.

This is the theology of high paradox, and it continues on in the Markan gospel. For the reader of this gospel enters into the passion narrative of chapters 14 and 15 through the gateway of the notorious chapter 13, sometimes called the Little Apocalypse.

This chapter is unique in Mark's gospel both in form and content. In form it is the only lengthy discourse in Mark, with Jesus speaking uninterruptedly on a single subject for some thirty verses, and there has been much discussion as to whether Mark in his redaction has incorporated here an already existent fly-sheet, or has himself brought together independent paragraphs on similar themes so as to construct a discourse. In content it is sustained apocalyptic prediction in the service of warning to disciples – the coming destruction of the temple, the appearance of deceivers, internecine warfare, the arraignment of disciples before the authorities, the manifestation of the mysterious 'abomination of desolation' in human form, unparalleled distress, the appearance of false prophets and false messiahs, and after cosmic chaos in which the only stability is that of the words of the speaker himself, the manifestation of the Son of man coming on the clouds with great power to gather the elect. This thought and language is at the greatest possible remove from what is natural or meaningful to us, but we are not here concerned with the problem which this chapter poses for the modern mind, but with the fact that Mark as editor and redactor has deliberately chosen to place it here as virtually the last words of the one whose suffering, scrutiny and naughting he is about to relate. The one who, once he is handed over, opens his mouth only three times in brief sentences, here speaks at length as privy to the divine secrets of the destiny of the universe, whose words are the sole permanent element in it, and in whose hands are the elect of God. The passion is thus not only the depotentiation of the one who acts with power, but also the silencing of the one who speaks with ultimate authority.[7]

The passion story which then follows is predominantly that of a Jewish matter. Previously, after careful preparation involving for the only time in Mark the use of the title 'the Lord' for Jesus (when the disciples, if asked about the requisitioning of the ass are to say 'The Lord has need of it', 11.3), Jesus had entered Jerusalem to a royal welcome and to shouts about 'the coming kingdom of our father David' (11.9–10). Perhaps two passages should be added here to the Old Testament background, the first II Kings 9.13: 'Then they hasted and took every man his garment and put it under him on the top of the stairs, and blew the trumpet and cried "Jehu is king"'; and the second I Macc.13.51: 'And Simon entered Jerusalem on the three and twentieth day of the month . . . with praise and palm branches.' The story continues as a religious story when the temple comes into the centre of it and remains there, though the matter is somewhat confused. For the violent action in the temple, which is generally called its 'cleansing', is said to have as its object, in accordance with words from Isa. 56.7, its universalization as a house of prayer for all peoples (11.15–18). This is, however, strange, since the starting point for the apocalyptic discourse of chapter 13 is the prediction to the hearers of its irretrievable destruction in their own generation (13.1f.). Further, having been arrested by agents of the chief priests, scribes and elders – there is no hint of Roman participation – Jesus is in the first instance accused on the charge of having said something like 'I will destroy this temple made with hands, and in three days I will build another not made with hands' (14.57f.). If he had said something of this kind it could have been the most radical and revolutionary thing he ever did say with respect to Jewish religion and life, and John has a variant placed in a quite different context in the form 'You destroy this temple and in three days I will raise it up', which that evangelist interprets of the resurrection (John 2.19–22). As they stand in Mark the words, particularly 'I will destroy this temple made with hands', are unintelligible.[8] They in fact evoke no reply from Jesus, are in any case said to be discordant and false testimony, and are not proceeded with. The trial continues on a religious note with the high priest's question, the reply to which occasions a ritual tearing of the robes and a judgment of blasphemy, which is the ground of a formal condemnation to death. The irregular, and in itself, not very probable buffeting by 'some', presumably members of the Sanhedrin, and by their servants, includes a covering of the face and the demand to prophesy. The mocking is that of a dummy prophet (14.53–65).

Compared with all this the Roman side of the story is abrupt and perfunctory as well as being obscure (15.1–5). It is abrupt when the high priests with the elders and scribes and the whole Sanhedrin hold a council (or make a plan) and hand Jesus over to Pilate, who asks the unprepared for question 'Are you the king of the Jews?' It is perfunctory in that Pilate, on receiving the apparently non-committal reply 'you say so', and observing Jesus' silence in the face of many accusations by the priests which are not specified, is content merely to ask the prisoner why he makes no reply. It is obscure because, in contrast to the five verses devoted to this crucial interview with the governor, there are nine verses connected with the question of the choice between Jesus and Barabbas. There is no firm evidence for any custom of releasing at the Passover a prisoner of the crowd's own choice, and it is unlikely in itself. Nevertheless, in Mark's account the fate of Jesus is sealed so far as the Romans are concerned over the question 'Who will you have, Barabbas (some manuscripts in Matthew have 'Jesus Barabbas') or Jesus who is called the Christ?' and when the crowd, which is brought in as an audience at this point, asks for Barabbas and cries out for Jesus to be crucified. There is thus no Roman trial and no legal verdict or sentence. Failing to elicit any defence from the prisoner Pilate throws the onus on the Jews, and though Jesus is put to death in Roman fashion it is really a Jewish affair.

From this point on the story is rapid and stark. The sentences are paratactic and staccato to a degree unusual even in Mark, and his somewhat rough Greek serves here the purpose of an unadorned realism. The isolation of Jesus is complete. Having begun with his prophesied desertion by the disciples (14.27, 50) and his denial by Peter (intercalated by Mark into the trial, 14.66ff.), it is further underlined when Roman soldiers offer him mock homage in horseplay (15.16–20), and when 'those passing by' (the meaning is 'anyone who passed by') together with the chief priests and scribes mock his impotence, the first throwing in his face the reputed words about destroying and rebuilding the temple, the second his claim to be the Christ (15.29–32a). It becomes total when both the fellow condemned mock him (15.32b), and speaking for the third and last time since his arrest he confesses the divine absence (15.34). Flanking this last utterance Mark places two events, of which the first is possibly and the second probably symbolic. There is a three hour darkness over the whole land, and the veil of the temple is rent from top to bottom (15.33, 38). Here the theme of the temple returns, and it is perhaps suggested that the presence of God, which the temple veil was to conceal from human eyes, is somehow in the death of Jesus actualized for mankind. Hence, at this point of complete isolation and depotentiation a representative of the Gentile world, a centurion, utters in his own fashion – 'Truly this man was a son of God' (15.39) – a kind of confession of divinity, which otherwise in Mark has been uttered only by the voice of God himself (1.11; 9.6) or by the demons as denizens of the supernatural world (3.11). This mysterious awesomeness continues on into Mark's only account of the resurrection (if his gospel ends at 16.8) when women, confronted by an empty tomb and an angelic messenger with a message for the disciples about the risen Lord and Galilee, flee in terror and remain silent from fear.

How Mark intends this story to be understood has already been seen in the Old Testament language with which the crucial points in it are underlined, so as to convey a strong sense of the action of God. At two points there is, further, the use of concentrated and suggestive metaphor to indicate that while in principle what is happening concerns Jesus and his disciples together, in effect it concerns him alone. Thus, in reply to a request from two disciples for places of honour in the coming kingdom mention is made of a 'cup' to be drunk and of a 'baptism' to be undergone. The first metaphor probably has an Old Testament background, though what it denotes precisely – suffering, judgment, wrath – is not clear. The second, 'baptism' or drowning in calamity has as such no certainly traceable background. And then, while the service of others is set out as the model for the greatness of the disciple, it is of the Son of man alone that it is said that this service through death is a ransom for many (10.35–45). When the metaphor of the 'cup' reappears in Gethsemane it applies to the struggle of the will of Jesus alone, and the disciples are markedly non-participants (14.32–42). Again, at the Last Supper 'This is my body' is expressive of the solidarity of the whole company, and the use of 'body' in this sense is without Old Testament background. 'This is my blood of the covenant' hints at the death of Jesus alone as a sacrifice inaugurating a covenant or relationship with God, and this is of an eschatological kind since he himself abjures wine until he shall drink it new in the kingdom of God (14.22–25). In the Gethsemane story that follows, where the language is violent ('he began to be utterly astonished and at a loss', 14.33), it is suggested that the inner moral content of this sacrifice is the surrender of the will. If it is asked for whom Mark wrote all this, it may be suggested that the manner of writing indicates that he has in mind those for whom Christian discipleship is likely to involve an extreme of persecution.

When the other synoptic account, the Lukan, is placed alongside Mark's it appears both as the same and as a different story. It is the same in being made out of Mark's and of material of a similar synoptic type. The extent of, and the relation between, these two ingredients are matters of debate between those on the one hand who hold that the admittedly complex evidence points to Luke having had to hand no continuous passion narrative other than Mark's, which he edits with some freedom and fills out with additional incidents, and those on the other hand who hold that, when the undoubted borrowings from Mark are removed, what is left behind is not a collection of separate units but a continuous narrative, and that this has been Luke's principal authority, being filled out from Mark when it needed it.[9] The matter is complicated, but it is not entirely academic. When in place of Mark's night session of the Sanhedrin (said by some to be in contravention of current Jewish regulations) followed by a morning session at which nothing seems to be done (Mark 14.53–65; 15.1), Luke has a single session (Luke 22.66–71), are we in touch with a source which here, and perhaps throughout, is historically more trustworthy, or with the result of Luke's editorial work in smoothing out an awkward story in Mark? Or, when instead of a two-part account of the denial of Peter which Mark places on either side of the night session, with Jesus out of sight in the high priest's house (Mark 14.54,66–72), Luke has a single smoothly written account of Peter denying his master in his presence with its affecting climax, 'The Lord turned and looked on Peter' (Luke 22.54–62), is this evidence of an independent source or of Luke's capacity for style and pathos?

Though it is the same story it is also a different story. The first difference is one of general perspective. Luke alone of the evangelists wrote a two volume work, which was something the others not only did not do but could not have done. For what they wrote about Jesus the Christ was single, ultimate and complete in itself, and each has in his own way so brought his book to a conclusion as to make it impossible for him to take up his pen again and write a sequel. Luke, however, is the historian of the Christian movement, of which Jesus the Christ, however complete and self-contained, is the founder, and which by reason of his passion, resurrection and ascension he sustains in the present and in the world. Further, within the perspective of the first volume the passion is not, as in Mark, the reverse of a series of acts of power. These Luke includes but along with much else, and the transition from the one to the other and from Galilee to Jerusalem, which in Mark is achieved in a few verses, takes in

Luke the form of a protracted journey of an itinerant teacher covering some nine chapters (Luke 9.51–19.28).

There are also differences of detail within the passion narrative itself, which at times are not unconnected with this difference of general perspective. There is first a difference in the structural balance between the Jewish and Roman sides. The Jewish side is reduced in size and scope. The charge concerning the temple does not appear in Luke's version of the trial. For Luke the temple, once it has been cleansed by Jesus, is taken over by him as the scene of his teaching ministry in Jerusalem, which occasions great popularity with 'the people', whom Luke here as elsewhere carefully distinguishes from their leaders (19.47f.; 20.1,37.; cf.Acts 2.47; 4.1f.; 5.12–26). This is no doubt related to the fact that Luke will introduce the question of the validity and permanence of the temple in Acts directly over the Hellenists, who make the first move in the direction of separating the church from Judaism, and indirectly over Jesus when the Hellenist Stephen is charged with having asserted that Jesus would destroy the temple (Acts 6.1–7.4). The double question of the high priest in Mark is in Luke two separate questions. To the first 'Are you the Christ?' the reply is not a categorical affirmative as in Mark, but is evasive: 'If I tell you you will not believe, and if I ask you will not answer'; though there is then added the statement about the Son of man, clearly derived from Mark but given a significantly different form. Instead of 'You will see the Son of man sitting at the right hand of God and coming on the clouds of heaven', which implies a manifestation to the high priest in his own lifetime, it is 'From now on the Son of man shall be seated at the right hand of the power of God' (Luke 22.66–71; cf. Mark 14.59–64). This is where in the Acts story Jesus is, directing the Christian movement for a more indefinite future, and it is here that Stephen, who is the only person to use the title 'the Son of man' outside the gospels, sees him, though admittedly standing and not sitting (Acts 7.55f.). To the second question 'Are you then the Son of God?' the reply is non-committal 'You say that I am', but is nevertheless held to be conclusive (22.70f.). The mockery is not by members of the Sanhedrin and their servants, but on the previous night by the Jewish guards, and it takes the form of horseplay; Jesus is blindfolded and is asked to guess who struck him (22.63–65). Again, it is possible to connect this with a dominant theme in the early part of Acts, that in the death of Jesus the

Jewish authorities were guilty of an act of injustice without basis in law, for which the resurrection offers a chance of repentance and forgiveness (Acts 2.22–37; 3.13–26; 5.30f.).

By contrast, the Roman side, so perfunctory in Mark, is in Luke, extended and formal. Without explanation the whole Sanhedrin uses what has happened at its own examination to bring before Pilate not unspecified charges but an accusation in threefold form – of perverting the nation, of forbidding the payment of tribute to Caesar, and of claiming to be an anointed king, and it is from the last of these that the question 'Are you the king of the Jews?', unprepared for in Mark, is now made to arise (23.1–3). There is some evidence for a threefold accusation as customary in Roman law, and it appears twice in Acts, once in the charge brought by an advocate against Paul in the presence of Felix that he was a mover of insurrection, a ringleader of the Nazarenes and a profaner of the temple (Acts 24.5f.), and again by implication when Paul in his defence before Festus replies as if to a threefold charge that he had offended neither against the law of the Jews, nor against the temple, nor against Caesar (Acts 25.8). Here the charges are all political and inflammatory. That Luke intended them as malicious follows from his having already included from Mark the question asked about the tribute money, to which the reply 'Render to Caesar what is Caesar's and to God what is God's' could only with perversity be interpreted as forbidding the payment of tribute (Luke 20.19–26; cf. Mark 12.13–17). After the non-committal reply, as in Mark, to Pilate's question and his first protestation of Jesus' innocence, the charge is renewed that Jesus is stirring up the people over the whole of Palestine by his teaching, beginning from Galilee and reaching to Jerusalem, whereupon Pilate, hearing that he is from Galilee, sends him to Herod Antipas, the tetrarch of Galilee and Peraea (23.4–7).

There then follows a comparatively lengthy, well-written but detachable narrative of an examination by Herod, in which Jesus remains silent, and which has no result except that Jesus is returned to Pilate dressed in royal robes (23.8–12). This is a curious incident, and there has been much debate about its probability.[10] Since Roman law required that a man should be tried in the place where the crime was committed and not the place of domicile there was no necessity for Pilate to send Jesus to Herod because he was a Galilean. It may have been that the Herods, who, as permitted their rule by the Romans, were pro-Roman even if often at odds with them, could be called in as assessors, as seems to have been the case with Herod Agrippa II, when at his own request he hears Paul's defence when staying with the prefect Festus (Acts 25–26). Here the object would seem to be to bring further testimony to Jesus' innocence from the angle of a coalition of the Romans and pro-Roman Judaism, and the two rulers are said to have become reconciled to each other over this issue. Pilate then summons the chief priests and rulers, and very oddly also 'the people', and twice more affirms Jesus' innocence, but he is overborne by their clamour, and delivers Jesus 'to their will' – a curiously forced way of saying that the Roman punishment of crucifixion is ultimately the responsibility of the Jews (23.13–25). It is difficult not to see here a preparation for the theme of *apologia* or defence in law which emerges in Acts and mounts to a crescendo over the figure of Paul. Wherever there is a disturbance in connection with the Christian movement, including disturbances with a supposed political flavour, it turns out to be the fault of the Jews, while the Romans say consistently that there is no case to answer. The Christian movement is not subversive; if it appears to be so, that is because of unfounded Jewish antagonism. This was an issue of primary importance to Luke, especially if his two volume work was not, like the work of the other evangelists, written in the first instance for internal consumption in the church but for the general public of the Graeco-Roman world.

From here on the story, as a result of additional material and of Luke's editorial work, continues to show significant differences. Jesus is not alone. Previously in Luke there has not been any prophecy of desertion by the disciples, and in the conversation Luke has supplied at the Last Supper they are assured of their future position by virtue of having remained with Jesus in his trials, and Peter's denial is as it were nullified in advance by the assurance that he is preserved from Satan's attack by the intercession of Jesus, and by the command once he recovers himself to strengthen his brethren (22.28–34). In Gethsemane, Jesus' separation from the disciples is less accentuated; he is strengthened by angelic succour (if this is in the text); he overrules their mistaken use of violence by healing the ear of the high priest's servant; and no mention is made of any flight on their part (22.39–53). So now, there is no mockery by Roman soldiers, and people move out to Jesus and he to them. On the way to crucifixion women mourn for him and are told to mourn rather for their children in view of worse things to come (23.28–31). He is followed by a large crowd, and while, as in Mark, the rulers deride his impotence, 'the people' only watch, and, having watched to the end, the whole assembled multitudes return beating their breasts (23.27, 35, 48). Only one of the fellow condemned derides; the other turns to Jesus for help and is promised immediate paradise with him (23.39–43). This introduces a motif common in later martyrdoms, that of the outsider who is moved by the martyr's patient demeanour, identifies with him by a confession of faith, and is himself drawn into the martyr's fate. Jesus moves towards the agents of crucifixion with the prayer 'Father, forgive them for they know not what they do' (if this is in the text), and moves with serenity towards God with 'Father, into thy hands I commend my spirit', and these two utterances provide a model in the death of the first martyr Stephen (23.34, 46; cf. Acts 7.59–60). This martyr motif reaches its climax when the centurion, observing not, as in Mark, the dereliction of Jesus and his great cry, but 'what had taken place', says not, as in Mark, 'Truly this man was a son of God', but 'Indeed this man was righteous (innocent)'.[11]

Thus the dominant note, which in Mark is mystery and realism, is in Luke pathos and humanity. And this continues on into the Lukan resurrection narratives, which are those of the appearance of a man amongst men, who travels and talks with them, and is reunited with them. As compared with Mark the use of Old Testament language is reduced in Luke. There is no prophecy from Zechariah of desertion, no scriptural words from the psalms in Gethsemane, no Isaianic 'blows' at the mocking. On the other hand the sense that the passion fulfils scripture is nowhere stronger than in Luke, not, however, in the course of the narrative itself, but from the lips of the risen Lord who explains it all. Twice, once on the Emmaus road and once to the assembled eleven, he is said to expound the whole of the Old Testament with reference to himself, and thereby to demonstrate how proper it was for the Messiah to enter into his glory by way of suffering (24.25–27, 32, 44–47). That is, the passion has been absorbed into the nature of things, and scripture shows its naturalness.

Further, Luke does not take over from Mark the episode of the request of the two disciples for places in the kingdom, with its reference to the cup, the baptism and the death of the Son of man as a ransom for many, substituting for it in the conversation at the Last Supper a briefer version in which the necessary humility of the disciple is grounded in the imitation of Jesus who is among them as the waiter at table (22.24–30; cf. Mark. 10.35–45). In the Last Supper itself – if the shorter text is to be taken as the original in Luke[12] – there is a cup for distribution followed by the broken bread, but no cup with covenantal and sacrificial words attached. Here, perhaps, we have that breaking of bread by which the risen Lord is recognized and known by the two disciples on the Emmaus road, and which the early church carries out in the early chapters of Acts (22.14–20; 24.35; Acts 2.42). Neither in this gospel nor in Acts is the death of Christ given sacrificial or atoning value. Finally in this respect, when Luke took over from Mark the first announcement of the passion and the consequent definition of discipleship as taking up the cross and following, he added to this definition the two words in Greek *kath' hemeran* (English 'daily'; 9.23). This became for Christian thought and piety perhaps the single most significant and influential editorial addition in the New Testament. For it took what in Mark still had the realism and horror of the gallows about it and made it domestic to the life of the Christian.

Here, then, are two different versions of the same event. In each of these versions the history in the event now includes history that has sprung from it, including the historical situation of the evangelist and of those to and for whom he writes. Mark's version is predominantly kerygmatic, and proclaims an isolated event done by God on a gallows in the midst of total incomprehension and as the sole basis of anything that may follow from it. Luke's version is predominantly didactic, with the cross, in Augustine's words, as 'the chair of the Master teaching', or a pulpit from which Jesus preaches his last sermon in terms of his previous teaching in Luke, 'Love your enemies, do good to them that hate you, bless them that persecute you, and pray for those who despitefully use you' (6.27f.). In Mark Jesus is the patient, though God is mysteriously active in his passivity; in Luke he remains the agent and his previous activity continues unbroken. In Mark the passion is something awesome and paradoxical, and bids men keep their distance in the presence of a sacrificial obedience to which they make no contribution. In Luke it has become in a Christian sense natural, and invites men to draw near, to embrace it as the love of God for sinners, and to imitate it. In Mark there is a discontinuity between the action of God and the actions of men, in Luke there is some continuity.

These two versions are not to be had simultaneously or mixed together, if it be the case that the historically conscious mind does not find conviction in a harmonized picture. Each has to be allowed to speak sufficiently for itself and in its own terms. It is, for example, presumably essential to what Mark thought he was presenting that Jesus should die in isolation with a cry of dereliction on his lips, and presumably it was also essential to what Luke thought he was presenting that he did not. Since, however, these versions are themselves evidence that interpretation of the event was an ongoing process, each may be seen to be valid and may be taken one after the other, even if they are not to be taken simultaneously. But then the question will be which is to be taken first and which second. In deciding that question a person might well declare his hand, and how he reads a great many other things besides.

4

The Passion of John

We do not live in a theological age like our forefathers who bequeathed to us our confessions of faith and our liturgies. As a result of a gradual secularizing of life and thought, and of a certain necessary dismantling of parts of the Christian edifice of the past, there is little theological language left in common and familiar to the ordinary person through which statements of scripture can be readily incorporated into a meaningful system of doctrine. The task of exegesis then becomes particularly difficult when the situation is such an open one, and when there are so few fixed points of reference for the translator and the interpreter. A notable feature in these circumstances has been not only the crop of new translations of the Bible – which can, indeed, accentuate the difficulties by revealing how much further removed than we imagined are the thought and language of the Bible from our own – but also the number of attempts to render the Bible narratives, especially the gospel narratives, in the form of drama, and one portion of the gospel narratives in the form of passion plays.

This is surely not to be regretted as though it trivialized the subject matter. The fact that the results are often mediocre argues no more than the mediocrity of most sermons. The sixteenth-century Protestant reformers in their anxiety to sweep away all vestiges of superstition perhaps went too far, and in opting for a sole diet of the word and preaching starved the soul, which hungers for elements of mimesis in its worship. Goethe, who hesitated over the proper translation of the opening words of John's gospel and finally came down on 'In the beginning was the act', affirmed that 'the highest cannot be spoken but can only be acted'. Hamlet's 'The play's the thing' can be given a serious connotation. In transforming a story into a play the dramatist is at least compelled to declare his understanding of its coherence and inner meaning, and in the process it may be discovered how far the story stands up and has authenticity.

There is, however, no need to transform the Johannine passion narrative into a drama. It is as it stands the archetypal passion play, and says a great deal of what it intends by being such. It achieves, possibly by accident rather than design, more of those unities traditionally required of the drama. Thus, there is a unity of time, with the long discourse of chapters 13–17, the examination and crucifixion taking place in a single day before the Passover. There is a greater unity of place, with so much of the action concentrated at the praetorium, the governor's residence. There the story has a *mis-en-scène*, as on a stage, with those who have brought Jesus forced to remain outside through scruples about incurring uncleanness for the coming Passover, and Jesus inside except when he is twice dramatically brought out for exhibition, Pilate acting as a kind of go-between. There is also, and this certainly by design rather than accident, a unity of theme. The motif of kingship, which makes a somewhat fleeting appearance in the synoptics in the abrupt question of Pilate and in the subsequent title on the cross, now becomes the dominant. There is also liberal use of dramatic irony, that theatrical device whereby an actor on the stage speaks better than he knows, or the opposite of what he intends, or unwittingly utters a truth which can only be recognized by the audience which is in greater possession of the facts.[1] The air is heavy with *double entendre*, and in John's passion story all the actors except Jesus move and speak as if in a dream.

Whether this evangelist had to hand an independent passion narrative remains a matter of debate. On the one hand it has been maintained, and is still maintained by some, that he is primarily indebted to Mark (and to some extent to Luke), and that the differences from these are largely to be put down to his own theological concerns.[2] On the other hand it has been powerfully argued that he possessed a passion narrative distinct from and independent of Mark's or Luke's. R. Bultmann sees the chief evidence for this as linguistic, claiming that a style can be detected throughout it that is significantly different from that of the evangelist himself.[3] C. H. Dodd's investigations are on a broader basis and more detailed.[4] He denies that all the differences from the synoptic accounts can be attributed to Johannine theology, and contends for a source both here and elsewhere in the gospel which reflects the interests of southern Palestine, and which could be in some respects superior to, and historically more trustworthy than, the synoptic sources. Even if this were to be the case, however, it has to be noted that it contributes comparatively little towards an understanding of the origins and formation of this gospel's picture of Jesus as a whole, or of how dialogues such as those with Nicodemus, the Samaritan Woman, with the disciples in chapters 13–16, or in the passion narrative with Pilate, came into being in their present form. For we do not have here one more variant form of the type of tradition that is visible in the synoptics. Rather there is here in the sphere of the New Testament something of a parallel to the question in classical studies of the relation of the original Socrates to the presentation of him in the Platonic dialogues. We are dealing here with an author who, with a comparatively poor command of the Greek language and with the most limited vocabulary of any New Testament writer, composed under the pressure of his subject matter what by any criterion is one of the most remarkable books ever written, whose language has a haunting quality and profundity the commentator seldom feels that he has plumbed.

In the Johannine passion narrative the structural balance is radically different from that in Mark or even in Luke. The Jewish side of the matter has almost vanished. This is related to the difference in pattern of the gospel as a whole. There is not here a ministry of deed and word in Galilee, with a transition, brief or protracted, to the passion in the form of a single doom-laden journey to Jerusalem. The public ministry covered by the first twelve chapters takes place in Judaea and Jerusalem itself with visits to Galilee. It is associated at times with Jewish feasts in Jerusalem – with the Passover (ch. 2), an unnamed feast (ch. 5), the Feast of Tabernacles (ch. 7) and the Feast of Dedication (ch. 10). The issues expounded or debated in it are religious issues, and they are expounded and debated in terms of the Jewish religion, though also – and this gives this gospel its special and often baffling character – in terms that suggest or evoke a wider religious background.

One incident belonging in the synoptics to the passion narrative, together with a version of the words about destruction and building of the temple, appears at the beginning of this ministry to mark at the outset the new order of existence Jesus brings into being (2.13–22). This public ministry in Jerusalem, though on occasion it can engender faith, for the most part meets with hostility and opposition, and it is characterized at its close as a ministry of rejection by quotations from Isaiah to this effect (12.37–43). In this way it comes about that this gospel is in some respects the most anti-Jewish book in the New Testament. While there is some measure of differentiation in the audiences, and reference is made to Pharisees and crowds, the interlocutors are generally designated 'the Jews'. This ethnic term is very rare in the synoptists, being almost confined to the title 'the king of the Jews'; in John's gospel it is used some sixty times. It is an extraordinarily generalizing and aloof expression; it lumps all together without discrimination as members of a people which is 'over there'. This anti-Judaism is not, however, anti-semitism, for what is said of 'the Jews' is also said of 'the world', a term denoting mankind. As it is said of the world that it does not recognize the Logos, that it does not come to the light, that it will seek Jesus without being able to find him, that it hates him and the disciples, so it is said of the Jews that they do not receive the Logos, that they are blind to the light of the world, that they will seek Jesus without being able to find him, that they desire to kill Jesus and will persecute the disciples. In 8.23 it is said to 'the Jews' that they are 'of the world'. The Jews in this gospel are also the world and represent it, and this is evidence of the evangelist's dramatic cast of mind. For 'the Jews', and to some extent, individuals in the dialogues such as Nicodemus and the Samaritan Woman, are not so much distinct personalities as *dramatis personae* who voice what Jesus is to correct or contradict.

The transition from this Jerusalem-centred ministry to the passion in the same place, and so from the Jewish side to the Roman, is effected quite otherwise than in the synoptists, and not without awkwardness and artificiality. It is done by means of the raising of Lazarus, an event unmentioned by them. In this gospel this is a climactic event in more senses than one. It is the last of the *semeia* (signs), which is John's word for what in the other gospels are called *dunameis* (works of power), and which places the emphasis on their significance rather than on the exhibition of power in them. It is the supreme *semeion* in being the revivification of a man four days dead – that is, already corrupting as well as dead – and its significance seems to be that the final and ultimate existence, the resurrection life, is resident in Jesus himself. It is, however, the report of this event that prompts the authorities to action. A Sanhedrin, oddly described as being composed of chief priests and Pharisees, formally devotes Jesus to death, and as he goes into hiding, orders are given for anyone knowing his where-abouts to give information so that he can be arrested (11.47–57). Further, Lazarus continues to influence the course of events. For it is noted in the story that follows, the anointing at Bethany, that the attendant crowd of Jews had come to see not only Jesus but Lazarus also, and a colophon is then added that the authorities had determined to put Lazarus to death as well (12.9–11). In the following episode also, the triumphal entry, not only is there a separate crowd described as 'that which had been with Jesus when he raised Lazarus from the dead', which gives its testimony to the kingship of Jesus, but the acclamation of the whole pilgrim crowd is said retrospectively to have arisen from their having heard about this *semeion* (12.17f.).

It is nevertheless difficult to see why the authorities should draw the conclusions they do from the report of this event, namely that since Jesus does so many signs all will come to believe on him if he is left alone, and 'then the Romans will come and remove (blot out) our place (the temple, or possibly Jerusalem, possibly even the priestly position) and our nation' (11.47.). In this way the narrative achieves a kind of transition from Jews to Romans, but it is forced, and its logic is not evident. It may be suggested that the dominant factor in this arrangement is the evangelist's dramatic concern to bring into immediate jux-taposition life and death, the judgment to death of the one who, as himself the resurrection, brings life from the dead. Certainly at this point John produces a piece of dramatic irony so heavy that he adds a note to explain it. In the Sanhedrin Caiaphas, described as the high priest 'of that year', argues that 'It is expedient (for you) that one (man) dies (on behalf of the people) so that the whole nation does not perish' (11.49f.). This is a maxim of poli-tical expediency to which there are parallels elsewhere,[5] but John adds that since Caiaphas was high priest of that year – which, since the high-priesthood was not an annual office, probably carries the meaning of 'that fateful year of judgment and sal-vation' – he did not say this of his own accord, but, reproducing the ideal conditions when a high priest would also be a prophet of

God, prophesied by divine inspiration (11.51f.). In doing so he unwittingly uttered what was to become the Christian soteriological truth that the death of Jesus was on behalf of the Jewish people, and the means of gathering into a unity the scattered children of God, meaning perhaps the Jews of the dispersion, but more probably both them and the Gentiles who should become Christian believers.

This formal condemnation of Jesus without trial is followed by three episodes – the anointing at Bethany, the triumphal entry, and the approach of certain Greeks (12.1–36). The first two have synoptic parallels, but in the reverse order. In the first the unnamed woman of the synoptic versions is identified with Mary, the sister of Lazarus, the objection to the wastefulness of the act is made by Judas, who is said to be a thief among the band of disciples, and the interpretation of the act by Jesus in relation to his burial is advanced into the story and is thus underlined (12.1–8; cf. Mark 14.3–9/ Matt. 26.6–13). The second episode, the triumphal entry, cannot have the same force as in the synoptics, since the arrival in Jerusalem is no longer the terminus of a journey from Galilee, the scene of the ministry. Jesus arrives from Ephraim, an unidentified place where he had taken refuge from Jerusalem and the authorities there (11.54–57; 12.19). The third episode, the approach of the Greeks, has no parallel in the synoptics, though it includes an equivalent in the Johannine manner of the troubling of soul and conflict of will in the synoptic story of Gethsemane (12.27). The request to see Jesus is not met with any direct response, but with the announcement that the hour of the Son of man's glorification has arrived, that a seed must die before it can bear fruit, and that if he is 'lifted up' – a cryptic reference to his death and the manner of it – his attraction will become universal (12.23f., 32f.). It may be suggested that the particular distribution of these episodes at this point and the way they are narrated proceed from the mind of the evangelist, and that before the saving events themselves he intends to express in symbolic terms through other events their inner meaning – Jesus dies, he is buried, he is exalted, and the fruit of it is the conversion of the Gentile world.[6]

These events, which in the synoptics belong within or on the border of the passion narrative, belong in John still within the public ministry of rejection, which closes at the end of chapter 12, and divides the gospel into two parts. The second part begins *in*

mediis rebus with a meal in progress, and is provided with a
solemn introduction which, while containing a chronological
element, is almost entirely theological. 'Now before the feast of
the Passover, when Jesus knew that his hour had come to depart
out of this world to the Father, having loved his own that were in
the world, he loved them to the end. And during supper, when
the devil had already put into the heart of Judas Iscariot, Simon's
son, to betray him, Jesus, knowing that the Father had given all
things into his hands, and that he had come from God and was
going to God, rose from supper . . .' (13.1–4). As chapters 2–12
have been an exposition of the statement in the prologue 'He
came to what was his own, and those who were his own did not
receive him' (1.11), so chapters 13–17 stand under the next statement there, 'But to as many as received him he gave the power to
become sons of God' (1.12f.), with this alteration that 'those who
were his own' no longer refers to Israel which has rejected, but to
the disciples who have accepted.

All that is to follow, the instruction of the disciples throughout
chapters 13–16, the Lord's prayer in chapter 17, as well as the
passion itself, proceed from the knowledge of Jesus of what is to
happen and of its significance. Out of this knowledge he washes
the disciples' feet, giving them effective cleansing and a paradigm of humility, and predicts, though not without disturbance
of spirit, the action of Judas. More, he sets this action in motion
with the gift of the sop and the command to act quickly. 'So, after
receiving the morsel, he immediately went out; and it was night'
(13.1–30). This is surely not intended as information about the
time of day. It is a moment of *frisson*, and the audience is to
shudder when Judas steps out of the circle of light, which at this
moment is concentrated on Jesus and his own, into the world and
its darkness. At this point Jesus speaks proleptically in the past
tense, 'Now has the Son of man been glorified, and God has been
glorified in him' (13.31f.). This proleptic tense governs the subsequent instruction of the disciples. In form there is nothing like
these chapters elsewhere. In subject matter there are parallels to
some of the themes present in the apocalyptic chapter 13 of Mark
and kindred synoptic material[7] but the language is transmuted,
and the coming eschatological events are spoken of as if from the
other side of an assured achievement and consummation. The
knowledge of God and the possession of the truth, the coming of
the Paraclete and preservation from the world, peace and love,

prayer and joy, are wrapped up in, and are the fruit of this achievement. This comes to a climax in the prayer of chapter 17, which is without parallel in the New Testament either in form or content, and which is hardly prayer at all in the ordinary sense of the term. Intercession for the disciples, for their preservation, their sanctification in the truth and their fruitfulness is included in, and based upon, the account which Jesus renders to the Father of an already completed mission. 'I have glorified thee on the earth, having accomplished the work thou gavest me to do . . . now I am coming to thee' (17.4,13). This prayer is 'a summary of the Johannine discourses, and in this respect is a counterpart to the prologue'.[8] Here the evangelist might have put down his pen, and in a sense a passion narrative is unnecessary to this gospel. However, he did not do so. He was writing a gospel, and the tradition required that he continue, as perhaps did also a conviction that meaning must cohere with event.

His passion narrative is, from its opening and throughout, a Roman affair, and it is Jesus who is in control of it. In the garden to which Jesus and his disciples repair (it is not named, nor is there any trial of the will there) he is arrested by a *speira* accompanied by Judas and servants from the high priests and Pharisees. This is a term for Roman soldiers, meaning either a cohort, which when up to strength numbered a thousand men, or a maniple of two hundred at full strength. Since their commander is called a *chiliarchus*, a leader of a thousand, it is probably the former. When in reply to Jesus' questioning they assert that they are looking for Jesus the Nazarean he says 'I am' – words which can simply be those of identification ('I am he'), but in the Bible can also be the language and title of God himself. At this the whole cohort retreats and falls to the ground as if at a theophany. To break this impasse and to get things moving again Jesus now has to do their work for them and to bring about his own arrest. Repeating his question he now speaks more plainly the language of identification, 'I have told you that I am (he)'. But in doing this he first lays down his own terms, and stipulates that the disciples are allowed to go free so as to correspond with the account he has previously rendered to his Father in prayer, 'Of those you gave me I have not lost one, save the son of perdition' (18.1–9; cf. 17.12). This is all highly dramatic, but historically quite improbable.

Jesus is then taken not directly to the high priest Caiaphas but to his father-in-law Annas (there may be some confusion here) and there the scene is as perfunctory as is the examination before Pilate in Mark. Asked about his teaching and his disciples he replies that he has always taught publicly and not in secret, and the information could be obtained from those who had heard it and knew. For this he is struck by a servant for insolence, but protests that it is a matter of truth or error. He is then taken to Caiaphas, but nothing happens there (Caiaphas has already had his say, 11.45–53), and he is taken from Caiaphas to the praetorium, where the remainder of the action takes place (18.12–14, 19–24, 28).

Pilate comes outside because the Jews through religious scruple cannot come in, and he asks the charge. This is not vague, as in Mark, nor explicit as in Luke, but evasive. 'If he were not an offender we would not have brought him'. On the basis of this reply Pilate hands the matter back to the Jews with the instruction to take Jesus and judge him by their own law (18.28–32). Here is the first crisis. This is a historical impossibility because, as the governor has surprisingly and somewhat laboriously to be reminded, the Jews do not possess the power of capital punishment, and it is assumed that Jesus must be put to death. It is also for the evangelist a theological impossibility, for Jesus must die in the manner he had foretold and for the reason he had foretold it – that is, by the Roman method of hoisting up vertically on a cross (to lift up), which could be a symbol of the exaltation to God that was its inner meaning, whereas to be knocked down flat by the Jewish method of stoning could not symbolize anything, at least anything to do with Jesus.

Pilate therefore goes back inside, and there is the first of the dialogues between him and Jesus composed around elements in the tradition. As abruptly as in Mark, Pilate asks the question, 'Are you the king of the Jews?' In reply Jesus himself asks whether the question is really his own or has been put into his mouth by the Jews. Pilate rejoins contemptuously, 'Am I a Jew?'. On this basis Jesus is prepared to discuss the matter in terms that are very common in the synoptic tradition in the form of 'the kingdom (kingship) of God' (though very rarely the kingdom of Christ), but that have appeared only once before in this gospel in the discourse with Nicodemus (3.3, 5). What is then said is mistranslated 'my kingdom is not of this world' and consequently misunderstood as having an entirely other-worldly sense. The evangelist here uses the preposition *'ek'*, which for him was one of the most important words in the language. It means 'out of' or 'from'. It is the preposition of origin, and throughout this gospel what a thing is is determined by its origin. Thus what is said is that the kingship of Jesus is in the world but does not derive its origin from the world and the world's possibilities. Otherwise it would have put up resistance in the manner of the world. 'But now is my kingdom not from there.' Pilate then repeats his question now shorn of particularism, 'You are then a king?' The reply begins from the tradition with 'You say that I am', but it continues with a deliberate contrast between 'you' and 'I' in the Johannine manner. 'I have had my origin (i.e. from God) for this purpose, and I have come into the world (i.e. from above) for this purpose, to bear witness to the truth'. The kingship of Jesus is the sovereignty of the truth. All that has been spoken of divine truth in the body of the gospel is effective in the world through the coming of Jesus into it. 'Everyone who is from (*ek*) the truth hears my voice.' Will Pilate then listen to Jesus, and so show that he is himself from the truth? That does not yet appear, for he is now given one of the best lines in the play, 'What is truth?' Without waiting for an answer to what was perhaps only intended as a rhetorical question he goes out by himself (apparently, for the stage directions are not always provided), and declares Jesus innocent. Reminding the audience of the custom of releasing a passover prisoner he suggests the release of Jesus, but the Jews reply, 'Not this man, but Barabbas'. In this way the first act is rounded off by advancing from after the sentence of judgment in Mark to before it a piece of the tradition in attenuated form (18.33–40; cf. Mark 15.6–15).

There follows the theme of scourging. In Roman law this could be administered either in lighter form as a warning preliminary to release (as referred to in Luke 23.22), or in heavier form after sentence and as the first stage of the punishment. Here it is neither and is misplaced, but perhaps deliberately in order to make the element of mockery central. The Roman soldiers dress Jesus in the purple worn by emperors in their triumphs, pay him mock homage as king of the Jews, and buffet him, perhaps in ritual game. Further, they plait a diadem of acanthus and put it on his head. This has probably been misrepresented in Christian art, and is really the halo-type crown of the radiant sun as depicted on the coins of hellenistic rulers.[9] That is, the scene is not one of torture; it is a charade. Pilate now goes out again, but takes Jesus with him in this guise, and makes a declaration which could be the height of irony. For its meaning could stretch between 'Look at the fellow!' to 'Behold, the man!', and 'the man' could in Christian vocabulary be an equivalent for 'the Son of man', the heavenly man who judges in God's name, to whom the judicial representative of the empire thus bears his unconscious witness (19.1–5).

The response of the Jews to this exhibition is a demand for crucifixion, which Pilate sarcastically grants in a form incapable of realization, 'Take him, and crucify him yourselves'. This impasse compels the Jews to show their hand. By their law Jesus deserves to die in making himself a son of God. This strikes terror into Pilate, either because of a pagan superstitious fear of encountering divine men unawares, or because 'Son of God' had become since Augustus a title of the deified emperor, or both. Returning inside he asks Jesus his origin, 'Whence are you?'. Here, once more, is the question of origins which is so important for the evangelist, especially in relation to Jesus, who in this gospel is the one who knows the whence and the whither of himself and of men. When, therefore, Jesus refuses any reply to this question, it is presumably because there is no language for answering it which would be intelligible to the pagan who has contemptuously denied that he is a Jew. There is, however, something that can be said that is intelligible in terms of the office he holds. When in face of a refusal to answer Pilate threatens that he has the authority of life or death, Jesus replies that the fact that Pilate is now standing in this position of authority over himself has its origin from above (it is permitted by the will of God), whereas the moral responsibility for this situation lies with those who have handed Jesus over to him. Pilate understands this quasi-religious issue to the extent that from this point on he endeavours to release Jesus. The question is whether he will be able to stand to his resolve (19.6–12).

Pilate now comes out again and expresses his conviction of Jesus' innocence, and the Jews then play their last card. To do so, they themselves move from the religious sphere to the secular, and for this purpose take up a pro-Roman stance. 'If you let this man go you are not Caesar's friend' [there is some evidence for 'Caesar's friend' as a technical expression for an inner circle of imperial advisers and for an imperial representative]. Everyone who makes himself a king [*basileus* = political pretender] sets himself up in opposition to Caesar.' The roles are now reversed. In place of the Roman governor offering the Jewish people the choice, 'Which will you have, Jesus or Barabbas?', the Jewish people offer the Roman governor the choice, 'Which will you have, Christ or Caesar?' This was to be the choice which faced Christians, perhaps already in the evangelist's own day. That is enough. Pilate brings Jesus out for the second time, presumably still dressed up. Place and time are carefully noted. The place is Lithostroton (in Hebrew Gabbatha), a paved area; the time is noon on the Preparation, the day before Passover. Pilate sits on the *Bema*, the official judgment seat (or, to complete the charade, sits Jesus on the judgment seat – the Greek could mean either), and says, 'Behold your king!' When they cry, 'Away, away, crucify him', and he asks 'Shall I crucify your king?', they reply, 'We have no king but Caesar.' Here the high point of the drama is reached, and some measure of theological thought and language is necessary to perceive it. The only claim to distinction of Israel, a geographically, economically and politically insignificant people on the outskirts of the empire, has been its divine election, and its *raison d'être* lay in its vocation to testify to the world in season and out of season that 'the Most High is sovereign over the kingdoms of men' (Dan. 4.32). When, therefore, over the issue of Jesus the Jews turn their backs on this vocation and speak like good pagan inhabitants of the empire, Israel commits spiritual suicide. At that point Pilate hands them Jesus for crucifixion (19.12–16).

To this he adds a codicil. Oddly he himself writes the *titulus* for the cross, 'Jesus of Nazareth, the king of the Jews', and does so in the two universal languages, Latin and Greek, adding in the circumstances Hebrew. To the request that it should rather read that he said he was the king of the Jews he replies, 'What I have written, I have written', and thus, in words sounding like official witness to a document, he unconsciously and too late testifies to the real status of the condemned (19.17–22).

At the crucifixion itself there is no mockery by anyone, no darkness, no rending of the temple veil. Jesus carries his own cross unaided, and his tunic is unrent. In a manner that *mutatis mutandis* stands nearer to Plato's Phaedo than to Mark's gospel Jesus makes his testamentary disposition from the cross by commending his mother and the beloved disciple to each other, utters the words 'I thirst' not because he needs drink but for the ful-

filment of scripture, and dies with the words 'It is accomplished',
recalling the prayer to the Father, 'I have accomplished the work
you gave me to do' (17.4). His legs remain unbroken, perhaps to
indicate that he is the veritable paschal lamb (Ex. 12.46), and out
of his body, when pierced, flow blood and water, the symbolism
of which is not evident. Thus, what in Mark is mystery and
realism, and in Luke is pathos and humanity, in John is majesty
and irony. And this continues on into his resurrection narratives:
the risen Lord makes himself known by calling Mary by name
and the sheep hears his voice; he imparts the Spirit by his breath
in imitation of God's creation of Adam, and is acclaimed by
Thomas with the highest christological title, 'My Lord and my
God', which echoes not only the opening words of this gospel,
'the Word was God', but also the title by which the emperor
Domitian had himself called, Dominus et Deus noster.[10]

In all this the evangelist paid a heavy price, the kind of price
any dramatist has to pay. It is hardly surprising that this gospel
early met with bitter opposition from those who must have
judged that, despite appearances to the contrary, it had come
down on the side of the Gnostics, who in their turn were wont to
complain of simple believers that they mistook the images of
reality for reality itself. One may legitimately ask with respect to
this gospel as a whole whether its Christ ever really has his feet
firmly on the earth, and of its passion narrative in particular how
the one who has already proclaimed himself to be the resurrection can be said to die in the ordinary sense of the word. The
evangelist undoubtedly walked a tight rope, and as he viewed
things in Christ was, apparently, compelled to do so. The matter
is delicate to assess and difficult to state, and the language for
stating it is not always adequate. Thus, at a crucial point in the
story crucifixion is said to be necessary rather than stoning for
Jesus' words ('I, if I be lifted up from the earth will draw all men to
me') to be fulfilled, words by which he 'signified', or 'indicated by
a sign' or 'symbolized' the manner of his death (18.32; cf. 12.32f.).
That is, 'lift up', which denotes elevation in space, and which
previously in the Christian vocabulary had been used for the
action of God in raising Jesus out of death and exalting him to
heaven (e.g. Acts 2.33, 5.31; Phil. 2.9), is now pressed back to
express the inner meaning of the cross as being itself this exaltation, which resurrection now comes not to reverse but to seal. It
is, however, essential for this theology that the physical elevation

shall have taken place, and it is this that words such as 'sign' or 'symbol' as they are generally used may fail to retain.

This use of the verb *sēmainein* ('to signify') as a hinge in the passion narrative directs attention back to the equivalent noun *sēmeion* ('sign'), which is John's word for the public ministry of Jesus as significant activity, and in this way passion and public ministry are in a sense more closely bound together than in the other gospels. The healing of a paralysed man points to the work of Jesus as sabbath work done along with God (5.2–29); the feeding of a multitude to the availability in Jesus of heavenly food (6.1–51); the cure of the blind man to the presence of the light of the world (9.1–34); the raising of Lazarus to the actualization of the life of the world to come (11.1–44). Again, words such as 'sign' or 'symbol' are adequate only if they do not dispense with, or dissolve away, the physical basis of the acts, which John seems to go out of his way to underline when he remarks that the lame man had been impotent for thirty-eight years, that the blind man had been blind from birth, and that Lazarus after four days in the tomb was already stinking. There is, it would seem, for this evangelist an ambiguous, teasing quality about the facts of human existence which is the jumping off ground for the grasp of spiritual truth. For in this gospel, called since Clement of Alexandria the 'spiritual' gospel, 'spirit' and 'spiritual' do not refer to what is without qualification good because it escapes from, or dissolves, the solid flesh. The flesh is human existence in its limitations, and what is born of, or has its origin in, the flesh is itself flesh (3.6). When its attentions are fixed upon itself, and its end is thought to be in itself, it is rendered sinful and dead. So the contrast is not between flesh and spirit, but rather between dead flesh and living flesh. For the Word has become flesh, and his flesh is living flesh since it is life lived in unbroken relation to the Father, who is both source and goal, the whence and the whither, and 'spirit' is the name for this relation. 'The words that I speak are spirit and are life' (6.64) because they continuously establish this relation. Hence in this gospel the road out of ignorance and the sinful misunderstanding of existence into knowledge and the truth is by way of faith, for faith in this gospel is largely the perception of who Jesus is, and that he is from and to God.

This ambiguous, teasing quality which inheres in the facts of human existence inheres also in the words and expressions to which they give rise. Characteristic of the dialogues of which this gospel is composed is that they so often hinge on the *double entendre*. A word or phrase used by Jesus to convey necessary spiritual truth is taken by others on the level of the flesh, as when Nicodemus understands being born 'from above' (Greek *anōthen*), which is necessary for entry into the kingdom of God, as being born 'afresh' which the Greek word can also mean. Or when the Samaritan woman takes the 'living water', of which Jesus speaks as her need, to refer to 'running water' which would save her trouble. This raises the question of the evangelist's irony. Is it a stylistic technique only, a verbal trick? Or is he driven to it by the truth with which he is wrestling?

Irony is a delicate and ambivalent instrument. It stands between satire and humour, and may be used in the service of either. That the Christian gospel is not in intention satirical is evident. What perhaps has not been sufficiently considered, except by one or two of the greatest theologians and then only fleetingly, is whether it is in its essence humorous. Again, the language available for the discussion strikes as inadequate. To say that life is in the end a joke and God the almighty joker would not answer. Nevertheless, it may be recalled that the greatest Christian poem so far written was called by its author *The Divine Comedy* (even if 'comedy' has here a somewhat different connotation), and in the view of some literary critics the development of Shakespeare's mind lay from light comedy of the *As You Like It* variety to tragedy, and then from tragedy into comedy again, but comedy of the *Tempest* and *Winter's Tale* variety, with its hints of the renewal of love by pardon and the transformation of the universe. Are there not hints of these things throughout this gospel, and may they not come to expression in Jesus' final word to his disciples, 'In the world you will have trouble. But cheer up! I have overcome the world' (16.33)?

The essence of irony may be said to be a congruous incongruity or an incongruous congruity. 'Its colourings may come from passing moods, or from a deep-seated habit of mind; its directions may obey the logic of a particular chain of events, or may originate in a vision of the universe which particular events are chosen to typify or represent'.[11] There can be no doubt which it is for this evangelist, for he has spread it consistently over the actions, words and passion of Jesus, and over these as the actions, words and passion of the one whom he believes to be responsible not only for the destiny, but also for the creation and existence, of the world. In him the incongruities of the temporal and the eternal, the fleshly and the spiritual, the sinful and the perfect, the false and the true, are congruously juxtaposed. To do this the evangelist has transmuted much of the earlier Christian thought and language. The previous tradition, as it is represented in various forms in the synoptic gospels, placed the ministry and death of Jesus in the framework of a passionate eschatology, or doctrine of the end, whereby his resurrection is seen as his deliverance from an extreme of humiliation and depotentiation, as the earnest of a coming judgment and destruction of the visible order, and of the divine consummation of all things at the hands of the Son of man coming on the clouds. This has largely, if not entirely, disappeared in the Fourth Gospel, to be replaced by a protology, a doctrine of the beginning, whereby the world's misunderstanding and misuse of its existence are exposed by the presence within it of its own author, who, as the man from heaven, holds it to its, and his own, source in the Father. Hence the use of two words concerning the passion that are peculiar to this gospel. It is spoken of in terms of a journey (*hupagein*). 'Now I go my way to him who sent me' (16.5, 10, 17; cf. 7.33; 8.14; 13.3; 14.4). This is not, however, a journey into death, which requires a violent change of direction to arrive at the goal, but is a continuation, now by way of death, of the direction that has been sustained throughout in coming from the Father and returning to him. It is also spoken of as a 'glorification'. This is the nearest that the Hebrew tradition came to ontology, since God's glory, his presence and power, is almost the equivalent of what the philosophical tradition was to call his being. When in the prologue it is said that 'the Word became flesh . . . and we beheld his glory, as of a unique one of the Father' (1.14), or at the first sign that Jesus manifested in it his glory so that his disciples believed on him (2.11), his whole fleshly existence is invested from the outset with the quality of divine manifestation. The same quality is asserted of that point in his existence where it appears least congruous, his death, as when it is said at the exit of Judas, 'Now has the Son of man been glorified' (13.31), or in the prayer, 'I have glorified you on the earth, having accomplished the work you gave me to do', and where the only glory still remaining unpossessed and to be asked for is the complete reunion with eternal existence – 'Glorify me with the glory I had with you before the world was' (17.4f.).

Hence, finally, the very plentiful but also peculiarly double-sided use in this gospel of the word *kosmos* (world). This is a philosopher's word for all that is considered as a single and coherent whole – the universe. It is absent from the Greek Old Testament before the Maccabean books and the late book *The Wisdom of Solomon*. It is a very rare word in the other gospels and in Acts. In the seventy or so instances in this gospel it is used in two opposite but connected senses. On the one hand the *kosmos* is what it is because it is the creation of the Logos, and the sending of the Logos or Son into it takes place because it is the object of the love of God (1.1–10; 3.16f.). On the other hand the *kosmos* for the most part does not recognize the Word in its midst, and rejects with murderous intent Jesus and his disciples, and has to be overcome. Since this perversion of the world from its proper nature reaches beneath the intellect to the heart and will, it requires more to overcome it than the exposure of its own mis-understanding of itself, to which the required response is faith. It requires the permanent presence to it, and the effective operation in it, of the divine love itself, which has been responsible for its existence and has established the law of its being. Goethe may have been thinking of this when he penned the words, 'Die to live. Know this, or else you are a stranger upon a dark earth.'

PART II

The Use of the New Testament

5

Hermeneutics

When a word shows signs of moving into the centre of a discipline, a question that may be asked, and perhaps ought to be
asked as soon as possible, is whether it refers to what is likely to
be a passing fashion, and if not (or even if so) whether it aims to
bring into the open something which lies concealed. The word in
mind in the sphere of biblical studies is 'hermeneutics'. This has
certainly become a modish word on the Continent and in
America in recent years, and may be on the way to becoming such
in Britain. It is a word likely to crop up in theological discussion of
all kinds, and when it does so it appears to exhibit elastic prop-
erties. What is it supposed to denote, and why has it become a
word which in some circles serves to focus the whole theological
enterprise?

The verb *hermēneuein* and its cognates have had a long history
first in Greek culture and then in theology. It would seem that
from the start they could bear one of two related senses, and that
the relation between the two senses could be significant. This
may not be unconnected with the curious career of Hermes, who
begins his mythological life as a wayside daemon, then develops
with his broad hat and magic staff into the herald of the gods, and
ends up as the tutelary deity of oratory, literature, arts and
sciences, and as the inventor of language itself. So the verb was
used by both prose and poetic writers for 'to utter', 'to proclaim',
'to state a message', and the Lycaonians dubbed Paul 'Hermes'
because it was he who did most of the talking. Since, however,
the message was often from the gods, whether in the form of
cryptic oracle or simply of poetry, what was said needed clarification for it to be understood, and the word took on the meaning
'to interpret', and in some contexts 'to translate out of one lan-

guage into another'. This ambivalence may be seen in Plato's brief dialogue the *Ion*, where he gives vent to his deep suspicion of poetry by having Socrates engage with Ion, a rhapsode or professional reciter of Homer, who also liked to give lectures on Homer. Socrates asserts that poets in their utterances are interpreters ('hermeneuts') of the gods, while rhapsodes are interpreters ('hermeneuts') of the poets to the audience; but poet, rhapsode and audience are all held together by a mysterious divine afflatus, as when a magnet holds a series of iron rings attached to one another by its transmitted magnetism. Whatever Ion himself may think, neither his reciting nor his lecturing depends on any art (*technē*), since he utters under divine possession and not with the aid of reason, and neither his reciting nor his lecturing impart any information, since he only knows what it is the poet is saying and not whether it corresponds with fact. Paul also knew of a special charismatic gift at Corinth called *hermēneia*, which consisted in the interpretation of what was spoken in tongues in distinction from the speaking in tongues itself, and he distinguished it from prophetic utterance on the grounds that the latter engaged the mind and built up the church.

Within the Christian theological tradition *hermēneia* settled down as a synonym for the exegesis of a now fixed, sacred and authoritative text. One may say 'settled down' for two reasons. Firstly, it came to be taken for granted that the text, the scriptures, added up to a single thing, with all the parts significantly interlocked to make a whole. Exegesis, whether of a historical, typological, but especially of an allegorical kind, proceeded from this conviction, and was successful in so far as it exemplified and reinforced it. If there was a distinction between exegesis and *hermēneia* it was that exegesis came to denote the actual interpretation of the text in this sense and *hermēneia* supplied the principles and rules for doing it. These rules can be seen emerging in the fourth century with the Donatist Tyconius and the monk John Cassian, to become later the four senses of scripture of the Middle Ages, to be revised in Protestantism according to the insights of the Reformation, and then to be taught there to theological students as one specialized sub-section of the biblical area of theology. Secondly, exegesis was closely related to systematic theology and was under its control. What the text had once said was assumed to be identical with, or in direct continuation with, what the doctrinal tradition within which the exegesis was being done was currently saying. There was scarcely any possibility of a gulf opening up between what the words of the text had meant to those who had written them and what they were to mean to those who were now using them.

Such a gulf only became a possibility as a result of the historical criticism of the Bible which came into being in the eighteenth century, and which has developed since then by trial and error and with ever sharpened tools to the present day. The gulf was possible both because such criticism sought to operate in freedom from the control of a doctrinal system, and also – and this was to prove far more important – because it coincided with, was itself part of, and made significant contributions to the development of, the historical method as such. As Mr A. J. P. Taylor has recently remarked, historical thinking and writing as we know them begin with the apperception that the past is really different from the present, and he judged the first English writer to possess this apperception to be Sir Walter Scott, whereas Gibbon, great as he was, did not yet possess it, so that for him the Emperor Commodus was still in the last resort an eighteenth-century gentleman with somewhat peculiar tastes.

In these circumstances a distinction became conceivable between the meaning of the text then and its meaning now. Exegesis and *hermeneia* could cease to be synonyms or to stand for practice and theory. In so far as the words were used at all, they could be divided between the twin activities of exegesis as clarification of what the writer had intended to say in his own time and situation, and hermeneutics as clarification and statement of what the text says with authority to the exegete's contemporaries. These activities could become widely separated, and there have been times when their separation has been experienced as a kind of agony, of which the present time is one.

These general considerations may be made specific by reference to that theological sounding-board the World Council of Churches. Under its auspices there appeared in 1951 a book entitled *Biblical Authority for Today*, one chapter of which, 'Guiding Principles for the Interpretation of the Bible', was the outcome of a conference of biblical scholars held at Wadham College, Oxford, two years previously.[1] It was an impressive work in harvesting much of the first-rate biblical scholarship of the preceding two decades, not a little of it associated with the great trio, C. H. Dodd, T. W. Manson and Vincent Taylor, but also with a

host of lesser figures. Part of its impressiveness lay in its confidence. This confidence was not asserted in the face of biblical
criticism but on the basis of it. Full acknowledgment was made of
the diversity and disparity of the traditions which an analytical
treatment of the Bible brought to light, but these were seen as in
the end coalescing in a more than formal unity. Old and New
Testaments were held together both historically by reference to a
line of significantly related acts of God, and conceptually by a
language expressive of the distinctively Hebrew understanding
of God and human life. The Bible was thus capable of being
expounded in its own terms and categories, and in these terms it
was directly relevant to the present or to any time. It was thus
possible to write books about 'Biblical Politics', or 'The Biblical
Doctrine of Work', or 'The Biblical Understanding of Sex'. The
problem created by the collapse of a doctrine of authority
imposed *ab extra* had been solved by an authority elicited from the
Bible itself *ab intra*. The gulf between exegesis and hermeneutics
that had opened up in the previous liberal era, with its concern
about what was kernel and what was husk, had been closed. Those
were the days in which it was good for a biblical theologian to be
alive.

Twelve years later, in 1963, at the Fourth World Conference on
Faith and Order at Montreal, all this came under heavy attack,
principally, though by no means solely, from certain pupils of
Rudolf Bultmann who had not hitherto taken part in World
Council discussions. The grounds of the attack were that the
supposed unity of the Bible which made it possible to entertain
something called biblical theology was far in excess of that with
which many biblical scholars actually operated in their work, and
that it involved a measure of harmonization which was inad-
missible. The presentation of something as *the* biblical view of
this or that, as was frequently made in World Council documents, rested upon a quasi-fundamentalist use of isolated texts.
With that humility and faith in work studies which are amongst
the most engaging characteristics of the World Council an investigation was initiated in five regional groups, two in the United
States, two on the Continent and one in Britain, which met over a
period of two years and had as their agenda not only the discussion of the subject in general but actual pieces of exegesis to be
done. The writer's membership of the British group was not only
for him a great privilege and pleasure but also one of the most

creative experiences of his life. This was the more so because the British group exhibited a wider spectrum of viewpoint than the others, though with hindsight this spectrum could with advantage have been made wider still by the inclusion both of a trained philosopher versed in the empirical tradition with its present concern about language (whether he himself belonged in that tradition or not), and of a trained literary critic who is used to living with literary texts and to asking about their meaning or whether indeed there is such a thing as *the* meaning of them.

The groups eventually pooled their findings and presented a common report in 1967 at Bristol. There could hardly be a greater contrast between this report and the book which had issued from the Wadham conference. For while it made a number of interesting and even penetrating observations it was able to offer only a single agreed statement, which was to the effect that the basis of interpretation is 'the generally accepted process of scholarly exegesis', by which was meant the methods of literary and historical analysis as they have been developed and are in use. There was no further statement in expectation that the common use of such methods would necessarily lead to a common understanding of biblical truth or of its authority or relevance. With regard to authority one commentator observed that it remained in the background as an unsolved problem. 'When we put the question: "What did the text say then, and what does it say now?", we have already assumed that the Bible is theologically relevant, and that what it says can and must be translated meaningfully. But this was exactly the assumption which was questioned by many in the English group.'[2]

Once more, then, the gulf was wide open, perhaps wider than before. What had happened that it should be so? Why the uncertainty in place of the previous certainty? Was it due to some widespread but inexplicable failure of nerve? Or to some change in the climate of opinion, with no more rationality to be given to 'climate' than to the English weather? Or to some swing of the pendulum with whose movement we ought by now to be familiar? Or was it rather that a fresh sensitivity about presuppositions betokened something deeper? Was it a sign that issues which had been there for some time had come nearer to surfacing, and that we have not yet plumbed the problems posed for theology by methods and techniques of literary and historical analysis and by the phenomenon of religious syncretism? A man trying to jump

his way out of a pit, and gathering himself for one supreme jump
and then failing, does not necessarily revert to his previous
position, but is compelled to take further stock of where he is. The
confident viewpoint of the previous decades, especially with
eighteen centuries of Christian and Jewish tradition behind it,
could encourage the conclusion that dispute about the authority
of scripture and about its unity and relevance, even if necessary
and perhaps purifying, was nevertheless short-lived, like an
attack of measles from which the patient will recover in good
time. So sudden a transition from certainty to uncertainty could,
however, pose the question at least whether such dispute may
not be on the way to becoming a permanent feature that has to be
lived with. If this were to be so it would be something new in
Christian experience.

The main issues would seem to be two. The first might be called
horizontal and the second vertical. The horizontal issue concerns
the extent to which the Bible has to be taken and read as a single
whole if it is to have anything approaching the authority and
force which have traditionally been assigned to it, and how that
extent of singleness is to be looked for, conceived and established. Undoubtedly the Bible offers in its own terms common
themes, motifs, organizations of thought and linguistic structures which go some way to bind its parts together. It could
hardly be otherwise when its documents come from those who
on any showing shared a considerable community of faith and
life. Though it must also be said that these themes and motifs are
not automatic in electing themselves as the means by which what
is central and what is peripheral may be detected, or as indicators
of how what is peripheral remains significant by some relation to
what is central. This is evident from the fact that the attempts to
write books with such titles as *The Theology of the New Testament* or
The Theology of the Old Testament – which only began to be made
again in the fifties of this century, and no one has so far had the
temerity to write *The Theology of the Bible* – inevitably involve great
difficulties, and meet with as much dissent as assent. In the
opinion of some the thing cannot be done. In the case of the Old
Testament it seems to require a prior decision on which theme –
creation, covenant, law, Israel, etc. – shall act as the co-ordinator
of the rest. In the case of the New Testament, when it is not
simply a study in depth of concepts lying side by side in the New
Testament but without much effort to relate them, it involves a

procedure by which one may legitimately make one's way from the synoptic gospels to John, to Paul, to Hebrews, to Revelation and back again. It is perhaps significant that the attempt judged most successful in the sense of being the most used and as being perceptive at so many points, that of Rudolf Bultmann, only manages to do this from the basis that Jesus does not belong to the theology of the New Testament, which is a basis many would deny him at the start.

It can hardly be denied that the so-called biblical theology of, for example, the Wadham Report seriously overplayed its hand in its endeavour to establish, admittedly with great linguistic, critical and theological acumen, an overall, organic, theological and therefore efficacious unity of Old Testament and New Testament, of prophecy and gospel, gospel and epistle, and so on; and that in talking in these terms of *the* meaning of a passage insufficient allowance was made for it to be interpreted in different ways by reference to the various levels or stages of tradition in which it could be placed. Indeed, the question could be asked whether, if the eschatology which was given such a prominent position in biblical theology was to be taken seriously, it did not, by its very capacity for directing attention to the incompleteness of all things, preclude a too great singleness or wholeness here as elsewhere. Hence it need not be simply one more surrender to the *Zeitgeist*, in this case of pluralism, but rather a deduction from the character of the biblical text itself, if we now have to be content with speaking of a plurality of theologies in Old and New Testaments and in the several books they contain. If so, would this not be something new in Christian experience? And would it not carry with it a somewhat different conception of theological truth, and of the kind of authority with which such truth asserts itself?

The second or vertical issue is that of historical and cultural relativism. This, of course, we have had to learn to live with for a long time now as it has emerged by stages as a consequence of that historical method which proceeds from a real sense of the difference between present and past, and at whose birth biblical criticism was in attendance, both contributing to and receiving from it. Again, however, it may be that it has emerged a stage further into consciousness as the result of a recent failure of a particularly vigorous effort to overcome it.

It goes without saying that for fruitful theological interpretation to take place there must be a measure of contact, of inner community, between the interpreter and the text. A considerable factor in the development of Christian theology has been the need and the attempts to state the major declarations of faith so that they speak to the age. To the extent that theology has consisted in the exegesis of scripture (Gerhard Ebeling, with somewhat typical exaggeration, has been prepared to say that it is nothing else, but one may instance the more modest claim of those whose approach to theology has given a prominent place to the study of how the fathers interpreted the Bible), this has meant the application of the biblical text to the needs of the age. Frequently, and from the earliest periods, the point of contact has been theologically secured by some doctrine of the Logos or Word of God. That is, because of its origin in the Logos, reality is always and everywhere basically the same. A more Protestant version of this might be that the Word of God, in announcing salvation and summoning to repentance and faith, addresses men whose basic needs are always essentially the same. A residual secular version might be that human nature remains basically the same. Whatever changes may have taken place, the interpreter still remains in the same continuum, shares a common framework or the same universe of discourse (however one may express it and proceed to delineate it) with those responsible for the biblical texts. One of the tasks of exegesis will then be to show that this is so, and in the process to demonstrate again the unity of scripture. This is what Origen set his hand to, and he was to be followed down the centuries by a host of others who held much the same conceptions and used much the same instruments as he. The prime exegetical problem will then be the gulf between God and man, and how the Word of God is to be discerned in the words of men. This was still the case for Karl Barth, and may account for what some would consider the failure of his theology on its exegetical side.

This is not, however, the exegetical problem as it is now widely felt, which is less the gulf between God and man than that between ancient and modern, between 'then' and 'now'. This is the gulf that has opened up, gradually, as a result of historical method and historical thinking, and more acutely as a result of inadequate attempts to close it, so that the interpreter is more conscious at many points, and those not necessarily peripheral points, of the distance which separates him from the text and of not sharing the same world with its authors. No doubt this can be over-stated, mis-stated, and all kinds of silly things can be said about it. It is a salutary reminder for cultural relativists that they are as much conditioned as anyone else. This, however, does not help anyone very much, as we still have to speak out of our conditioned existence and to make judgments as though they were important. The effects of cultural relativism can be mitigated by further knowledge, as for example by the realization that the plurality of theologies in the Bible itself reflects a cultural relativism. Thus it has been remarked that a gospel of the resurrection of Christ would have been impossible before the first century BC or AD, because previously neither the word nor the idea of resurrection existed, and the conceptions of life and death had hitherto been different. In practice its effects are commonly mitigated by the use of the Bible in liturgy, whether of the word or sacraments, where the congregation experiences some sense of continuity of discourse, and may find itself able to greet Abraham as its father; though it must be admitted that this is achieved with greater or less success so far as individual members of the congregation are concerned, and at a price that might not be able to be paid indefinitely. James Barr remarks in the course of a predominantly favourable treatment of the use of the Bible in liturgy: 'The more one hears of the exodus of Israel from Egypt as part of the liturgy for the baptism of infants in water, the less one is concerned to ask whether any Israelites ever came out of Egypt and, if they did, how they got out.'[3]

Whatever the qualifications and mitigations the gulf remains an acute one. Its acuteness is in part a boomerang from biblical theology. For it was a central tenet of that theology, on which it harped almost *ad nauseam*, that the core of the Judaeo-Christian tradition, the distinctive feature that made it what it was, consists in a revelation of God in a series of historical actions. Leaving aside the criticism which could be, and has been, made of the accuracy of this judgment itself, a concentration on the events as the medium of divine revelation could mean, and has meant, a concentration on what is relative and conditioned. That the problem is a practical one may be illustrated from two examples. The first is the commentary significantly entitled *The Interpreter's Bible*.[4] In the lay-out of this commentary the text is printed in English with a line drawn under it. Beneath this line is what is termed the 'exegesis', which is of a historical kind and is done with a high standard of competence by recognized scholars. Under the exegesis a further line is drawn, beneath which is what is called the 'interpretation', which is done by someone other than the scholar responsible for the exegesis. What makes this commentary difficult, even at times embarrassing, to us is the hiatus and contrast between the exegesis and the interpretation. A particularly ripe example is the comment on Mark 16.1–8, where the exegesis is what would be expected from a scholarly discussion of this very complex pericope, whereas the interpretation runs as follows: 'Now and then on the bulletin boards of post offices we see presented the face of a man with this warning, "Dangerous man at large!" That is the message of the resurrection.'

In the recently initiated commentary series to which the editors have deliberately given the name *Hermeneia*, in order, they say, to recall 'its rich background in this history of biblical interpretation as a term used in the ancient world for the detailed, systematic exposition of a scriptural work', the foreword contains the following paragraph:

> The editors of *Hermeneia* impose no systematic-theological perspective upon the series (directly, or indirectly, by its selection of authors). It is expected that authors will struggle to lay bare the ancient meaning of a biblical work or pericope. In this way the text's human relevance should become transparent, as is always the case in competent historical discourse. However, the series eschews for itself homiletic translation of the Bible.

Are not these words very bold indeed or naïve? For what is this competent historical discourse which, without resort to homiletics, can ensure that the text's human relevance (whatever is precisely meant by this term) becomes transparent? Was that what the authors of these commentaries – e.g. Dibelius on the Pastoral Epistles – thought they were attempting and achieving when they wrote? Might one not have to work very hard for such a result from some parts of those epistles? Might it not emerge from competent historical discourse that it had to be said of some passages that for us they had no meaning? And would not this again be something new in Christian experience?

In the light of these considerations it is not as surprising as might otherwise appear that there has emerged latterly a school, first in Germany under Gerhard Ebeling, Ernst Fuchs and Hans-Georg Gadamer, and then in dialogue with them in

America under J. M. Robinson, Amos Wilder, R. W. Funk and others, which places interpretation right in the centre of the theological enterprise and defines theology in terms of it. Such theologians do not write Theologies of the Old Testament or of the New Testament, but books with titles like *Das Hermeneutik*. By hermeneutics they do not understand a sub-section of theology or a department of exegesis but a way of doing theology itself, an activity which is co-terminous with theology. For them exegesis and interpretation are once more to be synonyms, and the gap in biblical scholarship is to be closed. The task which theology sets itself in examining the text has not been performed until something like the sermon has been reached. Only then is the intention of the text realized.

It would not be possible here to expound this position in any detail, if only because one is unable to follow much of what its exponents are saying. Being fathered by Heidegger – by the later Heidegger, it is said, rather than the earlier Heidegger with which one has become more familiar by way of Bultmann's demythologizing – its obscurity, indeed its jargon content, are high. It is difficult simply to read, let alone understand, some of what is written. Nevertheless, it would appear that important things are being said.

In contrast to the previous emphasis on history, on event, on acts of God and so on, prime place is given to language and to the consideration of what language is. This is promising. After all, a text, which is what we have to deal with, is in the first place, language; it is encapsulated speech. In so far as this school uses the word 'event' it tends to use it in the curious hyphenated expressions 'language-event', 'word-event', or 'speech-event'. This marks the conviction that it is language which makes things happen so far as a human being's understanding of himself is concerned. Man, it is said here, is a linguistic animal, and language is a, if not the, key to his existence. His speech is not an addendum to his living by which to be able to analyse it, describe it, make comments upon it or transmit information about it. It is the means of transmitting life itself from the past, of understanding it in the present, and of anticipating the future. The language of common parlance, of everyday usage, on which the empirical philosopher lays such stress, reflects and discloses how men have arrived at a *modus vivendi*; but they are not confined within this, for as men they are unable to remain in the past and simply to repeat it. They are open to the future, and have the property of attaining fresh understanding of what it is to be human. This fresh understanding, which is involved in the search for a true human life, is not something which precedes language and is then overtaken by it; it depends on some kind of language for its achievement.

If from this angle the question is once more asked what the point of contact is between the text and the interpreter, the answer given would seem to be twofold. Firstly, it lies in the observation that some texts are particularly rich in this kind of language, that is, language whose intention is not to analyse, describe or comment upon, but rather to proclaim and to communicate by proclamation, and thereby to create. And the Bible is the text which is richest in such language and is dominated by it. One may, perhaps, detect here an echo of Luther when he ventured the bold thesis – too bold for many – that the writing down of the gospels was an unfortunate even if necessary concession to human weakness, inasmuch as Christ and the apostles had not written anything but had only spoken; and that the gospels were not what they were intended to be until they were turned back again into the spoken word so as to continue to do what they had done in the first place by being spoken. Exegesis and hermeneutics are synonymous; the sermon executes the intention of the text.

Secondly, the answer lies in the observation that the biblical text does not intend to furnish facts or doctrines, whether these be taken as they stand or are given some kind of modern translation. What it contains is the same interest, the same basic concern as the interpreters. In this context Luther's words have been quoted: '*Qui non intelligit res non potest ex verbis sensum elicere*' – 'He who does not understand the subject matter cannot elicit the meaning of the words.'[5] This, one may suppose, underlay his preoccupation with justification by faith, not as a doctrine enunciated in scripture to be handed on doctrinally – which is what it tended to become in Protestant orthodoxy – but as a conviction that what Paul had perceived in his conflict with first-century Judaizers was basically the same *res*, the same subject matter, as that which was involved in Luther's own very different situation in relation to the medieval church. This could also chime in with one of the consequences of biblical scholarship as it has come to be practised in the preliminary stages of criticism and exegesis.

For in the past the biblical text has been used in exegesis primarily as a source book of theological information and knowledge. Its statements were taken separately as having a direct connection with the subject matter of theology. They could be gathered together to make up a doctrine of God and of his actions towards men, and could be handed over in this form to the systematic theologian for further more coherent and consistent expression. The common subject matter was then the doctrine itself, and the point of contact with the text was the acceptance of the doctrine as one's own. The modern biblical exegete, however, will be primarily concerned with the attempt to discern the situation of the writer of a whole book, to get into his mind, and to read the intention of any statement he may make in its relation to the whole of his text and to that situation. The common subject matter will then be the writer's intention in making the statements that he does, and the point of contact will be an appreciation of the situation as giving rise to precisely these kind of statements.

To quote by way of summary of what has come to be called (though not by its exponents) the New Hermeneutic from one who is both a representative of it but also not uncritical of it:

> From the standpoint of Biblical material, the word of God is the bringing of the text that was once proclamation into fresh proclamation, that is, into the situation where it again becomes faith. . . . The total theological enterprise is the clarification, that is, of true existence. It is not that faith informs theological reflection, but that theology is the articulate understanding and coming to understanding of faith. This means that the various theological disciplines cannot really be distinguished, though certain sharing of labours can take place. . . . Hence, exegesis is completed in proclamation. Historical disciplines, such as church history, disclose the history of interpretation of texts for the sake of disclosing past mistakes, true intentionality and meaning, and preventing the unintended and unreflective repetition of the past.[6]

It is too early to speak of success or failure in respect of this conception of hermeneutics. It has already been notably successful with those types of biblical material which are more closely and obviously concerned with the evocation of faith. Thus, its exposition of the speech of Jesus, especially of the parables, is amongst the best available, and it is illuminating in its handling of that particular, perhaps unique, form of communication which came to birth in the Pauline letters. On the other hand, it would appear to be markedly unsuccessful in treating events, or miracle, or the passion story, or the resurrection in so far as it is, even in Paul, expressed through appearances of the risen Lord, or doctrinal formulae – anything, that is, in which truth is objectified. This is, perhaps, to say that it suffers from a defect, inherent in whatever is begotten existentially, of unduly circumscribing the scope of experience, life and thought, and of operating in a kind of vacuum where language tends to be the voice of faith talking about itself. May not such a weakness, however, serve to raise again the question whether theology, including theology tied to biblical exegesis, can only function properly in close relationship with some kind of philosophy, in this case with a concern for the scrutiny of language, even if such a close relationship is at present hardly anywhere to be seen, and even if philosophers on the whole express disinterest in the kind of language found in the biblical text. Can theology ever go it alone? Is Ogden correct when he says that our theological resources fail because our philosophical resources fail?

Supposing, however, that this school were to be successful in its contention that theology is hermeneutic, and that in what biblical scholarship sets its hand to there is no stopping short of something like the sermon, might not the implication be that theology would have to go out of the university, both because the university, as it now understands itself, could hardly tolerate such an activity within it, and also because the specialization of disciplines which is now germane to a university, as it understands itself, goes beyond a mere division of labour, and would militate against, rather than foster, this form of study? Biblical scholarship as we know it was born in the universities, and could hardly have been born anywhere else. It grew up there, striving after an objectivity which should accord with the spirit of a university, and only in that context was it able to command, develop and deploy the resources it has done. May this, however, turn out to have been an episode in the long history of interpretation – an episode, no doubt, of great importance for theology and of considerable importance for the history of Western thought as a whole, but nevertheless an episode? This need not be a purely hypothetical question. It can happen that a class is engaged on some part of the syllabus, perhaps the history of biblical interpretation, and the discussion turns on whether biblical scholarship has any reference beyond itself. Someone may say, or rather cry out with some poignancy: 'We know that as a result of what we are doing here we shall never again be able to say in the pulpit "Jesus said".' Is this the kind of cry which it is proper to be uttered in the context of study at a university? If so, the question may be asked whether there are any other subjects of a kind that a similar cry could legitimately arise in the study of them, or whether theology is peculiar here and its vocation to be peculiar in this particular manner. If it is held not to be proper, then the problem is how to demarcate the areas of the subject in such a way as to see that it does not arise, and so as to ensure as far as possible that exegesis is studied in such a way that it does not issue in proclamation.

6

Queen or Cinderella

The position of theology in a university has seldom in modern times been without a certain tension. How this was already being felt by one acute observer in 1833, the year of the birth of the Oxford Movement in England, can be seen in the lecture, 'An Apology for the Study of Divinity', delivered before the University of Durham by Hugh James Rose.[1]

> Let me not be misunderstood. I am not wild enough to hope that in these days, even if I could speak with the tongue of men and of angels, I could convince the world that such a study deserves, and has a right to demand, the attention of *all* thoughtful and instructed men, however deeply I may be persuaded of the truth myself. I am well aware that the study which professes to discover nothing – I will not say which is not known to mankind at large – (for that would be an undeserved compliment to the age) but which might not have been known for above eighteen centuries to all who would exercise their powers upon the subjects to which it relates, can find little favour in men's eyes. I have heard it indeed asked, with a mixture of scorn and triumph, what is there to be *done* in divinity? And when they who pursue it must unhesitatingly confess that in this sense they have no mines to explore, and no inventions to hold up for admiration, no victories to achieve, and no triumphs to win, they must be content to hide their diminished heads in obscurity – to tread the silent and shady paths, and give up the broad way and the sunshine to the science of facts, which now walks abroad with the name of Philosophy boldly written on its brow.[2]

Believing it impossible, therefore, to commend anything to his audience unless it could be shown to be both practical and useful, Rose devoted his lecture to arguing that since, in fact, man is a creature of an all-wise creator, and the only one of his creatures made in his image, divinity, as the study of man's relation with

God, was the most practical and useful of all pursuits, and that the theologian uses every other study so, and only so, as to make it subserve this end. Divinity, he says, 'is the mighty ocean into which all the petty streams of human knowledge are to pour their tributary waters'.[3]

Rose in his lecture was still following the relics of a traditional schema even while he lamented its disappearance. In this schema, to quote Hastings Rashdall's summary of it at the end of his work on the Universities of Europe, 'theology remained the Queen of the Sciences . . . the architectonic science whose office was to receive the results of all other sciences and combine them in an organic whole, in so far as they had bearings on the supreme questions of the nature of God and the universe, and the relation of man to both . . . the ideal was one which cast a halo of sanctity over the whole cycle of knowledge'.[4] Thus in Rose's view natural science was entitled to respect and gratitude 'as a handmaid to theology, in pointing out the footsteps of God's love and wisdom in every quarter';[5] philosophy was to provide evidence of 'the wonderful adaptation of the Gospel system to the wants and requirements of man, and the crying witness thus given that both came from the same hand';[6] while history, which is only a handmaid of other studies and not a very important one in itself, gains its dignity only when seen through the eyes of the theologian as religion teaching by examples.[7]

The conception of theology ruling as queen of the sciences, married to philosophy, and prescribing for the graded hierarchy of subject children under her, had had, of course, a long and impressive history behind it, possessing, as Rashdall observes, and certain architectonic splendour, and a more than superficial plausiblity. Is not God, at least according to one venerable definition, 'that than which no greater can be conceived', and is not theology, at least by one possible interpretation of the word 'the speech of God'? Yet, at the heart of that gospel which theology exists to serve, there remains the paradoxical and haunting statement that the Christian disciple is called to behave in a manner the reverse of that of the rulers of the Gentiles who lord it over their subjects and exercise authority upon them. He is to be the servant of all and the minister of all; and it was always possible that the question might be asked whether this principle did not apply in the sphere of thought as well as in that of action. In any case the children had one after another come of age, having·established their claims to exist in their own right, and in competition with them theology had shown herself only too often to be something less than the speech of God; to be, in fact, an all too human speech about God. It was not, then, along the old paths[8] that theology was to go, but along the new and often zig-zig paths – some might call them a veritable crazy paving – which were laid down by the scientific spirit, especially as it was applied to that department of which Rose appears to have thought almost with contempt, the study of history. The truth which was to be left over from the conception of theology as the queen of the sciences, but which that conception had in part obscured, was rather that, as the study of man in relation to God, theology finds herself unable to function on her own, and is always driven to look for a partner before she can dance to full effect. It was, after all, this need which had originally led her in the second century to take up with philosophy at all, in order both to explain herself to herself and to make contact with second century philosophical minds. That partnership was now over, and another was in the making. Theology was to have a new partner which she was to be less able to dominate than philosophy.

It is widely supposed that the specifically modern scientific study of history was first elaborated on its own, and was then later applied, not without considerable reluctance, to the scriptures. This is not the case. The matter seems to have been both more complicated and more interesting than that. Indeed, Albert Schweitzer could go to the opposite extreme. At the beginning of his survey of the course of critical study of the life of Jesus from the publication of the work of Reimarus in 1774 to that of Wrede in 1901 he wrote:

> The problem of the life of Jesus has no analogue in the field of history. No historical school has ever laid down canons for the investigation of this problem, no professional historian has ever lent his aid to theology in dealing with it. Every ordinary method of historical investigation proves inadequate to the complexity of the conditions. The standards of ordinary historical science are here inadequate, its methods not immediately applicable. The historical study of the life of Jesus has had to create its own methods for itself.[9]

This is something of an exaggeration. Rather, it would seem, modern historical method and the critical investigation of the scriptures grew up alongside each other, sometimes in close connection with each other, each both giving to, and receiving from, the other. The foundations of modern historical method were already being laid by the philosophic spirit of the seventeenth century, although it was not until the nineteenth century that it was fully established.[10] Similarly, the first foundations of biblical criticism were laid, independently, in the seventeenth century with Richard Simon's three critical studies of the text, the translation and the interpretation of the New Testament respectively, and in the next two centuries, as the full complexity of the problem unfolded itself, theologians for want of anything ready to hand were often compelled to fashion for themselves and on their own the tools necessary to do the job. In this way they came to make important contributions to historical method in general. The story of this partnership has never been fully told, and indeed hardly could be, for much of it went on underground, and only occasionally does it come to the surface and become visible.

The first requirement of any historical study is an accurate text of the sources to be used. Scientific textual criticism of the New Testament may be said to begin with John Mill and his contemporary, Richard Bentley (of whom his patron, Stillingfleet, remarked that 'had he but the gift of humility he would be the most extraordinary man in Europe'). Bentley was, of course, like all professors in Cambridge at the time a theologian, but it was as an incomparable editor of classical texts that in 1713 he turned his attention to the text of the New Testament, to a task of which he himself said that 'nothing but sickness (by the blessing of God) shall hinder me from prosecuting it to the end'. The full Bentleian confidence breathes in what he wrote in his Proposals for Printing. 'The author believes that he has retrieved (except in very few places) the true exemplar of Origen, which was the standard to the most learned of the *Fathers*, at the time of the Council of Nice and two centuries after. And he is sure that that the Greek and Latin MSS, by their mutual assistance, do settle the original text to the smallest nicety, as cannot be performed now in any *classic* author whatever.'[11] In face of this confident beginning the question which faces any biographer of Bentley is why his interest declined and the great project remained unexecuted. It was not sickness. The likeliest explanation, on evidence which is not altogether clear, is that as he progressed Bentley began to see that the principles which he had laid down were inadequate to the complexity of the material, that he lost confidence, and that, in the search for additional help among the manuscripts, even the master lost his way in the mass of the evidence.[12] It fell to an admirer of Bentley, Karl Lachmann, to realize Bentley's design, and to illustrate 'not for the last time, the stimulus which may be given to Biblical criticism by the appearance in the arena of a scholar trained in other studies'.[13] It was not to a theologian, but to a philologist pure and simple, a scholar of the highest rank in classical and German philology, and one regarded in those spheres as the true founder of a strict and methodical system of textual criticism, that the credit has to be given for having made for the first time a clean break with the faulty text, based on a few late MSS, which, with the prestige of Erasmus and of the great continental printing houses behind it, had maintained itself as the Textus Receptus for three centuries. Yet even Lachmann was more daunted by the task in the New Testament that in the classical field. He set himself a limited aim of establishing, not the original text, but the true form of the text as it was current in the fourth century; to make the task compassable he worked with a somewhat mechanical method and on comparatively few texts; and in refusing to indulge in any judgment or emendations (with the admirable object of eliminating the personal equation) he over-simplified his task by ignoring an important factor, viz. that in the New Testament text more changes are made of a deliberate and intentional kind than is ever the case in classical literature. Hence, while Lachmann's influence on the general course of philological studies was probably greater than that of any other single man of his century, his work on the New Testament, great as it was, did not naturally and immediately lead on to the results which might have been expected from it. It was the theologians who further elaborated the science, and it was a classical scholar who, surveying in 1899 the advances made in classical studies, could write: 'The degree in which it [sc. textual criticism] has now approximated to the condition of a science may be seen, for example, in the chapters on "Methods of Textual Criticism" in Drs Westcott and Hort's "Introduction to the New Testament".'[14]

The restoration of a reliable text is, of course, only a pre-liminary. Historical science as we know it begins from the moment when the sources themselves are no longer taken as they stand and at their face value, or used, as Hugh James Rose would have had them used, as quarries for moral examples to be taken out of their context and applied universally, but when the his-

torian penetrates inside the sources, gets behind them, so that
they begin to talk, and to tell a story of the development of a
nation or a culture. Thus was brought about a revolution in the
sphere of historical understanding similar to that effected by
Darwin in the understanding of nature. Its results began to
appear in Niebuhr's *History of Rome*, and, in this country, in the
writings of a notable group of men – Thomas Arnold, Julius Hare,
Richard Whateley, Connop Thirlwall, Henry Milman and A. P.
Stanley – who have been denominated the Liberal Anglican
Historians.[15] This revolution in method and understanding was
associated, to a degree which we may now find surprising, with
F. A. Wolf's famous Prolegomena to Homer. Wolf's conclusions
had been that the Iliad and the Odyssey were the end products of
a process in which poems originally from more than one poet had
been handed down orally by rhapsodists; that after being written
down they had been polished by redactors to bring them into line
with the then accepted canons of literary taste; and that their
unity was not the unity of the original poems, but one imposed
upon them at a later date. Wolf's work aroused a storm of controversy, in which words like 'impiety' were thrown about, since
in classical culture Homer had always been the nearest thing to a
bible. Even Wolf himself spoke of his anger and regret that his
own work had destroyed his belief in a single Homer. But his
work on Homer was only part of a wider work in which he
conducted, as it were, a survey of the whole of classical literature
considered as material for yielding a reliable picture of Greek and
Roman life at the various stages of its development. The application of such a critical method would clearly be of decisive
importance for theology, for scientific criticism of the Bible begins
when the Old and New Testaments are no longer treated as two
parts of a single, indivisible whole, in which each is interpreted at
all points in the light of the other, both together providing the
groundwork of a doctrinal system, but are separated from one
another, and each is regarded in its own right; and when, the
process being carried further, the Old Testament and New
Testament apart are not treated as single, indivisible wholes, but
each book within them is regarded in its own right. That the
opposition to this would be even more bitter was only to be
expected, since the Bible was, after all, the Bible, its several books
being guaranteed as a single whole, and as scripture, by a doctrine of divine inspiration. It is, however, a moot question, and,

as it turns out, a somewhat amusing one, whether theology was not here first in the field. For in the year after the publication of Wolf's Prolegomena, 1796, Johann Gottfried Herder, court preacher and classical scholar, published a book in which he maintained two theses, the first, that the picture of Jesus in the synoptic gospels and that in the Fourth Gospel must be kept separate and evaluated separately; the second, anticipating in some measure by a century and a half modern methods of form-criticism, that the first evangelists were, so to speak, rhapsodists, who handed on orally independent units of tradition which, since they were passed on in the interests of preaching, had no biographical interest, and that for this reason the words of Jesus had been more faithfully preserved by them than the historical narrative. This sounds like Wolf applied to the gospels, and so it has been generally taken to be. But in the previous year, 1795, Herder, in an anonymous paper on Homer, had intimated that he had discovered the separate authorship of the Iliad and Odyssey when a boy, and that he had long held the view that their origin lay in the activities of the rhapsodists, thus implying that Wolf had plagiarized his ideas. If Herder's claim, which he did not retract in face of a counter-charge of plagiarism by Wolf, was just, then Homeric criticism and gospel criticism were even more closely united, originating in the same person.

Wherever the truth lay in this classical squabble,[16] it was without doubt in the biblical field that Wolf's method, once evolved, was chiefly applied, if only for the reason that classical literature has not much to offer of the same character as Homer, while the Bible has plenty. For the next hundred years it was applied, not indeed continuously, but by a succession of scholars, until in 1883 we reach another famous Prolegomena, that of Julius Wellhausen to the history of Israel – famous not because it was original (Wellhausen himself drew attention to his predecessors), but because it was the most lively, lucid and convincing account of the process by which the Pentateuch could be shown to be a composite production extending over centuries, its layers peeled off, and each layer assigned to a separate historical and theo-logical milieu. There is a charming and eloquent testimony to the partnership of theologian and non-theologian, and to the pioneering work of the theologian, to be found in a place where one would not naturally look for it, namely, in the dedication to Julius Wellhausen which that prince of classical scholars,

Wilamowitz, attached to his *Homerische Untersuchungen*. It is worth quoting at length, since, amongst other things, it contains acute observations on how matters stood at the time.

My esteemed friend, this book would belong to you, even if I were not expressly dedicating it to you. Firstly, because it was you who bade me write a book. . . . Secondly, I am glad to acknowledge whom I have to thank for the development of my mind, and this book is not the first place in which your influence can be traced. Finally, however, the subjects with which I am concerned in it are related as well internally as externally to those upon which you concentrated your own energies in the years we were together. The analysis of the Homeric poems is in the first instance, like that of the Pentateuch, simply a matter of philological analysis. And Bible and Homer must first of all be analysed and understood from within themselves; it is the manner of their tradition and the history of their text, which challenge comparison. Such analysis, however, could only be undertaken with any success when the modern world arrived at a historical sense in general, and at a sense for the evolution of race, religion and poetry in particular. This was first attained in Goethe's time, and Herder and Goethe took an intelligent part in both spheres to foster it; the latter was, through his preoccupation with Wolf's Prolegomena, led back to Moses. But it was Ilgen, whom you salute as one of the chief promoters of Old Testament criticism, who was at the same time one of the principal and most resolute representatives of the view which takes its names from Wolf.

Since a completely new understanding was necessary in order even to pose these problems, and since they concern the Bible and Homer, the twin roots of our whole culture, even a purely philological problem appeared as something revolutionary, and anyone who attempted to solve it had to contend with all the force of custom, superstition and inertia. Further development has shown, indeed, that the matter is something more than a philological investigation of sources. Now that the requirements of linguistic studies have made themselves more and more powerfully felt, it is no longer possible for any one man to research in both fields, or to pursue both studies at least on their grammatical and linguistic sides. I have not read your detailed analysis of the Pentateuch, and I beg you to leave my analysis of the Odyssey largely unread. Nevertheless, the course of the development of research has been, for all that, a parallel one, and will become even more so. The analysis of the Pentateuch has led on to an enquiry into the origins and development of the religion and culture of Israel, and the opening up of another tradition contained in the monuments has brought the history of Israel out of its isolation, and back into the context of the history of the East. The analysis of the Iliad and the Odyssey has developed into a history of the Greek epic, and must lead on to an analysis and history of the Greek heroic sagas, so as to be able, finally, to present the problem of a history of the Greek tribes down to the time when the Hellenic people arose out of them. Here also, fortunately, the accession of historical material is enormous and constantly increasing. Admittedly we, in the sphere of Hellenic studies, are only at the beginning of the road which Old Testament studies have already travelled. It is only gradually and painfully that I myself have worked my way through to a realisation of what the task is which lies before us, and the most I can hope to do is not so much to propagate it as to prepare for it. The present generation is not called to provide a Greek history for the pre-Attic period, not even a sketch of one. Sketches are dangerous, as they easily do damage to the whole. We are not, indeed, free to choose our work; we have to obey the demands of science, which are presented to us without consideration for the inclinations or convenience of mortal men.[17]

As Wilamowitz observed, the the analysis of the Pentateuch had opened out into a study of the history and culture of Israel. That is, a technical mastery of the sources is a preliminary to the proper use of them, and the proper use of them consists not in reproducing them, but in asking them questions which, once they are detached from the unity imposed upon them, they are capable of answering. It was the contention of R.G. Collingwood that this stage marked the real birth of scientific history. He distinguished between scientific history and what he called 'scissors and paste' history. In the latter the historian goes to his sources, collects from them his material, exercises his judgment in deciding what is trustworthy and what is not, and so writes his history; and what a critical method of analysis gives him is an increased capacity for deciding what is trustworthy and what is not, what is to be accepted and what rejected. But this attitude still remains one which is receptive towards the sources and which, in the last resort, incorporates their ready-made statements into a history of the period. The scientific historian, however, looks to his sources not for statements but for evidence, and if the question is asked 'evidence for what?', the reply is 'evidence for answers to the questions which the historian has already framed in his own mind', and by means of which he interrogates the sources. Question and evidence in history are correlatives; anything is evidence which enables you to answer your question.[18] I do not know how Collingwood's contentions are regarded by historians in general; I am here only concerned with them because it would appear that it was a theologian, and one who for many years dominated the theological scene, who first conducted his studies along these lines – Ferdinand Christian

Baur of Tübingen. Baur may well have learnt his method as a member of Niebuhr's seminar on Roman history. Starting from the conviction, for which there is at least some evidence in St Paul's fierce polemic in the Epistle to the Galatians, that the primitive church was dominated by a bitter conflict between Jewish Christians, who saw Christianity as a reformed Judaism within the Jewish Law, and Gentile Christians, who saw it as something radically new outside the Law, he approached the books of the New Testament as documents evidencing a kind of chain reaction in this conflict. In a series of penetrating studies written between 1831 and 1860 he set himself to interrogate the various New Testament books as to where they stood in this conflict until it was brought to a close by the Acts of the Apostles, which Baur placed in the middle of the second century, regarding it as an eirenicon written to show that Peter and Paul had been in harmony from the first. It is true that no one now holds Baur's views, at least in the form in which he propounded them. It is also true that Baur's relative failure draws attention to a fundamental methodological point, that if scientific history consists in asking questions of the sources, then the questions must be asked in the right order. Because he neglected the preliminary work of establishing, so far as was possible, the relative dates of the documents before he began, and because he adopted the view, well suited to his thesis but in fact untenable, that the gospel of Matthew was the only one written without bias, and that the gospels of Mark and Luke were dependent upon it and were written in reaction to it, Baur often asked the wrong questions at the wrong time, and so jeopardized his conclusions in advance. As he progressed he found himself more and more like an army whose position has been turned because its flanks have been left unguarded and it has lost touch with its base. It is further true that Baur was influenced by the current Hegelian philosophy, whereby Jewish Christianity was the thesis, Gentile Christianity the antithesis, and the resultant Catholicism of the second century the synthesis. Yet, for all this, Baur's whole approach to the New Testament has had permanent results, so that even at the present time those bold spirits who have begun again to embark upon the writing of a Theology of the New Testament – until very recently the last to be written in English was that of G. B. Stevens in 1899 – do not dream of assembling ready-made statements from the sources under various heads, which can be handed on to the

systematic theologian to carry the process further; rather do they
select what seems to them to be an, or the, original kernel of the
Christian faith in the New Testament, and go on to enquire of the
sources how far, and in what ways, this original kernel has grown
and developed, whether the basic ideas in it have held their
ground in the course of the development or have been deflected;
and the systematic theologian, being presented with such
results, is compelled to carry on his own studies on his own
subject matter in much the same way.[19] But inevitably the question is then raised of the nature of the forces in relation to which
the development has taken place. It was a serious limitation of
Baur and his school that, intent on the New Testament as the
record of a single internal development brought about by the
interplay of forces within the church itself, they assumed too
easily that the questions which they put could all be answered
entirely out of the New Testament itself.

Wilamowitz had further remarked that the source analysis of
the Pentateuch had had as one of its results the removal of the
Old Testament out of its isolation into the larger world of oriental
religion and culture. The New Testament was also to be taken out
of its isolation, and that by a further close co-operation between
theologian and non-theologian. It seems to have come about in
the first place as the result of certain boredom. Around the turn of
the last century a notable group of classical scholars – R. Reitzenstein, E. Norden, P. Wendland, E. Rohde, E. Schwartz, F.
Cumont, H. Usener and A. Dietrich – chafing at the somewhat
conventional round of classical studies and its restriction to the
so-called 'pure' classical authors, began to stray outside their
normal ground into the as yet largely uncultivated hellenistic
field, and to turn their attention to such writers as Plutarch, and,
in particular, to the religions of the Graeco-Roman world of the
first centuries BC and AD.[20] In the preface to his influential book
Agnostos Theos, which is an enquiry into the forms taken by
religious speech at that period, Norden tells what it was that set
him off on the trail. It was that 'in our seminar in the winter
semester of 1910–11 we were reading the Acts of the Apostles,
and there took place, as was to be expected, a lively debate on
chapter xvii; for, when it came to a scene which took place in
Athens, we philologists were determined not to defer to the
authority of the theologians, as we had done over the rest of the
book'.[21] For this group the New Testament was one document

amongst others in the comparative study of the religions of the Graeco-Roman world, and while they were united in acknowledging that it had been the theologian Eichhorn who had led the way in the comparative method,[22] it was the accession in a short period of such a wealth of talent from outside the theological faculties that brought about its rapid development. The questions which from their angle they were led to pose were these: Does the New Testament contain not one but two religions, the one, to be found in the synoptic gospels, Acts and some epistles, a semitic, hebraic, historical, prophetic, messianic religion of obedience to commandments (the Old Testament, in fact, brought to a fine point), and the other, to be found in the Pauline epistles and the Johannine writings, a hellenistic, oriental, unhistorical, mystical and sacramental cult of union with a dying and rising Lord (a particular variation of the popular pattern of religion in the Graeco-Roman world), and if so, how do these two religions belong together? To some extent these questions have haunted theology ever since.

It is, then, as a partner with the developing scientific historical method that biblical theology has in the last two centuries learnt again to dance, and some of the most important steps have been taken by the theologians. It has not been a case of submitting meekly and following in the wake of others; the theologians have often led the way. This is not because they have been particularly clever, but because their proper subject-matter, the scriptures, has by its very nature pressed harder upon them, and has held them consistently to the examination of exceedingly complex problems of historical study, which have necessitated ever more refined instruments to deal with them. Hence, merely in the pursuit of its proper work, the theological faculty has come over the years to find itself in possession of a linguistic discipline, a technique of source analysis and a training in the use of the historical imagination second to none. Indeed, for long periods it seemed as if theology, as such, had ceased to be written at all – at least such theology as would qualify for the shelves which the librarian so delightfully labels 'Outsize Theology' – and that the theologian had become content to be a special brand of historian. The contribution to theology of Bishop Lightfoot, whose name is attached to the chair which I have the honour, all unworthily, to hold, was largely that of a critical historian.[23] It has even seemed from time to time that the theological faculty was about to disappear inside the history faculty, and the question could be raised whether the existence of two faculties was not an unnecessary duplication. Further, theology itself in the process has become acutely aware not only of historical method but of historical thinking, and so of the historical basis of the Christian religion which is permanently fixed in its creed by the words *sub Pontio Pilato*. That Christianity is a historical religion, that the revelation of God is given not in propositions or doctrinal assertions but in events, these and similar statements have for some time now been the settled convictions of critical orthodoxy, and have passed as commonplaces into the textbooks. I wish, finally, to raise the questions whether they are not in some danger of becoming shibboleths, and whether there are not pointers in an opposite direction.

There is first the little matter of dates. No doubt dates are vulgar things, but a modicum of dates is a vulgar necessity for a historian. Thus, for example, it has been argued that one reason why our picture of what led up to the Arian controversy and the Council of Nicaea is so confused is not that the historians on whom we rely had no reliable information, for they appear to have possessed dossiers on the subject, but that, the contents of their dossiers being undated, they produced unreliable and contradictory accounts because they used the documents in the wrong order, and so made false deductions from them.[24] A glance at the article on The Chronology of the New Testament in any of the Bible dictionaries will show that the writer is attempting to make bricks without straw. Indeed, a recent one begins with the sentence, 'The reader is warned that no certain results will be found in this chapter.'[25] There is only one specific date in the New Testament, the sixfold date with which St Luke, in Thucydidean manner, begins his account of the ministry of Jesus in the third chapter of his gospel, and it is at least an arguable hypothesis that it would be easier for us to find room for such sequence of events as we have in the gospels if this date were abandoned as a well-meant but mistaken guess.[26] There is one thoroughly reliable fixed point in the New Testament, the mention of Gallio in Acts 16, but it was not intended as such by the author, and has only become so for us by the chance discovery of an inscription which fixes with tolerable certainty the dates of Gallio's proconsulship in Achaia.

But this objection may be brushed aside as trivial. Let us go a little deeper. Supposing we were to put the Bible into the hands of a competent person who had been thoroughly trained in historical method, and to ask for his considered report on it as a historical source. Would it be surprising if his report went somewhat as follows? The earlier books of the Old Testament are dominated by the figure of Moses, of whom it might be said, borrowing a sentence from one of the Schweich lecturers, that his existence appears to be like that of a lump of sugar in a cup of tea – the sweetness proves that the sugar is there, but it has now lost all recognizable shape;[27] that in the subsequent narratives of the historical books from Joshua to Chronicles court records appear to have been used, but are so deeply coloured by religious and theological interpretations belonging to later generations that it is not easy to see what they are good for; that the books of Ezra and Nehemiah are so full of holes that only by means of manipulation, rearrangement and guess-work can they be used as sources for the return of Israel from Babylon; and that only when he came to the first book of the Maccabees (assuming that his Bible contained an Apocrypha) did he find the kind of source with which he was used to dealing, and which he was accustomed to call historical – a source given to exaggeration, especially in the matter of numbers, as are most ancient sources, but, in the judgment of one of its commentators, the work of a man 'who writes as a historian, whose duty it is to record the facts without colouring them with personal observations', sober, matter of fact, his most striking characteristics being 'that the direct divine intervention in the nation's affairs is not nearly so prominently expressed as in the books of the Old Testament; and . . . that God is not mentioned by name in the whole book'.[28] This might be sufficient at least to put a question-mark against a too close entanglement of theology with history. Sir Edwyn Hoskyns, to the inestimable privilege of being whose pupil I owe both my first love for theology and also any sort of competence I may have in it, was known in moments of enthusiasm to assert a favourite thesis, that in New Testament thought the whole is contained within the part, by exclaiming 'the whole of the Gospel is contained in II Peter and Jude'. It would require even more hardihood to maintain that the core of divine revelation is to be found in the first book of the Maccabees. Indeed, it is stranger than that. For, if our enquirer were looking for the core of revelation, he would find a good deal of it, at least as the New

Testament sees things, in a book roughly contemporary with I Maccabees, the book of Daniel. Here are to be found some of the powerful images which dominate the New Testament, the kingdom of God, the one like unto a son of man coming on the clouds, the antichrist, but the message of this book is conveyed through religious romance masquerading as world history. Supposing we extend the enquiry to the New Testament to see where the balance lies. It would be evident from even a slight acquaintance with their writings that, in the hammering out of the distinctive Christian doctrines of the Trinity and the Incarnation which occupied the Christian fathers from the second to the fifth centuries, the decisive part was not played by the synoptic gospels, whose factual basis is not dissolved even under the most stringent examination, but by the Fourth Gospel, in which the glory of the heavenly Lord is always shining through the earthly incidents, and in relation to which the critical scholar will find himself, perhaps not infrequently, repeating the judgment made by Origen upon the discrepancies of the evangelists, that where possible they gave the truth both spiritually and factually, but that where it was not they preferred the spiritual truth, this spiritual truth being often preserved, so to say, in factual falsehood.[29] Further, the Christianity which made its way in the world from the second century onwards was, in considerable measure, the Christianity of St Paul, whose letters, at least, betray little interest in what we, as the result of the historical method, have come to call the Jesus of History. Such a survey could, no doubt, be both arbitrary and superficial, but it would, for what it is worth, point in a different direction from that in which we have been looking, and would almost postulate a theological Boyle's law to the effect that the content of divine revelation is in inverse ratio to the content of historical fact.

But, it may be said, this is to operate with a very narrow, wooden and out-of-date conception of history. What men believe, feel and experience is also history. That which can be known historically, says Collingwood, is that which can be re-enacted in the historian's mind, and the historian's task is to re-enact past acts in his mind, and to think for himself the thoughts which the acts express. The raw material of history is thought, and thought is an act of self-consciousness.[30] But it is precisely here that the problem for the New Testament theologian becomes most acute. For one of the results of the

application of the critical method has been to bring to light as the
dominant category of its thought the eschatology of the New
Testament, and eschatology is always an intrusive element in
history and a dissolvent of it. Towards the end of the Old Testament period the Jewish religion grew up, in the sense that no
religion can be said to be mature until it takes completely seriously the facts of evil and death, and is no longer content to offer
as a solution of the first a repentance of which men are only partly
capable, and of the second the assurance that a man lives on in his
family and his race. Hope now came to be set on a future event-
to-end-all-events, when that which had been partially revealed
in history would be given its final, permanent and satisfactory
form. This is the nearest approach that the most unphilosophical
religion of Judaism made to a metaphysic, and as it did so by
hypostatizing a final event in history its language inevitably
became more and more uncontrolled and bizarre as it tried to
imagine this event which would dissolve history itself. Judaism
survived by eventually disowning its eschatology, and because,
for it, the event did not happen. From a purely historical point of
view eschatology, if taken seriously, can hardly be regarded as
other than a species of lunacy, and as such cannot be re-enacted
in the historian's mind. Yet the New Testament is set within this
eschatological framework, which delineates the life, death and
resurrection of Jesus as the event which brings 'the fullness of the
times'. On the one hand, then, the Christian gospel is contained
in an event which is genuinely historical and in a life authentically
human; the very fact that its investigation has gone hand in hand
with the development of historical science itself, to which it has
made its own significant contributions, is a strong indication of
this. On the other hand, however, it escapes a purely historical
description, and the historical method does not suffice to penetrate to its heart.

Thus, in the first place, historical science, and especially the
school of comparative religion, while frequently illuminating
New Testament Christianity by placing it in a wider setting and
adducing significant parallels, does not succeed in accounting for
its peculiarity, or in explaining why it did not obey the law of
history and go the way of the other religions it so closely re-
sembled.[31] The student is forced back to the conclusion that in the
New Testament there has taken place a genuine act of what St
Paul calls 'new creation in Christ' in the sphere of thought and

belief as well as in that of life and morals. Secondly, it does not suffice because, if the subject matter of history is that which the historian is to re-enact in his mind, some at least of the New Testament would seem to be written in order to frustrate such a design. The evangelists – and this explains in part why their gospels remain *sui generis* as literature – would have regarded as blasphemous the idea that the Lord about whom they were writing was on all fours with, and moved on the same plane as, themselves, or that men could re-live in their minds what it felt like to be the Messiah. For all that he lived a historical life, he and they were separated by the span which divides heaven and earth, and the gospel was not something to be sympathetically understood and reconstructed, but to be believed and accepted. Thirdly, the New Testament does not leave eschatology where it found it. The effect of applying it to an actual event in order to declare the nature of that event seems to have been to work a certain transformation in men's minds, and to have carried them further along the road towards philosophy whither eschatology itself had been tending. 'Jesus came into Galilee saying "The time is fulfilled and the kingdom of God is at hand; repent and believe in the gospel" ' – this is how the gospel begins, as history in the framework of Jewish eschatology. 'In the beginning was the Word . . . all thing were made by him . . . the Word became flesh', and 'all things have been created through him and unto him; and he is before all things, and in him all things consist' – this is how it emerges, as a gospel set within a cosmology of uncertain provenance. At this point the historical method no longer suffices, and the theologian has to look around for assistance from another quarter.

Maybe already theology, sitting by the kitchen hearth – for she has learnt like the rest of us these days to take her meals in the kitchen – is beginning to cast appealing eyes in the direction of her old partner philosophy, but, so far, with little prospect of success. For philosophy is standing at the sink, and keeps his back resolutely turned. His dancing days, he says, are over, and he doubts whether it was ever anything but a child's pursuit. He must get on with his proper job, which, so far as one can see with his back turned, is to be scraping his pots and pans with the latest brand of detergent.

7

Christology and Theology

Among the first theological utterances I heard as a student at Cambridge were the two definitions with which Sir Edwyn Hoskyns chose to open his lectures on the Theology and Ethics of the New Testament. They ran as follows:

> The study of the theology of the New Testament is concerned with the analysis and description of that energetic and specific faith in God which controlled Christian believers in the first century AD, in so far as the books of the New Testament bear witness to that faith.

And:

> The study of the ethics of the New Testament is concerned with the analysis and description of the actual behaviour of those men and women whose thought and actions were, during the first century AD, controlled by specifically Christian faith in God, and of the nature of the forces which directed their concrete behaviour, in so far as the books of the New Testament bear witness to such behaviour and to such forces.

If this task has proved more difficult than was imagined, this may be due in part to the circumstance that much of the work on the New Testament in this century has been done in the midst of, and by way of, an acute controversy. Critical study of the New Testament had emerged for the first time from behind the closed doors of the theological faculties in Harnack's immensely influential lectures delivered in 1899–1900 to an audience drawn from all the faculties in the University of Berlin, and translated into English as *What is Christianity?*.[1] The general conclusion of those lectures was held to be that the application of critical methods to the New Testament uncovered a movement in which Old Testament prophecy had been reborn in Jesus of Nazareth, who, out of an intense communion with God, proclaimed the Fatherhood of God and the brotherhood of man. Here, indeed, was a recovery of the theological concentration of Judaism in a notable form, but it was a doctrine of the Father without a doctrine of the Son. It is true, as P. T. Forsyth pointed out long ago,[2] that such a summary was unfair to Harnack, for while he had written 'what belongs to the Gospel, as Jesus preached it, is not the Son but the Father alone', he had gone on to say, 'Jesus belongs to his gospel not as part of it, but as its embodiment. He is its personal realization and its power. And such he will always be felt to be.' Nevertheless, Harnack was generally understood in a reduced sense, and the popular version of this theology – for theologies come sooner or later to have their popular versions – was 'Christianity is the building of the kingdom of God'. Since that time a good deal of the investigation of the New Testament has been carried out in conscious or unconscious reaction from this view, and has laboured, and on the whole has surely laboured successfully, to show that a doctrine of the Son, of the messiahship, of the person of Christ, was integral to Christianity from the first. A notable contribution to this was the collection of essays by British and German scholars published in 1930 and entitled *Mysterium Christi*.[3] The popular form of this theology has tended to be 'Christianity is Christ', or, 'Christianity is the religion of a person'. But have not the 'christologians' succeeded only too well, and has not something dropped out in the process? At first sight it might appear hardly possible to exaggerate the Christ-centredness of the New Testament writings, and the place which christology holds in them. One has only to remind oneself of such simple facts as that to the outside world the most natural term for Christian believers seems to have been χριστιανοί, i.e. 'partisans of one called Christ', or that such a Hebrew of the Hebrews as Paul, in so short a time, could have so completely identified the Messiah with Jesus that the word 'Christ' almost ceased to be a title denoting an office, and became a proper name for Jesus. It is an indirect testimony to the impact made by Jesus upon the first disciples that, whereas Jews on the whole read off the person of the Messiah from a doctrine of the kingdom of God and of the elect, the early Christians came more and more to read off the kingdom of God and the elect from the person of Jesus. Yet, difficult as it may be to exaggerate this, it is possible to do so, particularly if the christology is treated as something on its own, and as existing, as it were, in its own right, for then it fails to evoke the whole majestic background upon which it is set and to subserve what Kierkegaard called 'the God-ness of God'.

How and why did Christianity spread so fast in the first and second centuries? In a far more lasting book than *What is Christianity?* Harnack summed up his own attempts to answer this question, and warns us how difficult it is to answer.

> How rich, then, and how manifold, are the ramifications of the Christian religion as it steps at the very outset on to pagan soil! And every separate point appears to be the main point; every single aspect seems to be the whole! It is the preaching of God the Father Almighty . . ., of his Son the Lord Jesus Christ, and of the resurrection. It is the gospel of the Saviour and of salvation, of redemption and the new creation. It is the message of man becoming God. It is the gospel of love and charity. It is the religion of the Spirit and power, of moral earnestness and holiness. It is the religion of authority and of an unlimited faith; and again the religion of reason and of enlightened understanding. Besides that it is a religion of 'mysteries'. It proclaims the origin of a new people which had existed in secret from the beginning. It is a religion of a sacred book. It possessed, nay, it was, everything that can possibly be considered as religion.[4]

If we isolate the first item in this complex we may ask, 'Did Christianity spread because it brought to men a doctrine of God, or because it brought a supremely powerful cult of Jesus as Lord, or because it brought both? And if both, how were they related to each other?' Behind these questions lies another: 'What did it mean to become a Christian in the early days for (a) a Jew, and (b) a Gentile?', and to become such, be it remembered, as in many cases to be prepared to suffer martyrdom rather than apostatize. We have not much material for answering these questions. The New Testament writings are too occasional in their nature, and what was written to serve the life, and answer the problems, of those who were already Christians will only by chance refer directly to the fact and experience of conversion. Our most direct source is the Acts of the Apostles, a book whose evidence is not easy to assess. We may leave on one side the question how far the preaching in Acts is a reliable summary of what apostles actually said, and how far it rather reflects what was happening in the author's own day in a milieu which had not yet, perhaps, abandoned, as the milieu of the Fourth Gospel would seem to have abandoned, all hope of converting the Jews. For the acceptance of such a book by the church in the second century may be held to show that its author was not just voicing his own conception of Christianity, and that his narrative was what the church wished to see in such a writing. We may not unreasonably assume that the author's conception of Christianity was the same as that of many other Christians.

In Acts 20.21 Paul is represented as stating, in a summary which could hardly be more condensed, the content of his mission. It had been the express affirmation ($\delta\iota\alpha\mu\alpha\rho\tau\upsilon\rho\acute{o}\mu\epsilon\nu\sigma\varsigma$) 'to Jews and Greeks of the repentance which is towards God and of faith towards our Lord Jesus'. This statement could be a *chiasmus*, in which repentance towards God applies to Greeks and faith towards our Lord Jesus applies to Jews, but it would be a violent form of *chiasmus*, and it is better taken as a summary statement of what the gospel aims at producing in both Jews and Greeks. In it theology and christology lie side by side, and the connection between them is not explained. Of the preaching to the Jews the author gives us his specimen in the speech of Paul at Pisidian Antioch in chapter 13. That it is intended as a specimen is indicated by the formal setting of the Jewish synagogue, in contrast to the *ad hoc* occasion of some of the other speeches. It is composed of two parts. The first part, which is picked up at the end, concerns the God of Israel; the second part concerns the work and person of Jesus. The first part consists of a carefully chosen selection from among the mighty acts of God in the history of Israel. The effective action of God has been exhibited in that he 'chose our fathers', 'exalted the people', 'led them out with a high arm', 'gave them inheritance in their land', gave them judges, a prophet, and a king, Saul, after whose rejection he 'raised up' David as king, bearing his own testimony to him that he had found 'David, the son of Jesse, a man after my heart, who shall do all my will', from which David a saviour was to be brought to Israel.[5] That this is a carefully chosen summary is suggested by the parallelism in thought and language between what is selected for mention and what is said elsewhere in Acts about Jesus as 'judge', 'prophet', 'king', and 'saviour'.[6] The writer has taken a step, though it is only a small step, in the direction of what we might call 'typology', using that word in its simplest sense; 'according to promise' is the writer's own way of expressing it.[7] When he makes Paul, although speaking to Jews, refer in a manner without parallel to 'this people Israel', he seems to be suggesting that there are now two Israels in existence, the historical people, whose rulers in Jerusalem failed to recognize the fulfilment of the promise, and 'the people', that is, Christians and those ready to become such, who alone are in a position to understand Jewish history for what it is.

This 'typological' Christian understanding of Jewish history is carried over into the second part of the speech, where it is taken a stage further, and the clue provided to this understanding. The connecting link is David. This second part consists of a christological statement of the career of Jesus in terms of David and his psalms. From David's seed, according to promise, God has brought a saviour to Israel. After the announcement by the Baptist of the imminent arrival of the Messiah, and with the coming of Jesus, the message of salvation is brought to Israel (that is, to the speaker and those who will listen to him). The inhabitants of Jerusalem and their rulers failed to recognize him (or 'it'), fulfilled the scriptures by condemning him, secured his death at the hands of Pilate, and (so the text seems to say) actually buried him. But God raised him from the dead and he appeared to those who now witness to the people. This act of resurrection is described by a forceful word ($\dot{\varepsilon}\kappa\pi\varepsilon\pi\lambda\dot{\eta}\rho\omega\kappa\varepsilon\nu$), not found again in the New Testament, as the 'through and through' fulfilment, the fulfilment without remainder, by God of his promises. That it is final, complete, and permanent is established by three quotations, two of them being from David's psalms – 'Thou art my son, this day have I begotten thee', 'I will give you the holy things of David which are faithful', and, with a play on 'holy' so as to interpret 'the holy things' as meaning resurrection, 'Thou wilt not suffer thy holy one to see corruption'. Again the selection, both of what is mentioned and of Old Testament texts, is significant, since for the writer this is the barest summary of what is already known to his readers from the gospel tradition about Jesus. There is sufficient evidence, though it is not abundant, in rabbinic Judaism and in the gospels themselves, to establish that already in pre-Christian times 'the son of David' was a messianic title, but, as Lohmeyer remarks in his study of it, the title was formal and external, conveying little more than royal descent.[8] It was not one which had a formulated *schema* attached to it. What the Davidic Messiah would be like or would do was uncertain. The title was thus wide open to interpretation, and the content given to it will depend on the particular facets of David's career, and the particular utterances of psalms (which are presumed to

be David's) which are seized upon as significant. Here we seem to
see the actual career of Jesus giving shape to, and providing the
content of, Jewish messianic expectation, at the same time as the
Christian christology is itself being shaped by Jewish messianic
expectation. There is mutual interaction, the Old Testament supplying the form, and the gospel story, even while being interpreted with reference to the form, supplying the form with content. Thus, in this speech, what is thrown into prominence is
David's accession to the throne as the result of the divine rejection of Saul, and this is because the career of Jesus is marked by
his resurrection; and his rejection by the Jewish authorities
implies their rejection by God. Moreover, David is 'a man', 'a
man after God's heart'. It is sometimes said that the descriptions
of Jesus in the speeches of Acts as 'a man who went about doing
good' (10.38), 'a man approved by God (2.22), or as 'the holy and
righteous one' (3.14), are the relics of an early and simple christology of a man who was raised to messiahship, which was later
complicatéd by a doctrine of pre-existence. This may be so, but it
is not necessarily so, if these expressions are the product of a
christological interpretation of the man Jesus in terms of the
David-Messiah, since I Sam. 13.14 had characterized David as 'a
man after his (i.e. God's) heart'; and the psalms, which were
taken to be the personal utterances of David himself, speak often
of 'the righteous' and 'the holy'. As Lohmeyer observes, David is
distinguished as the prophet of the last days (as in Acts 2.29)
because it was David's seed and throne which were to be the
content of the last days,[9] and the supposed authorship of the
psalms by one whose career provided something of a model for
the Messiah enabled the first Christians to use the psalms in such
a way as to show David speaking of a true and deathless king, a
holy one and son, of which he himself was the type and shadow.

Two points may then be noted about this speech. First, the
appeal to the Old Testament aims at establishing the continuity
and identity of Jesus with the agelong purposes of God. This is an
obvious point, but it perhaps needs to be made, as in some
modern writing the idea of fulfilment is interpreted as aiming to
establish the newness and uniqueness of Jesus, his messiahship
as such. Thus it is sometimes said that the first Christians
believed themselves to be the new Israel. But the word 'new' is
never used in conjunction with Israel in the New Testament.
There can be a new covenant with Israel, a new commandment

given, a new Jerusalem and even a new creation, but not a new Israel, and this may account for Luke's curious hovering in this speech between 'Israel' and 'this people Israel'. The Old Testament is used here to show Jesus as not being a figure in his own right, but as one who is in the closest connection with the purposes of God. Secondly, the continuity of God's purposes is a continuity of power. This binds the two parts of the speech together. In the first part God is the subject of a series of verbs expressing his redemptive and providential activity – he chose the fathers, exalted the people, led them out, took the land from the Gentiles, gave them judges and a prophet, and raised a king. In the second part the emphasis, as always in Acts, is on the resurrection, which, as has been said, is the out-and-out fulfilment by God of his promises. Therefore the speech can come to rest, quite naturally, with a double point – belief in Jesus and belief in God. Belief in Jesus – 'by him every one that believeth is justified from all the things from which you could not be justified by the law of Moses'; belief in God as powerful – 'behold, ye despisers, and wonder and perish, for I work a work in your days, a work which ye will not believe if one relate it to you'. Here we have theology and christology no longer simply lying side by side, but effectively, if still simply, combined, the latter subserving the former. Jesus is so closely identified with the purposes of God as the David *par excellence* that he can be identified with the work of God; in his person salvation is given, and faith can be in him. On the other hand, his career as Messiah is of such a kind that it does not stand in its own right, but requires resurrection to establish it, so that through him faith passes to, and comes to rest in, God as the living and active God.

What was involved in the preaching to, and conversion of, Gentiles is not so easy to ascertain. The evidence is more indirect, and it is made more dificult to interpret by our uncertainty in many cases of the precise composition of the Christian communities to which New Testament writings were written. The two occasions in Acts when Paul preaches to the Gentiles are, perhaps, less representative than the more formal address in the synagogue at Antioch. In the first, at Lystra, there is an exhortation to turn ($\dot{\epsilon}\pi\iota\sigma\tau\rho\dot{\epsilon}\varphi\epsilon\iota\nu$, almost a synonym for $\mu\epsilon\tau\alpha\nuο\epsilon\tilde{\iota}\nu$ 'repent') from 'the vain things' (i.e. powerless and dead things) to a living God, whose attribute 'living' is based upon his act of creation, his sustaining of creation, and, by implication, his judgment which he has delayed to execute. In the second, at Athens, the exhortation is to repent from the man-made worship of man-made gods to that of the known God, who is 'known' by virtue of his act of creation, his lordship over, sustenance, and disposition of, the world, and the kinship of human nature with him in that it also is living; and the exhortation to repentance is based on the appointment through resurrection of a man to judge the world. There is little christology here, and what there is is not explained. There is insistence on 'repentance towards God', but only an echo of 'faith towards our Lord Jesus', although the general impression left by Paul's preaching at Athens is said to have been that he proclaimed Jesus and the resurrection. There is, however, this connection between the preaching to Jews and the preaching to Gentiles, that both are intended to lead to faith in, and adherence to, God as the living God, the God of creative power. The gospel is so formulated that Jesus is neither added as lord to the pantheon of gods nor is he merely one of the prophets of the one God. In the section in his *Theology of the New Testament* in which he deals with this subject, Bultmann states that the 'Christian missionary preaching in the Gentile world could not be simply the christological *kerygma*; rather it had to begin with the proclamation of the one God.'[10] The Christians, he says, took over the hellenistic Jewish propaganda for monotheism which had preceded them in the field, and he adds that I Thess. 1.9, where Paul asserts that at their conversion the Thessalonian Christians had turned from idols to God to serve a living and true God, indicates that in his preaching to Gentiles Paul began with the proclamation of the one God. It is very probable that something of this kind did happen, that the Christians found themselves the residuary legatees of the Jewish mission, and that they reaped abundantly where the Jewish propagandists had so laboriously sown. This Jewish mission was, in the early days, a far greater *praeparatio evangelica* than those factors which are generally listed in the opening chapters of Church Histories. But I am not clear that Bultmann is correct in his assessment here. In the first place, the situation at Thessalonica is obscure. Both the story in Acts and the Thessalonian epistles themselves would lead us to expect a church there which was predominantly Jewish, but these are strange words to be addressed to erstwhile Jews, and there is no hint that Paul is at this point addressing only a Gentile section of the Thessalonian church.[11] In the second place, if what we have maintained so far is correct, the preaching to the Jews did not consist simply of a christological *kerygma*, but of a christological *kerygma* so closely tied to the Old Testament as to be the means of awakening to its fullest extent the faith in the living God which was latent in Judaism. In the third place, Bultmann does not here quote the passage from I Thessalonians in full. It is an important passage, as being the only explicit statement in Paul's epistles of what conversion had actually involved. It runs: 'You turned (ἐπεστρέψατε) from idols to God to serve a living and true God, and to wait for his son from heaven, whom he raised from the dead, Jesus, who delivers us from the wrath to come.' The style and structure of this sentence[12] suggest that it is meant to be a unity, and not a loose conjunction of two statements. Monotheism stands together with a christological statement of the resurrection of Jesus, the man, as son, to be the coming judge and the saviour from judgment. Is it, then, sufficient to say that Paul added the preaching of Christ to a preaching of the one God, or were these two preachings more closely related, the one securing the other? In a later discussion of the whole passage, Bultmann admits that it shows that Christ belongs within the eschatological *kerygma*.[13] But how does he so belong? According to Bultmann Christ's judgeship simply lies alongside God's judgeship, and no attempt is made to reconcile them.[14] But is this so? In Romans 14, where Paul is concerned with the relation of the strong and the weak in the matter of eating, he moves backwards and forwards between the judgment of Christ and the judgment of God. Receive the weak brother, he says, because God has received him; each must stand to his own master because the Lord has made him able to stand; if we eat, we eat to the Lord because we give thanks to God; whether we live or die we live or die to the Lord, and we must all appear before the judgment seat of God. But in the middle of this passage occurs: 'Christ both died and lived again, that he might be lord both of the dead and living'. The lordship of Christ, and therefore his position of judge alongside God and in God's name, are the fruit of his death and resurrection, and the resurrection of Christ from death is always for Paul the energetic act of God by which he establishes himself as God. Indeed, at a later point Bultmann admits that the message of the raising of Jesus from the dead was a basic constituent even of the *kerygma* to the Gentiles, pointing both to I Cor. 15.1ff. as tradition to that effect, and to the probably pre-Pauline formula in Romans 10.9: 'If you confess with your mouth that Jesus is Lord, and believe in your heart that God raised him from the dead, you will be saved'. Indeed, 'who raised him from the dead' is in Paul, in other New Testament writers, and beyond in the apostolic fathers, the specifically Christian designation of God, by which he is now known pre-eminently to be God.[15] But resurrection carries with it lordship, and the position of judge and saviour. Thus resurrection, lordship, judgeship, repentance, and faith towards God belong to a single complex. It is perhaps significant that the Epistle to the Hebrews lists, as belonging to elementary Christianity, repentance from dead works, faith towards God, resurrection from the dead, and eternal judgment.

If something of this sort was the basic pattern of primitive Christian faith, we may ask whether it proved capable of maintaining itself as it began to be filled out, and whether it allowed of internal development without serious distortion, particularly when attention came to be fixed upon the person and work of Christ. It would seem that we can see this happening in such a writing as the First Epistle of Peter. It has often been observed that this epistle exhibits a remarkable comprehensiveness in the way that it includes within a short space and in a balanced whole the various facets of Christian thought which in other writings are found in isolation or are treated as special themes. E. G. Selwyn refers to it as 'a microcosm of Christian faith and duty' having a 'synthetic character', and to the qualities of its author, which enabled him 'to represent and to combine features of Christianity, and indeed of religion generally, which are commonly recognised to be fundamental though they are often found in isolation'.[16] Those who believe the epistle to be by the apostle will explain these features by the nearness of its author to the early pattern of preaching; but they would not be surprising if, as seems more likely, the epistle is a later work, and its writer is meeting the needs of his readers by putting what he has to say into the form of an address modelled on what was said to converts at baptism, since sacramental and liturgical material tends to be conservative and to preserve earlier modes of thought. In the exordium to the epistle we see the basic pattern we have referred to preserved even while it is in the process of being expanded. God is blessed as the God who has begotten Christians to a hope which is living by raising Jesus from the dead; this hope is for a heavenly inheritance for those who by the same power of God are preserved in an attitude of faith to look for the final salvation, to be manifested at the revelation of Christ, on whom they believe; this salvation was the object of the prophets' inquiry, who were speaking of the suffering and consequent exaltation of the Messiah. Through the blood of Christ, who was foreknown before the world (here is a development of the christology, though it does not necessarily imply pre-existence), they have been delivered from their previous worldly and idolatrous life, and through Christ are believers in God as the God who raised him from the dead and exalted him, the end being that their faith and hope may be in God. This is to be born not of corruptible seed, but of the word of a God who is living and abiding (to follow Hort's interpretation). Here faith in Christ is, indeed, central, but it is the means by which faith comes to rest finally in God, so that one commentator can declare roundly: 'Clearly the thought of this writer is not Christocentric but theocentric; it begins from and returns constantly to the thought of God as Creator, Father and Judge.'[17] Further, it may be noted that this pattern maintains itself at a point where it might have been expected not to do so. I refer to the passage, 3.18–22, concerning Christ's preaching to the spirits and baptism. Even if this passage is not, as Windisch proposed, a baptismal hymn to Christ, it is rhythmical in structure and hymnal in tone, and Christ is introduced as the subject of a series of verbs which depict an earthly, followed by a more-than-earthly, career. It was precisely such christological hymns which could lead to, and be the expression of, a concentration on the figure of Christ alone, setting forth his earthly and heavenly career by itself, and without any close connection with an explicit doctrine of God, and this might especially be the case when the appeal to prophecy was replaced by a doctrine of pre-existence.[18] We have an example of this, perhaps, in I Tim. 3.16, where without any close connection with the context, occurs the hymn: 'Great is the mystery of godliness [i.e. our religion]: he who was manifested in the flesh, justified in the spirit, seen by angels, preached among the Gentiles, believed on in the world, assumed in glory.' Even here the words 'justified' and 'assumed' may still indicate that Christ is the passive object of the action of God. In the christological hymn in Phil. 2.5–11 we have a form halfway towards this. In its first part, the descent, Christ is the subject of the verbs

– 'being in the form of God' he 'emptied himself', 'took the form
of a slave', 'humbled himself'. In the second part, the ascent, God
is the subject of the verbs and Christ is the passive object of his
action – God 'highly exalted him', 'gave him the name' which all
are to worship to the end that through the universal acknowledgment of the lordship of Christ God may be worshipped.
In I Peter 3.18ff. we have a form in which the christology is still
closely knit with the theology: Christ suffered once for sins to
conduct us to God, having been put to death in the flesh and
brought to life in the spirit; and the reality of baptism as the
pledge made to God from a good conscience is established by the
resurrection of Christ and his exaltation at God's right hand to be
the ruler of the spiritual universe.

It would take us too far afield to consider in any detail the
epistles of Paul, although it is in them that the most significant
developments in christology can be seen to have taken place. It
was probably Paul who 'first threw into such sharp relief the
significance of Jesus Christ as a Redeemer, and made this the
central point of Christian preaching',[19] so that it was possible for
scholars of an earlier generation to declare, with some plausibility, that he had transformed an ethical, prophetic, and messianic gospel into a sacramental, mystical, and salvatory cult of
the Lord Jesus. It may suffice here to make three observations,
which could be greatly expanded, with reference to Paul's person, his theology, and his ethics respectively. In his study of the
word 'apostle' in Kittel's *Wörterbuch*, K. H. Rengstorf treats Paul
as the classical example of an apostle, since he is the only one
concerning whose apostleship we have direct information.[20]
While his apostolic consciousness, he says, is completely determined by his encounter with Jesus on the way to Damascus, so as
to differentiate him from the other apostles who gave themselves
to Jesus only after many hesitations and a long period of edu-
cation, his understanding of his apostleship is determined by the
idea of God which had governed his life from the beginning, and
which now for the first time assumed absolute supremacy, a fact
which Rengstorf accounts for by the parallel which Paul draws
between himself and the supremely God-conscious prophet
Jeremiah. 'The subject of the process, however, was God rather
than Christ, though it was certainly Christ who encountered and
addressed him.'[21] It would thus be quite inadequate to Paul's
thought to say that as a Christian he had added to a previous

satisfactory belief in God a belief in Jesus as the Messiah; rather had belief in Jesus as Messiah brought to light for the first time what belief in God really was, and had made it operative. This governs Paul's theology and ethics. We surely misunderstand Paul's doctrine of justification by faith unless we see it as essentially a doctrine of the power of God which brings into being for the first time, over the death and resurrection of Christ, faith in God of a total kind. This is clearest in Romans 4, where the archetypal nature of Abraham's faith for all men of faith is argued over the figure of the archetypal Israelite. The faith of Abraham was not faith in general, but the quite specific faith that God was able to accomplish the particular thing which he had promised, the blessing of the world through Abraham's children, and it comes into being in the face of what was, humanly speaking, an impossibility, because of Abraham's own deadness so far as begetting, and the deadness of Sarah's womb so far as conceiving, a child were concerned. Abraham's faith, then, is faith in God as 'he who raises the dead', and who does so by a power similar to that used in creation – he calls things that do not exist into existence. Then Paul makes one of those sudden jumps which admit us into his mind; and the point to which he jumps is the point where, for him, this power of God has been preeminently shown, and where, therefore, total faith is evoked, that is, the resurrection of Jesus by God from the non-existence to which he had been brought by the sin of men. It was not written just for Abraham's sake that faith was reckoned for righteousness, but for the sake of us, 'the believers on him who raised Jesus our Lord from the dead', which Jesus 'was delivered up because of the sins we have committed, and raised with a view to our being justified'. It is, therefore, essential to Paul that the messiahship of Jesus shall be of such a kind that his sufficiency is seen to be not of himself but of God. Indeed, for the relationship of Jesus to the Father, Paul is content with the single word 'obedience' (ὑπακοή), with a strong sense of subjection, and while he does not explicitly say that the resurrection is Jesus' own justification by God (justification, that is, from death not from sin), he seems to imply it when, in Rom. 6.6ff., he first makes the rather curious statement that 'he that has died is justified from sin', and follows it up by saying that Christ dies no more, having been raised from the dead, and that the death he died he died to sin once and the life he lives he lives to God. Paul's ethical analysis of human life is governed by the antithesis of κατὰ σάρκα and κατὰ πνεῦμα. There is an Israel 'after the flesh' and an Israel 'after the spirit'; there is a life of men lived 'after the spirit' and a life of men lived 'after the flesh'. To live 'after the flesh' is to live out of the sum of purely human possibilities and to believe in their adequacy; to live 'after the spirit' is to live from the mind of Christ, and that means from the sufficiency which is God's alone. But behind this analysis of life lies such a christological statement as that which opens the epistle to the Romans, that the gospel of God, promised beforehand by the prophets, concerns God's son, who was 'after the flesh' of the seed of David, and who was declared, or established, son of God with power 'after a spirit' of holiness, by a resurrection from death, which generates obedience in faith. In the classical description of the Christian life in II Cor. 4, life lived from the sufficiency which is God's is further defined as 'bearing about in the body the putting to death of Jesus that the [resurrection] life of Jesus may be manifested in our bodies'. For Paul the greatest miracle of all is the moral miracle of freedom from sin, and it is brought about by the same energetic power of God as that which raised Jesus from the dead and summoned light out of darkness. As Goudge remarks, commenting on the opening words of the second epistle to the Corinthians, 'the God and Father of our Lord Jesus Christ', it is not only the fatherhood of God which is revealed through the Son, but equally the godhead of God.[22]

What of the gospels? The appearance of the gospels was a moment of decisive importance, because in them the work and person of Christ were presented in the form of an extended narrative, or series of narratives, and once they were in circulation attention would be fixed, to a degree perhaps unparalleled before, upon the figure of the Messiah himself. The whole material before the eye would be christological. Certainly what we read in Acts and the epistles hardly prepares us for the appearance of the gospels as we now have them, and it is at least conceivable that they might have been written otherwise. To judge from Mark's gospel it was possible that they might have approximated, as do some of the apocryphal writings, to hellenistic 'aretalogy', a class of literature dealing with the exploits of gods, sons of gods, prophets, ascetics, or other holy or ideal men, in which one scene is strung after another with no particular connection, except that they relate to the same person.[23] The fact that, while exhibiting certain features of this literature, the synoptic gospels are on the whole so different in tone is, I would suggest, due to three causes. Firstly, the Old Testament language in which the stories are told, or with which they are interspersed, helps to tie them back to the Old Testament conception of the one God who manifests himself in power and action, and prevents them from escaping from the bounds of Jewish monotheism. Secondly, the compulsion which the evangelists feel to bracket this succession of narratives between, at one end, the story of the baptism of Jesus (or his birth), and at the other end, of his resurrection, with the transfiguration in the middle. No doubt we find these particular stories especially difficult, because the 'mythological' element in them is so pronounced, but to the evangelists they are essential, since it is precisely these stories which secure that the figure whose career is being narrated shall be seen κατὰ πνεῦμα, that is, as the God who stands behind him sees him, and as the instrument of that God. Thirdly, the whole narrative of incidents, miracles, parables, and sayings, is so told as to move towards crucifixion, ratified by resurrection, and so the Messiah is not presented as an independent 'lord' in his own right, upon whom attention comes to rest, but as one who is Messiah because he is *capax resurrectionis*, and faith in him issues in faith in the God who stands behind him. Is this last a construction of the evangelists, perhaps imposed upon their material under the influence of a conception of the gospel which had been formulated in missionary and other preaching? We are hardly in a position to say, but there are not wanting elements in the teaching of Jesus, and in his conception of his work and person, which would answer to such a construction, and which may lie behind it. In his teaching I mean especially his insistence that God shall be God; that nothing shall obscure the full force of God's commands; that the meaning and worth of anything – prayer, fasting, almsgiving – is the meaning and worth which they have for the God who sees in secret; that the kingdom of God already at hand is God's, and therefore must wait upon God to be brought in power. In his conception of his person and work I mean that we have not got rid of the sense that he regarded his passion, to be ratified at the hands of God, as the goal to which his ministry moved, when we have written off as *vaticinia ex eventu* such predictions of death and resurrection as are contained in Mark 8–10. There remain other, more enigmatic, sayings, such as Luke

12.50: 'I have a baptism to be baptized with, and how am I straitened until it is accomplished', or Luke 13.32–33: 'To-day and to-morrow I cast out demons and perform cures, and the third day I am perfected. But it is necessary that I go on to-day and to-morrow and the next day, because it is impossible that a prophet perish outside Jerusalem', which set the ministry in the context of that to which it is leading. There is the definition of that ministry in terms of a Son of man who is authentically human to the point of total rejection by Israel, but is to come in triumph before Israel's God; there is his confidence of a vindication which must remain obscure as to its details precisely because it is known to the Father alone. These are indications that he thought of himself as occupying, of necessity, that position before God which it was the set purpose of his authoritative words and actions to insist that all men should occupy, and as being the only one who did so. It is in the combination in one person of such a complete identification with the purposes of God that there is no hiatus between him and them, and a complete subordination to him whose purposes they remain, that radical faith in God is born.

The Fourth Gospel, as so often, seems to stand at the end of a development which it profoundly illuminates. For, on the one hand, we have in this gospel in narrative form a Christ-centredness every whit as intense as anything in the Pauline epistles. All those things for which men rightly long – life, light, truth, food – are mediated solely through Christ, because they are resident in him. This is stressed all the more if, as Bultmann contends, the 'I am' in the great 'I am' sayings is to be construed as predicate and not as subject – 'the living bread, it is I'.[24] Here, if anywhere, we might expect the gospel form to run off into the earthly story of a divine hero, who in his own person performs wonders and dispenses wisdom; and it must be admitted that it comes within an ace of doing so. The picture of Jesus in the Fourth Gospel is very different from that of the other three. It is in some respects that of a hierophant, and the fourth evangelist undoubtedly leans heavily on one side of the double-sided truth that Jesus is human and divine. On the other hand, no book in the New Testament stresses more strongly the subordination of Jesus to God and the Father. It is impossible to maintain that the Fourth Gospel is an interpretation of the earlier tradition in terms of some fixed non-Christian mythology, if only for the reason that the christology is still subservient to something beyond itself. For all that he is the mediator of all things, Jesus is only so because he makes himself nothing that God may make him something. This is especially clear in one important respect. While for the earlier theologians the phrase 'who raised him from the dead' has become almost a title for God, and serves to secure a proper understanding of the earthly career of Jesus by reference to the divine action, resurrection, which stands at the end of it, this is replaced in the Fourth Gospel by the phrase 'he who sent me'. It is difficult to reproduce in English the full force of the expression ὁ πέμψας με πατήρ, in which the participial 'having sent me' has become a verbal adjective, denoting a permanent attribute by which, through Christ, God is known as God. This 'mission' from God is in the Fourth Gospel drawn into the earthly career itself, is put constantly into the mouth of the Lord, and is made to govern the whole narrative. In this gospel the humanity of Jesus is not found in his hungering or weeping, or even in his rejection, but in the fact that he was sent into the world and into the flesh, and the earlier episodic gospel material has been so recast as to make clear that the life which is being narrated is the one life which constantly, and in all its parts, points to its transcendental ground, and which, apart from this ground, would fall into a hundred discordant fragments. At the same time as all things are resident in Jesus, who is the mediator of them, he is himself, as it were, transparent, so that faith in him, which is at the very core of this gospel, passes immediately into faith in him who sent him.

It may be concluded, then, that there is convergent testimony in the New Testament that early Christian experience was in the first place theocentric, in the sense that Christians claimed to have a direct relationship with God and to know his power, and that it was also christocentric; that faith swung between faith in Christ and faith in God, and yet was felt to be one faith, since the former always reinforced the latter. That this faith continued to be operative can be glimpsed in the worship, credal formulas, and life of the post-apostolic church; that it tended to fall apart in conscious theological thought is due to the particular situation in which the theologians of the second and third centuries generally found themselves. They were not writing as missionaries or pastors but as apologists, who were on the defensive on two fronts as they faced, either the whole system of popular poly-theism embodied in a persecuting state, or the Jews, from whom they were now separated as enemies. Hence a great deal of

Christian literature falls into two unconnected groups, even when it comes from the pen of the same author, πρὸς Ἕλληνας and πρός Ἰουδαίους, and the problems with which each is concerned are treated in isolation. In the face of popular paganism it is faith in the one God which is argued, but with a public ignorant of the Old Testament it is argued on popular philosophical grounds, and the christology, in the form of a Logos doctrine, is something of an incidental feature, and in the end an encumbrance until subsumed into a doctrine of the Son. In face of the Jews, with whom the area of debate was the Old Testament and its proper understanding, it was the christology which was argued, but, on the whole, in a somewhat wooden manner, which stopped short at the attempt to show an exact equivalence between Old Testament predictions and the events of the gospel, and which hardly led to a fresh apprehension of the one God through his Messiah. It was the later theologians of the Nicene period who went some way to recover the unity, albeit in their own terms, which were scarcely able to do justice to it. They found the New Testament embarrassingly Arian, as indeed it is, if its statements are taken separately and out of their context in the whole, and are read in isolation on the background of a largely philosophical conception of God; but they held to the conviction that the gospel is one of divine power and action wrought between Father and Son, and they concluded that, to be maintained as properly divine, it required a divine agent as the correlative of a divine actor.

In his contribution to the symposium *Mysterium Christi*, which, as we have said, was influential in recovering the centrality of the christology in the New Testament, Hoskyns permitted himself in a concluding paragraph some reflections on the wider implications of his subject.[25]

> This rehabilitation of the Christology is, however, not merely a piece of New Testament exegesis which challenges the adequacy of the ruling reconstruction of the development of primitive Christianity . . . it has implications for Christian Theology and for philosophy which vitally affect the doctrine of the Incarnation. The New Testament scholar, who is also a Christian, cannot patiently permit the dogmatist or the philosopher to expound the doctrine of the Incarnation on the basis of an analysis of human nature illustrated by the humanity of Jesus. He was unique; and this particularly rivets the Christian doctrine of the Incarnation to the Christology . . . and presents awkward material to the philosopher who is operating with a rigid doctrine of evolution.[26]

It is clear where the shoe was pinching. Christian thinkers are always likely to be people in search of some all-embracing category of thought by which to be able to grasp their faith as a whole and to bring it to bear on human life; and this is all the more likely when critical methods have, as it were, de-canonized the scriptures, and destroyed their purely formal and external unity as scripture. At the time when Hoskyns was writing, attempts were still being made to restate Christianity in terms of evolution, with Jesus as the highest point in an evolutionary process, and it was the christology which cried out loudest against such attempts. That danger is over. But is there not now a danger, as a result of the very success of the 'christologians', of an attempt to capture Christianity for a different category of thought, which may obscure the particular character and force of the christology? In a sociologically and ideologically conscious age the dominant category of thought is 'history', and it is noticeable that those theologians whose thinking is most 'christological', Barth, Tillich, and others, are also those who bid us see Christ as 'the centre of history', as 'the turning point of history', and the Gospel as providing us with 'the clue to history', with a 'proper interpretation of history', and promising us 'a philosophy of history'.[27] These are large claims, and it is not clear whether the language in which they are made is meant to be taken as precise. Thus the only precise meaning of the word 'centre' is a point equidistant from all points on a circumference, and this would seem to involve us in a circular view of human life which is certainly not that of the Bible. The only precise meaning of 'turning point' is a point at which something takes a radically new direction, but this would conflict with the view that the direction which things take in Christ is the direction which has already been given them in Abraham. It must surely be left to the historians to debate whether it is proper to spell history with a capital letter, and to mean any more by it than the sum of memorable events and their effects, open to a variety of interpretations by the historians, for the Bible itself does not supply a category called 'History'. It is sometimes said that it does so, in that it contains what is called a *Heilsgeschichte*, a 'sacred history'. But, strictly speaking, *Heilsgeschichte* is not Christianity but Judaism, in the form that history continues in a straight line to the final kingdom of the Son of David, which can be read off from the historical David. We have argued earlier that the figure of David did, indeed, provide early

Christian preaching with an important type, but also that what governed the use of the type, and gave it its Christian meaning, was the wholly unexpected cross and resurrection, which served to shatter the Jewish conception of sacred history. According to Mark this conception had already been undermined by Jesus himself when, on the eve of the passion and at an important moment, he is represented as passing from defence to attack, and as posing the question so frequently misquoted as 'What think ye of Christ?' and misunderstood as referring directly to himself. The question was 'What think ye of the Messiah?' and it was a technical question of theology. Whatever else is implied in the dilemma which is posed in the words, 'If David in the spirit calls him Lord, how is he his son?' they cannot be construed otherwise than as calling in question the idea of messiahship as the historical fulfilment of the sacred history which stretches from King David, and as making room for messiahship of a different kind to be established by the cross and resurrection. This is the messiahship of the Son of man, and even from this messiahship the last traces of historical schematization were to be removed by the non-occurrence of the *parousia*, and by its loss from Christian consciousness, in the form in which the first Christians held it, beyond recovery. Thus the Messiah, while using historical means, escapes from the control of history, and the gospel was able to break out of the envelope of Judaism and to become the faith for man as man. That the Messiah is an historical figure is of immense and permanent importance, because he is thereby established as truly human, and attention is fixed upon what men do and are. It is of equal importance for men that the Messiah is that particular historical figure through faith in whom God is established to be God.

8

Parable and Dogma

The Ethel M. Wood lecturer is instructed that he is to avoid subjects which are controversial. Strictly interpreted this might be held to preclude any theological lecture whatsoever. What was probably intended, however, was that he should avoid matters of denominational dispute, and with this he now has no difficulty in complying, inasmuch as denominational dispute has as good as disappeared from the theological scene. This disappearance registers less a fundamental change than a shift of the location of controversy to within theology itself, which continues to exhibit, if not acute conflicts, at least considerable tensions. One such tension, which is indeed to be expected at a time when predominantly analytical methods of study are overtaken by strong movements in the direction of synthesis, is that between biblical and systematic theology.

The biblical theologian is not infrequently aware of the systematic theologian breathing down his neck in pursuit of a body of biblical material that shall be sufficiently coherent for the purposes of a systematic theology, and he is not insensitive to the exasperation he arouses when he fails to produce it. He knows that he must appear awkward and unco-operative, constitutionally incapable, it would seem, of giving straight answers to plain questions, but in this he cannot entirely help himself. For he finds himself faced with unresolved tensions within the diverse biblical material itself. It is, for example, simply a matter of fact that in the constitution of the gospels there is such a hiatus between the narratives of the passion of Christ and the accounts of his Galilean ministry in respect of persons involved and issues at stake, that it is hardly possible to show the one as patently the outcome of the other, so as to provide, if required, a firm his-

torical as well as theological basis for a doctrine of the death of
Christ. Another such tension, emerging where least to be
expected and where the gospel material is commonly supposed
to be at its most straightforward, arises from the presence of so
much parable in it.

Parable, when to what is specifically so called is added what is
of the same kind even if not so designated, forms such a substantial and pervasive element in the synoptic gospels and their
individual sources that it has to be reckoned with in any systematic presentation of the gospel. Whether such a pre-
dominance of parable in teaching was a unique phenomenon at
the time cannot be said with certainty, since causes were not
operating to secure the survival of the same amount of the utterances of a Hillel or a Shammai as of Jesus, but it is unique in
relation to what has survived. Once past Nathan's parable to
David the scholar has to scratch hard over the extensive area of
the Old Testament to find parallels; the intertestamental literature including that of Qumran does not add a great deal, while
the rest of the New Testament, including the Fourth Gospel,
adds hardly anything at all. What is the explanation of this, and
what was the place of this concentrated element of parable in the
wider context of the synoptic gospels and of their 'gospel'?

Until the end of the nineteenth century there was hardly any
problem here. In that allegorical exegesis which, despite occasional protests,[1] had reigned supreme from the time of Origen
both as a method of interpreting the Bible and of securing its
unity and coherence, parable, with which this mode of exegesis
was in any case felt to have a natural affinity, was subject to a
process of decoding into doctrinal statements already established
on other grounds. To refer yet once more to the hackneyed
example of Augustine's interpretation of the parable of the Good
Samaritan, which he would seem to have received from tradition,
and which, even if over elaborate, may be taken as representative
– the man going down from Jerusalem to Jericho indicates the fall
of Adam, the Samaritan is Christ, being placed on his ass means
being united to the incarnation, the inn is the church, the inn-
keeper St Paul (perhaps an individual Augustinian touch here),
and the two pence the sacraments. Here then there were being
taught by Christ in advance and in encoded form for future
decipherment some of the fundamentals of Catholic Christianity
as it was to emerge, and this had been the parable's purpose.[2]

Why there should have been this curious arrangement in which fundamental theological truths had to be secured by being uttered twice and in two such different modes, once explicitly in the doctrinal language fitted for them and then over again in the language of cipher, is a question which does not seem to have been discussed as such. To judge from scattered statements part of the explanation might have been that for scripture to be cryptic corresponded closely with its nature as a religious book, while there are occasional hints that this might have been God's way of giving professors of theology something to occupy them.[3]

All this was brought to an end by Adolf Jülicher's book *Die Gleichnisreden Jesu*.[4] It is unfortunate that this book was never translated into English and was known by most only at second-hand from summaries of its conclusions in other books on the parables, so that its full measure was seldom taken. For it could be said in retrospect that it was responsible for one of the deepest scars left by biblical criticism on the body of Christian tradition. This was not by reason of its governing principle that a genuine parable has a single discoverable point (a principle that has had to be modified at times though it has on the whole weathered well); and still less by its Aristotelian-type logic which was manifestly not a key to the thinking behind the parables; but rather by its opening up a vista of a Christian tradition that was marked from the first by two forms of statement, the doctrinal and the parabolic, distinct in form and distinct perhaps also in origin, and so raising the question of how they belonged together if the one was no longer to be simply subsumed in the other. Exploration of the subject since Jülicher has shown how complex it is at every stage, and how difficult it is to be precise at any point.

In the first place there has been a fresh appreciation of the profusion and variety of the material to hand. It is characteristic of the Old Testament that it says what it has to say with a veritable riot of figurative speech and a minimum of technical religious language. The word *'mashal'* and its synonyms, which underlie the *'parabolē'* of the gospels, cover a wide range of utterance varying from, at the one end, the brief and self-explanatory proverb, through manifold forms of extended metaphor to, at the other end – and this is most surprising – the riddle or enigma. Such figurative speech was evidently most at home in the Wisdom tradition, where the mood is more universalist, static and tranquil, and the emphasis is on how things are in virtue of the

divine creation and regulation of the world and by providential
instruction. But it was not absent from prophecy, which is more
particularist, dynamic and turbulent, and is concerned more with
what things are to become through divine judgment and restoration; nor in increasingly bizarre form from prophecy's extension
in apocalyptic. Moreover, Wisdom could be identified not simply
with divine instruction in general but with the Torah, which thus
takes on the cosmic status of Sophia,[5] and Moses could be
regarded as a wise man as well as a prophet; and by the first
century AD there had emerged into prominence the scribes, who
were exegetes of scripture, and especially of the Torah, and who,
to judge from the exiguous evidence available, would also on
occasion use parable.[6] When, therefore, in Matt. 23.34 Jesus,
speaking apparently as the divine Wisdom, is made to say: 'Behold, I send you prophets and wise men and scribes', or when
Paul in I Cor. 1.20 asks the rhetorical question: 'Where is the wise
man, where is the scribe?', were these intended as individual
designations of distinct figures, each recognizable for what he
was partly by the way he spoke in pursuit of a particular vocation? Or could they overlap, or flow into one another, or even
become synonyms? And could a single person be all at once, or
sometimes one and sometimes another? These are difficult questions to answer. The biblical critic will be, or ought to be, haunted
by the fear that they are maladroit, that his method may be
seriously mishandling his subject-matter, and that by processes
of dissection and dismemberment he may fail to grasp what is a
rich and subtle living whole. Nevertheless, he can hardly help
asking them if he has amongst his tasks to bring each of the
diverse types of material in the gospels into the sharpest possible
focus in order to understand it the better, and to determine how
they belong together in relation to a single person, in the hope of
arriving this way at an identity for Jesus, or at least for his voice,
behind the inevitably composite Christ of a systematic theology.

Thus, was Jesus a prophet? Competent studies have arrived at
the conclusion that he was, and was recognizable as such, on the
basis not only of statements in the gospels about him or by him,
but also of similarities as to modes of speech and dominant
concerns between some strands in the synoptic sources and the
Old Testament prophetic literature.[7] But what is the relation of
these strands to other strands? Is it to be concluded that he was
'amongst other things' a prophet, and if so what are these 'other

things', and how is he a prophet 'amongst' them? In particular, when he spoke in parables was it *qua* prophet and in the service of prophecy, or in the service of some other things? Rudolf Bultmann, whose overall designation for Jesus was that of eschatological prophet, also judged some of the parabolic material – though not the majority of the parables proper – to have been wisdom sayings in general circulation which the tradition came to place in the mouth of Jesus.[8]

Or was Jesus a rabbi? Here the evidence is more fugitive and inconclusive, and even the propriety of the use of the word 'rabbi' in the question is debated.[9] But it is possible to point to similarities of form in the gospel picture of the 'teacher' or 'master' accompanied by his 'pupils' or 'disciples', as well as, occasionally, to similarities of content of teaching. The question could be specially pertinent in relation to parables, since, as P. Fiebig and others have shown, the closest parallels in form to at least one type of gospel parable – the type introduced by a question, 'To what is it like?' or 'With what shall we compare it?' – and to some extent in content in the use of certain stock figures – father and son, king and servants, invitation to a feast, etc. – are to be found in parables recorded as told by rabbis. But for the rabbi, it would seem, the parable was a tool of exegesis which he used in the exercise of his vocation, and the 'it' in the formula 'To what is it like?' pointed to a passage in scripture which required the parable to illuminate it or resolve its difficulties. Is it then to be concluded that 'amongst other things' Jesus was an exegete or scribe despite appearances in the gospels to the contrary? Along this line of enquiry the hypothesis has been advanced that the parables are to be understood as a kind of rump of Jesus' synagogue sermons, what was remembered from his exegetical preaching, and that the lectionary passages prescribed for reading in the synagogue should be combed to see how far individual parables could best account for themselves as having originated as suitable illustrations for a preacher expounding this or that combination of Old Testament texts.[10] Such a hypothesis will have difficulties of detection of its own over and above those attached to any theory of gospel origins based on appeals to the Jewish lectionary, but it could not be ruled out in advance. For it at least takes its starting point from observed parallels with one type of Jewish activity at the time, the scribal and exegetical, and could be held to provide a more intelligible setting for the

parables than the wandering preacher or the lakeside pulpit of
the gospels.

Variety of a different kind, and with it added complexity, is
introduced by critical analysis, whether operating at the source-
critical, form-critical or redaction-critical levels. For this brings to
light forces that have been at work modifying parables in their
shape, and consequently in their intention, in the course of a
living and moving tradition which, up to and including the writing of the gospels, did not consist solely in the repetition of what
had been uttered in the past, but also involved, naturally and
very properly, the application of what had been said to subsequent and significantly different situations as an authoritative
and contemporary word to those situations. Thus, at the level of
selection and redaction it can hardly be coincidence that the
predominant, perhaps exclusive sense to be given to parable in
Mark's gospel is that of 'enigmatic saying', and that this accords
with the note of secrecy and mystery pervading that gospel. Or,
that the more elaborate paradigmatic type often regarded as the
parables of Jesus *par excellence* – the Good Samaritan, the Prodigal
Son, Dives and Lazarus – and those in which the characterization
is achieved by the use of monologue or soliloquy by the principal
figure – the Prodigal Son, the Unjust Steward, the Unjust Judge,
the Rich Fool, the Pharisee and the Publican – are all confined to
the material peculiar to Luke's gospel.[11] All three levels of analysis could be involved in assessing so brief a parabolic saying as
that about the lamp, according as it appears in the form 'Does a
lamp come in order to be placed under a bushel or under a bed,
and not in order to be placed on a lampstand?' (Mark 4.21), or
'They do not light a lamp and put it under a bushel, but upon a
lampstand that it may light all that are in the house' (Matt. 5.15),
or 'No one takes a lamp and covers it with a vessel or puts it under
a bed, but upon a lampstand for all who enter to see the light'
(Luke 11.33), in order apparently to make the respective points
that a present and puzzling obscurity of the word heralds a future
revelation (Mark), that the disciples as the light of the world are to
behave as such (Matt.), and that truth will out (Luke).

What is bound to strike here is the fragility of the instrument.
Some might prefer to say its elasticity. Once metaphor is
extended beyond the proverb which, by reason of a succinctness
of expression, is able to maintain its shape in all weathers, but has
not yet arrived at some recognized form – the epigram, the hymn,

the lyric – where it is sufficiently controlled by rules, it is at its most fragile and vulnerable. It is a delicate construction of the mind, which may indeed have some rules of its own – the rule of only two, or at the most three, figures in a story, for example – but these may be inadequate to protect it once it is launched on the wind and is at the mercy of the elements. The man who chooses to talk consistently in parables must surely recognize that in doing so he is putting himself and the truth at risk, and if he lives to see what is done with his parables he is likely to find himself from time to time expostulating: 'Clumsy oaf! That is not what I said or meant at all.' Nevertheless, he may still maintain that for all its fragility no other instrument will do for the particular subject in hand.

This consideration sharpens the original question of the place of parable in the context of the gospels and the gospel, for this now becomes the question of the co-existence and co-ordination of two kinds of language and of what they are fitted for, the language of 'is like' and the language of 'is'. The language of parable is analogical and suggests; the language of theology is substantial and states. The language of parable is random, being drawn from here and there in human life; it is light of touch, indirect in manner, oblique in reference, delivering a glancing blow at its object, and even in the form of extended metaphor or narrative never wholly loses the quality of simile – 'the kingdom of God is like . . .'; 'Listen. A man had two sons . . .' The language of kerygma, even if it is parabolic in the sense that all language about God or even about life in depth has to be metaphorical, goes beyond this and belongs to the privileged vocabulary of theology; it is heavy in character, direct in reference, and aims to secure its object – 'The time is fulfilled, the kingdom of God has drawn near . . .'; 'Jesus is Lord'; 'You are the body of Christ'.

These two languages may co-exist, but it is not immediately evident how they are to be co-ordinated if the one is not simply a function of the other. So, some of the more massive theologies of our time, which have been centred upon the proclamation of objective saving events – such as, for example, the salvation-history of Oscar Cullmann or the dogmatics of the later as compared with the prophetic exegesis of the earlier Barth – have found themselves unable to make much use of the gospel parables. R. W. Funk poses the problem sharply when he writes:

The *Gattung* gospel tends to make *explicit* what is only *implicit* in the parable – and thus violates the intention of what may be the dominant mode of discourse in which Jesus taught. One could put it more incisively: the mystery of the kingdom held in solution in the parables precisely as mystery, tends to be profaned, made public, by the *Gattung* gospel. If we permit the 'gospel' to be defined by Jesus' parables, the question then arises: has the *Gattung* known as 'gospel' not already transgressed the intention of the 'gospel' as defined as parable? [12]

This question has commonly been regarded as resolved by the emergence of what might be called a critical orthodoxy on the subject. This has largely come about by an unusual consensus of German and British scholarship in two books, C. H. Dodd's *The Parables of the Kingdom*[13] and J. Jeremias' *The Parables of Jesus*.[14] The governing principle of both is that when the proper surgery has been performed on them the parables are shown to have their sharp point in relation to the basic message of Jesus as this can be reconstructed from elsewhere in the gospel material. They are comments upon, ancillary statements of, and in particular defences of, some aspect of that message and of the situations which it had brought about. Thus Dodd, convinced on other grounds that this basic message was one of 'realized eschatology', that is, that the consummation of all things, of which the kingdom of God was an image, had arrived without remainder in the actions, words and presence of Jesus, found this confirmed in the parables themselves, once they had been docked of all futurist references, which represented the later adaptations on the part of those who were unable to hold on to this central conviction and had reverted to a more traditional attitude orientated towards the future. In parables of seed and harvest the emphasis was to be seen as falling on the harvest as a symbol of the present time of salvation, the sowing having already taken place in the past history of Israel. Shorn of hortatory or moralizing conclusions or of allegorical elements within them parables of wealth, of payment, of reckoning, etc., appear as pointers to that unique crisis with which the contemporaries of Jesus were confronted simply by belonging to that generation. Jeremias, whose book builds upon that of Dodd and is a very learned refinement of it, was convinced on other grounds that the basic message of Jesus was one of an eschatology in the process of realizing itself – that he had brought about a situation which was already critical in the present moment but was also at the same time impending and looked to a future fulfilment; and he found this accent in the parables, again when pruned of later accretions or transformations, and with it the authentic voice of Jesus. In detailed expansion of this general position Jeremias succeeds in bringing all the parables or parabolic sayings into a unity under an umbrella of some eight aspects of the ministry and message of Jesus – the Great Assurance, Now is the Day of Salvation, God's Mercy for Sinners, the Imminence of the Catastrophe, the Challenge of the Crisis, Realized Discipleship, the Via Dolorosa of the Son of Man, and the Consummation.[15] It follows that the parables contain an implicit christology, a hint at least of the person of Jesus himself, which some scholars have wished to see as explicit.[16] Thus, not by allegorizing but by critical dissection, the hiatus between dogma and parable is overcome. The dogma is the eschatology, and the parable assists, substantiates or defends it.

Central to this reconstruction is the search for the *Sitz im Leben* of each of the parables, meaning by this technical term of form-criticism the particular circumstances or aspects of the ministry of Jesus, in distinction from the circumstances of the early church, which give it its sharpest point. It could be said that in this way it renders the parables expendable, when they are attached inseparably to, and are exhausted in, a historical situation which was unique and unrepeatable – the arrival or approach of the kingdom of God for a certain generation – and which, moreover, was itself to be overtaken by a further situation, the death and resurrection of Jesus, which was then to constitute the core of the proclamation of the gospel. This, however, would not necessarily be a valid criticism, for it could be maintained that it is of the nature of parables to be expendable, and that the speaker intended them to be so once they had performed their limited and ancillary task.

The correctness of the analysis may indeed be questioned in some instances, though whether they are of a sufficient number to lead to a serious modification of the reconstruction as a whole would be a matter of detailed examination. Here a single brief illustration must suffice, though it concerns a passage which is important for any consideration of the subject, the collection in Luke 15 of the three parables of the Lost Sheep, the Lost Coin and the Prodigal Son, introduced as a reply to an objection from 'the

Pharisees and the Scribes' (whoever is precisely intended by these somewhat stock figures) to Jesus' association with sinners. Jeremias, like others before him, has no difficulty in showing that Matthew's parallel version of the parable of the Lost Sheep is secondary in comparison with Luke's, and illustrates one of the laws of transformation in being told to disciples and by means of a moralizing conclusion applied to the behaviour of Christians to one another. He is, however, here as elsewhere content to take the Lukan version as it stands, despite its interpretation that there shall be more joy in heaven over one sinner repenting than over ninety-nine in no need of repentance,[17] which is awkward in two respects. For it introduces a concept of the righteous without need of repentance which it would not be easy to locate elsewhere in the message of Jesus, and which, while it might have a certain plausibility in the parable of the Lost Sheep, since straying sheep was a biblical image for sinners, would be wholly artificial in the plainly twin parable of the Lost Coin, since lost coins were not such an image and could hardly be such. And secondly, this interpretation is a deflection from the action common to both these parables, which is the indefatigable search by the person concerned for that which is too valuable to afford to lose. Further, the following parable of the Prodigal Son has suffered a similar deflection, and hence an assimilation to the previous two parables, by the addition after 'This my son was dead and is alive' of the words 'was lost and is found', since these do not correspond to anything in the action of the parable. Thus it is possible that the original intentions of these parables were other than they are now made to appear, and that the polemical setting arising from the circumstances of the ministry of Jesus to which they are now addressed has been the creation of Luke or of the tradition he has used.

A more general, and possibly far-reaching criticism could be made that in this reconstruction the term *Sitz im Leben* is being used in a significantly different sense from that which it originally has in form-criticism, where it refers to the situation which best accounts not for the content of a passage but for the particular form of utterance the passage takes, whether that form be regarded from an aesthetic or a sociological point of view. For, whatever the subsequent use made of parable in the tradition, it is not obvious, nor perhaps likely, that it elects itself as a form of utterance for proclaiming an eschatological message or for defending it. That it could be so used appears from such passages as 'Those who are whole have no need of a physician but those who are sick; I did not come to call the righteous but sinners', or 'If I by the spirit of God cast out demons, then indeed the kingdom of God has come upon you. How can anyone enter the house of the strong man and despoil his goods unless he first bind the strong man and then he will despoil his goods?'[18] But these are generally instances of a brief parable or parabolic saying firmly geared to a context and forming a step in an argument. It could be otherwise with the longer self-contained parables, which are sometimes ill-fitted to this purpose even in their present contexts, when indeed they have one. The judgment that all parables are combative in character may be a correct one, but it may be still an open question why they are so.

It is in part dissatisfaction with this strictly historical interpretation which has led more recently in some quarters to a different approach. It may be called broadly speaking literary-critical, though it is for that reason in its own fashion theological. It argues for a relative autonomy for the parables and for sufficient attention to be given to what they are in themselves as internal organic unities of form and content apart from any immediate reference to anything outside themselves. This is not unrelated to the marked preoccupation with language and its possibilities that is widespread in philosophy of more than one kind from the analytic to the existentialist, in anthropology and some of the sciences, in literary criticism and in theology itself, especially where it is concerned with hermeneutics and the relation between what the text meant for the writer and what it may mean now. Man is a linguistic animal and his existence a linguistic existence. Language does not simply clothe thought; it may precede and determine it. Integral, perhaps original to language is metaphor, which is not an ornamental form of expression for what could be equally well or even better said otherwise, but is itself a mode of enquiry into the world and of cognition. In Middleton Murry's words, 'Metaphor is as ultimate as speech itself and speech as ultimate as thought.'[19] It stands permanently alongside the conceptual and univocal language of discursive reason, and is not there simply to be displaced by it. Insight and understanding of existence proceed from movements of the imagination which take shape in fresh combinations of words whereby they can convey more than they ordinarily do. Parable is extended metaphor, a possibility of speech to be considered in its own right along with other possibilities – the poem, for example, or the novel – and it involves a coherent and self-contained organization of form and content through which something is seen anew. It must be respected and received in the first instance for what it is, and due regard should be paid to the fact that it is found so plentifully at the heart of the gospel traditions.

So along this line the philosophical theologian P. Ricoeur observes of the parables of Jesus that they are 'a language which from beginning to end thinks through the Metaphor and never beyond', and reaches the conclusion that in them as a whole we are given 'more to think through than the coherence of any concept offers', and that 'taken together they say more than any rational theology'.[20] Dan Otto Via's book on the subject, both in its general treatment and in exegesis of individual parables, rests on the conviction that the parables are aesthetic objects which by speech and action dramatize man's existential possibilities.[21] In having their own distinctive characters and their autonomous world they resist more than do other types of gospel material the efforts of evangelists to make them part of, and subsidiary to, the structure of a gospel as a whole. In her exploratory and engaging study, *Speaking in Parables*, Sallie TeSelle claims for the Christian tradition from Jesus in his parables, Paul in his letters and Augustine in his *Confessions* 'through to the present day' a vein of what she calls 'intermediary theology'. This has always been indirect in its method, reflecting upon and grasping its object by way of metaphorical clarity and precision, and it remains for that reason foundational, capable of renovating thought and language including what she calls the 'tired clichés' of Christianity. It lies somewhere behind systematic theology, though precisely where and how is the problem.[22] The way from the one to the other may be, as R. W. Funk remarks, 'circuitous and tortuous'.[23]

A literary critical approach of this kind may well appear strange to biblical scholars, whose own disciplines may not have prepared them to assess it, and it has weaknesses of its own. The parable may prove too small a unit for such large deductions to be made from it. Exegesis here will be more than ordinarily bedevilled by whether the text to be expounded is the text as it stands, which may have been partly spoiled by later adaptation, or some hypothetical reconstruction of an original aesthetic object. And it leans heavily on existentialist modes of thought.

Nevertheless its concentration on the character of parable as the main clue to its understanding may be valid and may have an important contribution to make. As an alternative to the existentialism I would like to suggest, though very tentatively, that in what some scholars have called 'the language event' of the gospel there were, from the first, two languages and not one, that parable was one of these, and that it performed within the strategy of the gospel as a whole the functions of a kind of natural theology. This is, of course, a question-begging term. I use it only as better fitted than existentialist modes of expression to focus that appeal to the natural order which is of the essence of parable, and I would stress 'a kind of natural theology'. For in those doctrinal systems which have admitted it, natural theology has tended to consist in a somewhat formal argument to the existence, nature and activity of God from certain regular and approved aspects of nature. This would not answer to the logic of the parables. It will depend here on what is to be meant by the word 'natural'.

That the raw material of the parables of Jesus is the observable world of daily life is a point made, if only in passing, in almost any study of the subject, and sometimes deductions are made from this fact.[24] It can strike with greater force when it is made intuitively by the non-professional, as in Pasternak's *Dr Zhivago* when the character Uncle Kolya observes: 'It has always been assumed that the most important things in the Gospels are the ethical teaching and commandments. But for me the most important thing is the fact that Christ speaks in parables taken from daily life, that he explains the truth in terms of everyday reality'; then adding as his deduction, 'The idea that underlies this is that communion between mortals is immortal, and that the whole of life is symbolic because the whole of it has meaning.'[25] The point deserves to be dwelt upon. The language of the parables is entirely secular – with the possible exception of Abraham's bosom in the parable of the Rich Man and Lazarus. This is even underlined by the rare instances of God appearing within the parable, for in the parable of the Prodigal Son what prevents a straight identification of the father in the parable with God is the fact that God appears alongside him in the son's words 'I have sinned against heaven and before thee'. Moreover, it is a wide range of daily life that is drawn upon. Simply to list the characters in the parables and their actions shows, at least in comparison

with such contemporary parallels as we possess, a relative pau-
city of stock figures and situations and a high proportion of what is
fresh and unexpected, which might suggest the observation of a
roving and catholic eye. It is important at this point, however, to
avoid sentimentality and not to draw superficial conclusions
about the secularity of the gospel. For it would seem that there is
seldom a straight carry-over from what we would call the natural
order into the parable. Even in the appeal to the organic processes
of nature there is evidence of invention and contrivance. It is the
smallest of seeds that produces the largest of trees; an enemy
sowing tares in another man's field corresponds to no known
agricultural behaviour and is fantastic; and there are still some
who remain unconvinced by Jeremias' argument from rabbinic
sources that ploughing after sowing, which he finds implied in
the Parable of the Sower, was good Palestinian practice.[26] The
statements that the birds of the air do not sow or reap nor the lilies
of the field toil or spin only make their point by being from one
point of view ridiculous.

The natural here would plainly have to be expanded to include
human nature, to which the majority of the parables refer, but
again not for the most part human nature in its normalities or as it
were on its best behaviour. Rather the opposite – 'which of you
will not get up at midnight if not because he is your friend at least
because of his need?'; the judge who is the negation of what being
a judge is in respecting neither God nor man and who satisfies
the widow's demands simply to get rid of her; the steward whose
shrewdness consists in swindling his way to security on the backs
of his master's debtors; the owner who breaks all known rules of
business in paying all workers the same irrespective of man-
hours; the banker who renounces the rules of banking by can-
celling a debt large or small; the epicurean complacency of the
successful farmer who feels he can relax when his barns are full;
the absentee landlord who sends one rent collector after another,
undeterred by the fact that they are all beaten up; the *bouleverse-
ment* of the rich man and Lazarus; the cartoon of a Pharisee and a
publican at prayer. Johannes Weiss spoke in this respect of the
strong element of the grotesque.[27] This would appear to be too
frequent to be simply fortuitous, and to lie too near the basic
structure of parables to be put down to superficial deformations
brought about in the course of tradition. The natural then would
have to be expanded to take in a large measure of the contrivance

of art. While the parables never fall outside the sphere of daily life
they are often based on daily life as it is pushed to its limits. Hence
C. H. Dodd's well-known statement that from them we can
better reconstruct the background of petit bourgeois and peasant
life in Palestine than for any other province in the Roman Empire
except the Egypt of the papyri[28] is less helpful than would be a
careful observation of the highly artificial situations which are
constructed upon that background. Or as G. Eichholz observes in
his essay with the intriguing title *'Das Gleichnis als Spiel'*,[29] in
comparing the exegesis of Jeremias and Schlatter of the Parable of
the Good Samaritan, the speculation of Jeremias whether the
story reflects an actual occurrence on a specially dangerous road
is of minor importance. It could have happened between almost
any two points on almost any road in Palestine. What is of crucial
importance is the evidence of constructive art in the deliberate
juxtaposition of priest, levite and Samaritan, much as if a modern
story began with 'There was an Englishman, a Scotsman and an
Eskimo'.

Once more the critic, be he now three parts literary critic, has to
make a judgment. Are these characteristics of the parables, supposing them to have been accurately detected, due to the pres-
sures of a dogma – justification by faith, the operation of divine
grace, the presence of the kingdom or of divinity itself in the
ministry of Jesus and its attendant circumstances – so that the
choice of figures and the construction of stories are determined
by that? Or do they have an independent origin and stand more
in their own right as so many mirrors held up to the life from
which they are drawn, and as statements of how things are for
this observer? If they are combative in intent, is it because they
seek to establish theological positions that have already been
taken up but are being called in question, or because they seek to
undermine the normal and accepted and to gain a new perception of the world by appeal to the world? Are the parables
defences of a gospel full-shaped, its end wrapped up in its beginning, or are they a preamble to it while it is still taking shape?

If it is the former then the task of the exegete could be to
complete the work which the tradition and the evangelists for
some reason only managed to get half done, to close the gap and
to draw the parables right inside the kerygma of saving history,
and in this way to have something to offer to the systematic
theologian. Since the gospel is in the end Christ, and the parable

is a function of the gospel, perhaps the Good Samaritan is after all Christ. If it is the latter then the task might be to keep them apart, concluding from the partial failure of the evangelists that there was something about the parables which continued to resist their doctrinal intentions, and then to allow each form of utterance, parable and kerygma, to have its own force. And the force of the parabolic element might be held to lie less in the constant repetition, exposition and application of the parables of Jesus than in an inducement of men by the parables of Jesus to a way of perception, and so perhaps to parables of their own. This need not mean that parable and gospel are not related. They will be related in emanating at whatever remove from a single person, and to be unified in thought is part of the definition of being a person. Exploration of their relationship and of their need of each other might be one avenue to the understanding of the New Testament. It could, however, mean that despite heavy appearances to the contrary in the gospels themselves the mission of Jesus was not from the first and always a single, uniform and univocal phenomenon, but was at least two-pronged in its approach.

The point at issue may be illustrated in conclusion by a brief reference to the Fourth Gospel, which here as elsewhere proves illuminating and baffling. For what is to be made of a writing which may legitimately be classed as a gospel in being a narrative of the acts and words of Jesus and of his death and resurrection, but which contains neither the Greek work '*parabolē*' nor a single parable of the synoptic type, if we exempt the buried instance of the Shepherd and Sheep in John 10.1–6 (Jeremias calls it simply 'a bad parable') which is called by the author a '*paroimia*', a synonym for '*parabolē*'. Part of the answer is suggested by the only other passage to use this word '*paroimia*', John 16.25–30, where towards the end of the last discourse Jesus observes that he has spoken to the disciples in parables (*en paroimiais*), but that the time is coming when he will no longer speak to them in parables but will tell them plainly (*parrēsia*) of the Father; and on what he then proceeds to say the disciples comment that now he speaks openly and not in parable. That is, there are no individual parables because all the words of Jesus in this gospel are parable; only parable now has to mean something like the cryptic operating as the symbolic. And not only his words; for in this gospel also the actions of Jesus are designated '*semeia*', with the emphasis on their symbolic and significatory character, and the same character belongs to his death. In this way diverse materials are assimilated to one another and are woven into a whole, which is reinforced by literary media, such as the use of the verbal *double entendre* and the theatrical device of dramatic irony.[30] All is now figurative, but that now means that all is religious, expressed in the language of 'is' rather than 'is like', and applied directly to Jesus and his circumstances. This is the more so if Bultmann's view is correct that in the 'I am' sayings the 'I am' is not the subject of the sentence but the predicate – 'the living bread it is I' – for this presupposes the existence of supernatural entities (heavenly bread, living water, true light) with which Jesus now identifies himself. In this way the Fourth Gospel becomes a powerful coherent unity, and as the history of the church in the following centuries was to show it offered itself more immediately for the development of articulated and systematic doctrine. But can it be denied that in the process of its composition daily life and the observable world have slipped away and are nowhere to be seen?

PART III

The Christian

9

The Christian Past – Tradition

The unknown author of what for want of a better name we call the
Epistle to the Hebrews, as he is reaching the end of his exposition, suddenly and unexpectedly pens an ejaculation which may
be rendered, 'Jesus Christ, yesterday and today the same, and to
the ages' (Heb.13.8). It is an ejaculation, for it has no verb and no
connecting link with what has preceded, and is thus in marked
contrast to the flowing and articulated style of this 'epistle'. It is
sudden and unexpected, since it is hardly accounted for either by
the exhortation which the author has just been giving his readers
to imitate their past leaders, or by the warning against false
teaching that he is about to give them. For these reasons some
have taken it to be a credal or liturgical formula which was current
in the author's church, and which he is quoting here. And if
words like 'yesterday' and 'today' strike as too prosaic for a
formula, one could refer to the ancient Egyptian so-called Book of
the Dead, where one who believes himself united after death
with the divinity Osiris is to be found saying, 'I am yesterday,
today and tomorrow'. But whatever its origin or its precise purpose in its context, the ejaculation can stand, and has stood, by
itself as a weighty and highly compressed statement of the core of
Christian belief. And even if the main issues of theological and
religious discussion have now begun to move away from the field
of the New Testament, a Christian could still do worse than to use
this statement as a means of examining himself as to his Christian
faith, and to ask what would have to be true for this statement to
be true for himself.

First, the Christ of yesterday. Much has been written in this
century about the historical element as that which is most dis-

tinctive of the Christian religion. Biblical criticism and the modern study of history came to birth at the same time and grew up together, sometimes as part of the same process. Christians have thus, along with other men, become increasingly aware, not only of the historical method of study, but of the historical way of thinking about human life, and of both the stimulus and the difficulty which they occasion for faith. The difficulty has been expressed in what has become a stock phrase, 'the scandal of particularity', which, even if he did not invent it, Gerhard Kittel illustrated in a notable essay when he wrote, 'That which we name humanity and human history is just a formless mass of innumerable lives which have run their course, and it resembles a great heap of sand. Can we dare to select one grain of sand and claim for it uniqueness and particularity?'[1] But the ejaculation of the author of Hebrews goes even further than this, and expresses the essence of Christian faith more completely, and for an historical age more scandalously. For it asserts of one who bears a personal and historical name, Jesus Christ, that he has a persisting and permanent identity. The difficulty here has recently been stated by Gunther Bornkamm.

> For the historian the frontier separating yesterday from today and tomorrow is in principle closed. Significantly, he speaks of 'what has passed', defines its place, and sets it in an already existent body of coordinates of time and space, though he does take into consideration the influence of past on present and future. And if he transmutes the abiding part of past history and its great figures into conceptual, moral and religious truths divorced from time and history, this is no accident.[2]

The ejaculation is not, however, speaking in our modern historical terms, but in those which had been current in more than one milieu for the description of God. Of Zeus it had been said that 'he was and is and will be'. In Revelation 'the Is, the Was and the Coming One' is an expression for the divinity. Jewish rabbis, meditating on the words in Exodus 3.14, 'I am he who is' were wont to find in the being of God all the tenses of the verb 'to be' combined. Thus to say of Jesus Christ that he is 'yesterday and today the same, and to the ages' was one way of asserting his divinity. But even this definition was not of God as he is in himself, but of him as he is turned towards men, as he is the subject of human thought and is apprehended under the categories of time. And it could belong also to a definition of man

that he is a being with a consciousness of past, present and future
– a consciousness, it may be noted, which is frequently experienced and heightened in prayer – and that in some way past,
present and future co-exist and cohere in man. To say, then, that
Jesus Christ is 'yesterday and today the same, and to the ages'
could be to speak of his humanity as well as his divinity, and of
the one as a diagram of the other. And to explore how, in Christ,
past, present and future belong meaningfully together without
being dissolved into one another could be a prime task of
theology in any generation. Hence we find Karl Barth, in the
volume of his *Dogmatics* which deals with Creation, heading his
exposition of 'man in time' with a section on Jesus, Lord of
Time.[3]

Already for the author of Hebrews, writing we do not know
precisely when, there was a Christ to whom the word 'yesterday'
was to be applied. How far back this 'yesterday' stretched from
the point of writing, and what it comprised or had to comprise by
way of actions, words and experiences of Jesus known to his
readers, we cannot say, any more than we can say this for other
expressions of Christian belief represented in the New Testament
documents. Not even a gospel, which was a single narrative of
such actions, words and experiences, need have been thought of
by its author or by its original readers either as all that a Christian
needed to know, or as what he must know to be a Christian. Only
with the growth and formation of the New Testament canon of
scripture, with the Old Testament canon to back it, did Christians, for whom the boundaries between past, present and future
had been to some extent blurred by the possession of the Spirit,
begin carefully to distinguish between the present and the past.
From then on a quantum, as it were, of past event was supplied as
the basis of a present faith, and one of the tasks of theology was
then to labour to show that this quantum was all of one piece, and
that even the Christ of yesterday had been indeed the same
Christ throughout.

But what is the character of this quantum so that Christ may be
perceived in it and confessed through it as 'the same'? It is this
question that historical analysis caused to be posed afresh and to
be answered in new and disturbing ways. The purpose of literary
and historical criticism is, by the use of techniques of examination
suggested by the nature of the material itself, to get behind the
finished documents, and if possible to see them in the process of

coming to be. The New Testament documents being what they are, this may operate in a number of ways. In the case of the gospels it operates most immediately at the editorial level, and even at this, the latest and most literary stage, it may disclose the coming to be of a Christ who is certainly modified, and possibly more richly apprehended, by subsequent interpretation. For example, to place alongside one another the three parallel accounts of the confession of Peter at Caesarea Philippi (Mark 8.27–9.1; Matt. 16.13–28; Luke 9.18–27) is to see aspects of Christian belief and spirituality, if not coming to birth, at least emerging into the open. This is so because for Matthew it is not simply a matter of reproducing what lay before him in Mark, but of a significantly modified version in which 'the Son of man' is first a substitute for the first person singular ('Whom do men say that the Son of man is?' in place of Mark's 'Whom do men say that I am?'), and is then said to have a kingdom in which he will be seen coming, whereas in Mark what will be seen is the kingdom of God coming in power; and Jesus is now acclaimed not only as the Christ but by his later Christian title 'the Son of God', on the basis of which, in a passage probably intruded into this context, there is promised the construction of the church on Peter. For Luke it is more a matter of reproduction of what he had in Mark, but the prophecy is now that they will see the kingdom of God and not its coming in power, which would not accord with the conception of the kingdom of God in Acts; and by the addition of a single word fraught with consequence for Christian life and piety the test of discipleship in taking up the cross in the wake of Jesus is now said to be a 'daily' occupation.

This is not an isolated example. Similar phenomena requiring a similar appreciation appear in other parts of the Galilean story; or in the discourse on the last things, which in Mark 13 is controlled by the prophecy of the abomination of desolation, in the parallel Matthew 24–25 by the coming of the Son of man, and in the parallel Luke 21 by the destruction of Jerusalem. Or it can be seen in the parallel but distinctive narratives of the Passion. But this leads to a stage further back behind the work of the editors, where modifications of a common original can no longer be detected in the process of emerging on the written page, but must be presumed on the evidence to have already taken place. So with beatitudes common to Matthew and Luke – whether they are four or nine, in the second person ('blessed are ye . . .') or the third person ('blessed are those . . .'), less religious or more religious ('poor' and 'hungry' or 'poor in spirit' and 'hungry after righteousness'), and addressed to disciples as a way of life or to the public to call them to discipleship. Or with the Lord's Prayer, longer and more liturgical and Jewish in Matthew, more succinct in Luke but again containing Lukan interpretation in the word 'daily' added to bread. Or a parable of a shepherd searching for a lost sheep, which is plainly being put to a new use when in Matthew it teaches the divine care of the little ones in the church, and is not necessarily serving its original purpose when in Luke it refers to the repentance of the sinner.

But this leads further back still, to where there are no parallels left for comparison, and each separate unit has to be assessed on its own. The very fact that so much of the first three gospels is of a kind that permits, even demands, this kind of treatment, because it consists of units which have once stood on their own, is itself significant. It prompts the questions whether these units survived because they were specially memorable, and whether part of their being memorable was because they bore particularly closely on some circumstances of Christian faith and living to which they were intended to be a guide, and whether these subsequent circumstances have themselves made a contribution to the form in which a narrative, a parable, a saying or collection of sayings had been handed on. Whatever happened did not happen in a vacuum, and at this point other classes of writing in the New Testament – epistles, Acts, Revelation – come into consideration. For they fill in the vacuum in part, and document some of those circumstances of Christian faith and life as they had developed in new conditions. They furnish some glimpses of the workshop in which gospel material received its shape and point in the service of this faith and life. One tool in this workshop would undoubtedly have been what the Jews termed 'midrash', an expression for various types of interpretative work, one of which was the rendering of a story in its repetition more coherent with later convictions and attitudes. Attention is, therefore, drawn to those stories of strong doctrinal content which also serve to organize the whole gospel material as a single narrative – stories of birth, baptism, temptation, of transfiguration, passion and resurrection – which are also those in which wide and significant variations are to be found. Having reached by this route the smallest units into which the material may legitimately be analysed, it is then necessary to retrace one's steps, and to attempt to appraise how each individual evangelist, by his selection and arrangement, his framework to and articulation of this particular kind of material, has arrived at his individual presentation of it for whatever purposes and audience he had in mind, until the process was arrested by the official authorization of his work along with that of others. This is the route which critical analysis of the gospels has learnt to take in response to the nature of the material which is being examined.

What is of primary importance in all this is not so much any particular findings as the fact that the gospel material as a whole becomes alive and moves under the fingers; and in this movement some elements appear as having given birth to others, with which they are now blended. Particular findings in biblical criticism are seldom assured. They are always, in principle, open to revision by the same methods as have produced them, or by other methods deemed proper, and they are frequently so revised. There is ample room here for differences of judgment, and little likelihood that some slide rule can be constructed for reading off as fixed quantities what is original in words and actions of Jesus, and what is adaptation through reaction to and application of them in developing circumstances. But if the material is what it is, in part at least because it is detected to have been from the first in movement, then something of importance about it may be lost if this is allowed to disappear from view. For it poses acutely the questions how far and in what way the material, both in its component parts and as assembled into continuous wholes, presents a recognizably or significantly different person. These questions have been there from the beginning. The early church, in principle, abjured the idea of a composite Christ when it rejected a single harmonized edition of the gospels in favour of the co-existence of four separated gospels. In practice, however, they were in their separation and co-existence used very largely in a harmonistic fashion, and this was unavoidable so long as all statements, whether historical, doctrinal, descriptive or interpretative, were taken as the same kind of statement on the same level. If historical criticism has made that impossible, it is because criticism involves, indeed largely is, discrimination, and such discrimination judges a composite Christ to be, from a historical point of view, chimerical.

In his Gifford Lectures, *Symbolism and Belief*, Edwyn Bevan

posed the problem in his characteristic way. He contended that a
religion which consisted of the words of the speaker without his
person could readily be dissolved into mere symbolism without
great loss, but that Christianity could not be so dissolved because
it has to do with a person still active. If what is meant by Jesus
Christ is the influence made by his personality as shown in the
records of his sayings and doings, then the crucial question
which all talk of his words without his person overlooks is, 'What
has happened to Jesus since? Has he ceased now to exist, just as
the old horse we may have seen last year in a neighbouring field?
Or does his spirit still exist, but only as one among a crowd of
discarnate spirits in the unseen world?'[4]

'What has happened to Jesus since?', meaning since his death,
is a question which begins to be answered in the New Testament
itself in ways which were to be determinative. In that Christian
experience for which the Pauline epistles are evidence 'what had
happened to Jesus' was that he had become the heavenly lord of
an earthly community of believers – though 'happened' could be
applied only to his resurrection, since this was the action of God
towards him, and in the rest he must be supposed to be the agent
and not the patient. In this community his word now ran (though
how this was related to the words he had once spoken is seldom if
ever clear), and he was explicated through this community as his
body. The believers both benefit from, and in some way share in,
what he was and is, and are shaped by dying with him and rising
to new life with him. In attempting to expound these Pauline
insights, and in wrestling with such pregnant statements as 'As
in Adam all die, even so in Christ shall all be made alive', or 'You
are all one man in Christ Jesus through faith', or 'If any man is in
Christ there is a new creation', the modern expositor of Paul finds
himself compelled to use expressions of Christ like 'corporate
personality', 'representative man', 'inclusive manhood', even
though he is hard put to make sense of what he is saying. These
cumbersome and barely intelligible expressions intend to describe a two-way but also one-sided process. What the believers
are is the effect upon them of 'what has happened to Jesus
since', but one of the things that has happened to him is that he –
his words and actions, passion and resurrection – now incor-
porate the experience of others than himself.

Here, as so often, the Fourth Gospel moves into the centre of
the picture. This is so because the actions, and indeed the death

of Jesus, are presented consistently in this gospel under the
modality of 'signs', which point beyond their physical event to
eternal realities to be apprehended, and because there is much
consideration throughout of the relation between seeing and
believing. It is also the case because in the long discourse of
chapters 13–17, so unlike anything in the other gospels and
distinctive even in this one, the question of the past and the
present, of discontinuity and continuity is a central concern. In a
series of contrasting figures – sorrow and joy, tribulation and
peace, travail and birth, entry and departure, going on a journey
for a little while and returning to take up an abode, judgment and
vindication, Son and Paraclete – the double truth is wrestled with
as it affects the disciples. The life of Jesus is a genuine historical
event in coming to an end in time, in being distanced and falling
away into the past. Its coming to an end brings sorrow to a
particular group of people, in a way it cannot do to others,
through the absence of one who has been so significantly present. It is the departure by way of death of one who had arrived
on the scene of the world. It is a separation and removal of the
direct contact of sight and speech in such a way as to leave them
behind in the world bereft of what these things have been. It is,
however, an event for which it is fitting that it should happen in
this way so as to produce the results proper to it. These are, first
and observably, the future results in the disciples themselves –
the greater works they will do, the fact that he will be seen in
them, and their entry into all the truth under the guidance of the
Paraclete. But more important, and as the basis of these things,
the past of Jesus in which the disciples have shared, limited as it is
and for all its finality still indirect, can lead to, and bring into
union with, that which it cannot comprise or hold as immanent in
itself – namely, the joy which cannot be taken away because it
belongs to the divine, the glory which is the divine presence
itself, and the mutual abiding through the Paraclete of the disciples and Jesus. The word 'abide' in this gospel stands not for
some supra-temporal reality which persists, but for the present
state of that which has been past. There is in this gospel a
confident statement through the person of Jesus of the contingency and transience of past events which does not issue in
either a pessimistic leap out of this world into some other world of
spirit, or in an optimistic prophecy that history somehow weaves
itself automatically into a harmonious whole without any judg-

ment being passed upon it, but in what is creative of the deepest possible things. But it has to be noted that such a confident statement is only made through the medium of a Christ who cannot be recognized, when compared with the Christs of the other gospels, as in any immediate or obvious sense 'the same'. If the word 'incarnation', suggested by 'the Word became flesh', is used to express what is meant by Jesus Christ, it will have to include at some stage, and possibly very early on, the flesh or historical existence of the believers as one of its constituents.

Is there an overall term capable of denoting such an authoritative historical phenomenon, which is found on analysis to be from the beginning and so constantly in movement, and in its movement so fertile? The term which suggests itself is 'tradition'. This, of course, has serious disadvantages, both from its use in common parlance and as a technical term with a past history in theological controversy. In common parlance it tends to stand for what is mechanically reproduced by an inert conformism, for what is lifeless and fossilized. In theological debate it has done service as a second source of Christian truth, a twin with or ancillary to scripture, and as such either to be welcomed or repudiated. Can the word be rescued at this later date, and refurbished so as to fit the facts? For it does, after all, express something in which people are commonly engaged, whether in family, school or university, or in social and political affairs; while the processes of handing over and receiving, which constitute it, are already there however far we can penetrate into the origins of the Christian gospel. As J. R. Geiselmann has noted in his study of the subject, there is a certain ambivalence in the term and in what it signifies.

> To 'transmit' may mean to make known a doctrine, to teach, to observe a rite, to hand on what has been announced in a precisely fixed form, to train people to act in a suitably practised way (not unlike putting into effect a police regulation). But to 'hand on' may also mean to appeal to the inner consent of the heart and understanding, the inner adhesion of the mind, to an attitude which is a personal expression of conviction. And again 'to receive' can mean the purely passive acceptance of what one allows to flow over one because one cannot prevent it, but may also mean the spirited reception and personal assimilation of the gift of God. Yet there is no impassable gulf between mere conformity and genuine tradition and the corresponding attitudes. The one may lead into the other.[5]

T. S. Eliot once drew attention to a feature of the artistic tradition, that to remain in the tradition the artist has to do something fresh. He who merely imitates the past does not remain in the tradition.

> We may expect the language to approach maturity at the moment when it has a critical sense of the past, a confidence in the present, and no conscious doubt of the future. In literature this means that the poet is aware of his predecessors, and that we are aware of the predecessors behind his work, as we may be aware of the ancestral traits in a person who is at the same time individual and unique. The predecessors should be themselves great and honoured; but their accomplishment should be such as to suggest still undeveloped resources in the language, and not such as to oppress the younger writers that everything that can be done has been done in their language. The poet, certainly, in a mature age may still obtain stimulus from the hope of doing something that his predecessors have not done; he may even be in revolt against them, as a promising adolescent may revolt against the beliefs, the habits and the manners of his parents; but in retrospect, we can see that he is also the continuer of their traditions, that he preserves essential characteristics, and that his difference of behaviour is a difference in the circumstances of another age. . . . The persistence of literary creativeness in any people, accordingly, consists in the maintenance of an unconscious balance between tradition in the larger sense – the collective personality, so to speak, realised in the literature of the past – and the originality of the living generation.[6]

With a more specifically theological reference Georges Tavard concludes his study of the seventeenth-century controversies over tradition in France and England with the judgment that 'what we have to do with is a past moving and dynamic, the chief characteristic of which, when seen from the point of view of development, is no longer its preservation as a deposit but its preparation of a future', and he pleads for the working-out of a theology of tradition which shall be 'une théologie du devenir et d'avenir'.[7]

The New Testament writings will have a special position for the Christian which cannot be completely covered by the word tradition. Nevertheless, since they also appear as a particular form of tradition, it is not easy to define the special nature of that position in terms appropriate to the writings themselves. Thus, they do not on examination appear to have the character of foundation documents transmitting a faith once delivered to the saints, and to be handed on as a kind of package or baton; nor do they contain a single corpus of consistent belief from which everything else then unfolds. If their special position is held to lie in their comparative proximity to the events of which they speak, what is to be meant by proximity will need to be further defined, and in such a way as not to exclude the possibility that a form of tradition may have no less authoritative insights for being at a greater remove in space and time. If this proximity is specified as that of eye-witnesses to the events in all their contingency, it has to be borne in mind that this is not stressed in the documents themselves, and appears to account very little for their being the kind of documents they are. On the rare occasions it is mentioned it is given an extended meaning not ordinarily present in the idea, as when Luke refers to the sources of his material as being 'eye-witnesses and ministers of the word', or when the author of the first epistle of John begins with 'What we have heard, seen, looked upon and handled concerning the word of life'. That is, what is witnessed to is not the event simply, but the event as it has been assimilated as word, and reflected upon. This can affect the way in which the documents are approached. If they are approached as title deeds, then they are likely to be treated primarily as documents providing fixed norms for direct transference and use, and their interpretation will tend to be the interpretation of written texts. But if they are approached as a particular form of tradition, transmitted and received in the fullest sense of the words, then the goal will be not the interpretation of written texts, but of the experience they document. The past has to be recalled and recreated in its reality as the past in order to be entered into before it is available in the present.

There is opened up here an aspect of the tension between the Christian faith and the world which has, perhaps, received insufficient attention. The modern world is characterized as modern by a deep sense of awareness of the past, and also of awareness of a fundamental break with it. The very word 'modern', from the pejorative sense which it had in the Middle Ages and beyond, has become a word of approval expressive of a radical discontinuity with reference to what has gone before. There are, no doubt, many reasons for this of a physical and intellectual kind which have been spelt out, though it can still be a matter of debate when and how the break came about in such a way that all before it came to seem to belong to another world continuous with the Stone Age. The study of history was itself a contributory factor, since it came into being through an exercise of autonomy which criticized actual traditions, and came to engender a critical stance towards all tradition as such. When combined with other elements in human nature this could become an ingrained mood of suspicion towards, impatience with, and even hatred of the past as meaningless waste. It may be that our hyper-critical attitudes, our negations and deep resentments, have some of their roots here. The drive of Christian faith is, however, different. It also desires, or should desire, to be modern, in the sense that God is God of the world and of the now. It has also shown itself to be not without considerable resources of criticism both of itself and of the world. But its initial impulse towards the past must be to embrace it and to love it, for it is there that it finds the Christ of yesterday in the significant experience of those who in their own times have lived in faith, or, as it has been put, 'from the centre'. 'I believe in the communion of saints', in either of its two possible meanings of the fellowship of believers or participation in holy things, is an integral part of the creed, and could for some people at some times become its opening clause.

This is not, however, to say that tradition is brought down on our individual or corporate heads like a ton of bricks, or is to be received as a solid block of authoritative wisdom. This would be untrue to the tradition if it is to be one 'du devenir et d'avenir', a genuinely living historical tradition directed towards the past and the future and not primarily towards the past and its origins there; and if the purpose of receiving it is not to reproduce the statements of authoritative texts, but to share in the experience to which they point. It would in any case be impossible, since we now receive it only as a fragmented tradition; and this could have implications in more than one sphere.

The most immediate of these is within the sphere of the Christian churches themselves. Engagement in the oecumenical task, when it is more than a huddling together of dwindling communities for greater warmth, or the attempt to weld together inherited authoritative structures, can lead to the discovery that doctrines, forms of expression and institutions which were crucial for Christians in the past for their apprehension of God in Christ, because they were part of the manner in which they apprehended everything, are no longer really alive in the tradition or credible. Apostolic succession and a canon of scripture, Filioque and monophysitism, justification by faith alone and the predestination of the elect, sacrificial atonement and various forms of infallibility, these and much else are found to be crumbling, or to have already crumbled, to dust, as does a skeleton when the lid is taken off a coffin. In their place, but still as expressions of identity with the experience they documented, a fresh plurality of gifts is to be looked for, and of interpretations attempting to encompass Christian truth. And these are likely to be less precise and to be couched in more parabolic language, and they will probably be without the same kind of consensus as was deemed necessary before. No doubt some of the norms by which various forms of the Christian tradition have been able to recognize their identity may be by-passed, but the search could still be for a tradition which, in being transformed, has coherence with the experience of the past.

But there is also the wider and stranger sphere beyond the inner circle of the Christian churches, that of other religions. This is now forced on the attention of the Christian, and not simply from outside by the pluralist form which society has taken. For at least since the time of Paul the church has been a body with the whole world on its conscience, and its performance in this sphere has surely been its weakest point, and is most in need of transformation. After a brief period when it was possible for some to hold, like Justin, that there had been anonymous Christians before Christ and outside the immediate Christian sphere, the church settled, with few exceptions, to an attitude of exclusiveness and hostility to other religions as being demonic parodies of the true. Then for geographical and cultural reasons it settled into an attitude of isolation; and when this was removed, into an attitude of spiritual imperialism. Now that the missionary enterprise in this last form is as good as over, the question is posed afresh whether Christ is in any way to be discovered to have been present yesterday in traditions with other religious origins and names.

Finally, there is what one might call the human tradition. This is too large to specify, though at times it can be fairly well recognized and identified, at least in retrospect. For the Western Christian has to ask himself how it has come about that over the past century or so much of the poetic tradition, the philosophical tradition, the social tradition, and other traditions concerned with the nature of man and the fullness of his life, have come to exist and operate outside the Christian tradition, in separation

from it, and often in opposition to it. Has this been due solely to
perversity or sin? Or is part of the story that the Christian tradition has proved too inelastic, and has failed to discern here also
the Christ of yesterday? If this is so, it is only the Christian
tradition that will wish, or be able, to do anything about it.

10

The Christian Present – Existentialism

The most mysterious aspect of the mystery of time is the present. If defined, as by Sartre, as 'the infinitesimal instant, the nothing-ness, between the future which is not yet and the past which is no more',[1] it is difficult to think or talk about in a rational way. It would seem that it has to borrow from the past and the future on either side of it before it is sufficiently framed to be looked at. Hence some philosophers have spoken of the 'specious present', meaning by that a sequence of originally separate events when they are apprehended as a single whole at a particular instant. The author of Hebrews appears to have been not unaware of this problem in his own way when, in the course of applying the injunction of Psalm 95, 'Today, if you will hear his voice harden not your hearts', to the day to day life of his readers, he adds the qualifying words 'as long as it is still called "today" .' Neverthe-less, these conceptual difficulties do not prevent us from talking about the present, nor from having a lively sense that we are talking about something. This is nowhere more evident in our own time than in the prevalence of philosophies labelled exis-tentialist, as well as in the discovery of existentialist elements hidden away elsewhere, even in the most unlikely places.

It would not be possible to do justice in a short space to these existentialist modes of thought – some would deny them the name of philosophy on the ground that the language they use is too inflated and imprecise. They are varied in their origins and styles. But in all their varieties they would seem to have certain features in common which are given greater or less emphasis, and these would perhaps be not unfairly summarized as follows. As the name suggests priority is given to the present, or the whole concern is with it. That I exist, am here, is the most immediate form that consciousness takes; it is a consciousness of the present in the present. What is to be looked for is a directness and immediacy of experience, and this must inevitably be impatient of taking the long way round. In contrast to any idea that I am a man by reference to some common thing called human nature, which can be detected and then stated in general terms, I am to become what I may be in the present moment. This is not the fruit of rational reflection, explanation or abstract theory, which is arrived at from an observer's position and with the aid of objective norms or some overarching meaning to life. It is, rather, the result of a passionate concern of the individual self to establish meaning for himself. He has to be prepared to do this in a present which is naked, since the world and its past are wholly ambiguous and without any reliable indications of a whence or whither. They are even absurd, the absurd being phenomena for which there are apparently no adequate causes. With these it is impossible to identify. Existence as meaningful living, whether in personal relationships or in creative activity, has to be established over against the world as something alien. There is thus an extreme disjunction between the two orders to which a man belongs, the order of reality and the order of value. Value therefore has to be created and affirmed by the individual for himself by means of what still lies open to him, and that is his decision and his choice. Such decision and choice have to be made in crucial situations, even if they involve the anguish of choosing in the dark and in face of the threat of nothingness, which in the end is symbolized by death. But such decision and choice constitute a man's freedom and responsibility, if they are such that the whole self is engaged in making them, and is totally committed to them in action. This is the only absolute there is. Along this way alone is a man disclosed to himself, and can he realize who he is. He may thus experience an existence which is authentic in being genuine to the facts, and which is legitimized not by external standards but from within.

By way of negative reaction to much of this, with its tendencies to irrationalism and to paradox run wild, even at times to hysteria and morbidity, it has been objected that it arose in the highly exceptional circumstances of extreme crisis and disruption associated with the rise and fall of Nazism in Germany and all that went with that, or with the collapse and occupation of France. The objection is correct as a statement, but is not therefore decisive. It cannot be ruled out in advance, least of all by a Christian, that circumstances of acute disruption may be occasions of deepest insight into how things really are under the surface. Similar notes have been sounded too often and from too many quarters for that. For the period of late antiquity one could not do better than refer to the Wiles Lectures given in The Queen's University of Belfast by Professor E. R. Dodds under the significant title *Pagan and Christian in an Age of Anxiety.*[2] It is discovered to be a recurrent and not simply a current condition that Yeats voiced when he wrote:

> Turning and turning in the widening gyre
> The falcon cannot hear the falconer;
> Things fall apart; the centre cannot hold;
> Mere anarchy is loosed upon the world,
> The blood-dimmed tide is loosed, and everywhere
> The ceremony of innocence is drowned;
> The best lack all conviction, while the worst
> Are full of passionate intensity.[3]

It is, moreover, an open question whether there are now factors not previously present which could bring about a permanent condition of absurdity, of phenomena without adequate causes – on the one hand in man's awareness of himself, as he looks backwards, as the product of an evolutionary process, about which he has to ask whether he is more than a speck in the cosmic dust, and on the other hand, looking forward, the permanent threat of destruction.

There are, moreover, too many echoes of this way of thinking in the Christian tradition itself for a purely negative attitude towards it. Passion in theology and philosophy, inwardness and immediacy, truth as personal and subjective and as rooted in decision and commitment, the urgency of the present moment – these have a pedigree in Christianity itself which reaches further back than Kierkegaard, the so-called father of existentialism, with whom indeed it took a special form in his native reaction to a desiccated Protestant scholasticism. They are repeatedly recognizable, and extend back by way of figures like Pascal and Augustine into the New Testament, to Paul and John, for both of whom faith has been described as consisting in 'an energy of the whole nature, an active transference of the whole being into another life'.

A more damaging criticism of contemporary, or what might be

called unsupported existentialism, would be that it so isolates the self as to render it incapable of ever emerging from a closed circle of subjectivity, and is for that reason out of touch with the facts.[4] But then the question posed for the Christian is what a supported existentialism might be. What public and shared facts, and what kind of relationships with whom, are required to evoke and sustain faith, decision and commitment? How much does the present have to borrow from the past and the future in order to be meaningful? And in relation to the Christian tradition this question might take the form of who Christ is that it may be said of him that he is not only yesterday but is also today 'the same'. In pursuing these questions into the heart of the gospel material, which is the mainspring of the tradition of the Christ of yesterday, we run straight into paradox. For there the significance of the present moment is largely conveyed by what, to the modern historically conscious mind which has recovered it, appears most alien, remote, unintelligible and useless, and what the Christian mind down the ages has had the greatest difficulty in knowing what to do with – namely, the eschatology.

Eschatology is a doctrine of the last or ultimate things. So long as it remained close to Old Testament prophecy it expressed these things in the language of time and history as decisive acts of judgment and restoration by which the God of Israel was to effect his purposes for Israel, and through Israel for the world. Apocalyptic, which is often loosely used as a synonymous term, is a particular kind of eschatology, which is to be distinguished from the prophetic at least in principle, however difficult it may be to make the distinction in certain instances. Prophetic eschatology remains within the sphere of history, even if language is strained to keep it there, and God's coming consummation of things is supported by, and to some extent read off from, previous patterns of events apprehended as a single whole and as witnesses to his activity. Apocalyptic, arising in a period which was felt to be one of extreme crisis, sees a radical breach between what is, has been or ever shall be in the historical sphere, and what must nevertheless be. It speaks of two ages and operates on two levels. Correspondingly it affirms a future revolution of divine action which is to be direct and total, and does so in cosmic terms drawn from myths of primordial events concerned with the fate of the world. There is to be a warfare between heavenly protagonists of good and evil, a universal judgment on all history, which is now divided into significant epochs, and a life which negates death by resurrection.

To penetrate into the heart of the gospel material is to be compelled to come to grips with this eschatological mode of thinking. Mark introduces his account of the ministry of Jesus with the compendious statement that he came announcing God's gospel to the effect that 'the time is filled up, the kingdom of God has drawn near; repent and believe in the gospel'. Whether this highly compressed summary was ever spoken by Jesus, or – since the evidence that he ever used the word 'gospel' is slender – is a later Christian epitome of what his message was taken to be, it brings into juxtaposition the eschatological future and the present moment, and the one as the basis of the other. The appointed time and its filling up belonged to the vocabulary of apocalyptic, as did also 'the kingdom of God', though this could function in other modes of thinking also. 'Repent', or rather the turning round which would be better conveyed by conversion, is a radical demand for a decision involving the whole person, while the expression 'believe in', which is unique in the New Testament with reference to the gospel, speaks of a personal commitment.

That Mark's sentence is a genuine summary is indicated by the considerable amount of material in the synoptic gospels which in one way or another treats of the kingdom of God. What is the purport of this material? Here one has to record it as a fact, melancholy or otherwise, that this question has turned out to be one of the most problematic in New Testament study, and has turned out to be so because of the nature of the material itself. For, into whatever strands of tradition a literary or non-literary analysis divides up these gospels, two kinds of statement about the kingdom or sovereign rule of God are found juxtaposed and unreconciled. There is, on the one hand, the kind of statement to the effect that it has by divine action overtaken history, and is manifesting its results. On the other hand, there is the kind of statement to the effect that it still remains in God's future, though in an imminent and not a distant future. So, in Mark's gospel Jesus knows that God has already given to disciples the secret of the kingdom and that a pious scribe is not far from it, but also that there are some who will not die before they see it come with power (Mark 4.11; 12.34; 9.1). In the material common to Matthew and Luke appeal is made to exorcisms of demons as evidence that the kingdom has indeed come upon his contemporaries in the defeat of the supernatural realm of Satan, yet in the Lord's Prayer disciples are to pray for its advent (Matt. 12.28; Luke 11.20; Matt. 6.10; Luke 11.2). In material peculiar to Matthew the publicans and harlots are said to be going into the kingdom in advance of the religious leaders, but the kingdom is like those found watching and ready for a bridegroom despite his delay (Matt. 21.31; 25.1ff.). In the material peculiar to Luke the kingdom is not to be searched for with scrutiny since it is there in their midst, but a parable is told to discourage the idea that it was on the point of appearing (Luke 17.21; 19.1ff.). A not dissimilar result is reached if the material is approached along some other line than that of its division into sources, and is considered by way of its classification into the different genres of parables, dialogues, commandments of law, words of exhortation or instruction.

In face of this evidence attempts have been made, naturally enough, to bring some consistency and coherence into it by seeking to establish one element at the expense of the other, to show one to be original and the other secondary. So it has been argued that Jesus' own consciousness of how things stood is to be seen in the announcement of a future but imminent kingdom, and that the conception of a present and already operative rule represents the reflection back into his time of the subsequent Christian experience of living in the more immediate presence of God consequent upon his resurrection and the possession of the Spirit. Or, contrariwise, that the announcement of the presence of the kingdom and its operation was his own understanding of the state of affairs, but that this proved too much to hold on to in the face of subsequent events, and the later Christian mind fell back into the more familiar mould of Jewish expectation of the future, and this reversion has coloured the tradition. That the logical contradictions can only be avoided if it is assumed that 'Jesus combined the coming age as the, for the present, distant future with the near future of the Kingdom of God in such a way that the power of this Kingdom of God "pioneered a way" for itself in the conduct of Jesus', or that in view of the available evidence 'consistency should be found in the opposite direction, namely by recognizing that Jesus perceived the Kingdom of God as having already come' – these two opposing conclusions have both had their eminent representatives and continue to do so.[5]

But it has further to be noted that neither of these two positions has been able to succeed in driving out the other, and in holding the field to the exclusion of the other. Unless, then, the gospel tradition is to be held at this central point to be altogether incoherent, it has to be entertained as a serious possibility that these two positions have somehow to be held together in tension. The result would be that, while we are frequently unable to arrive in respect of particular statements at a precise understanding of what is being said, we nevertheless receive a strong impression that the truth is being uttered by this interlacing of the future and the present, and is being uttered in such a way as to bring it to bear with full force in the present moment to an audience which is for this very reason addressed as 'this generation'. What is being declared to them as though they were the last generation of all, in terms of the kingdom, is the structure of reality, how things are as Jesus sees them. This is not, however, by means of theoretical explanation or of an appeal to general norms, but rather by demands for concrete action in particular circumstances, for action which is often in contradiction with what has hitherto obtained, and which is proper and good not of itself but in virtue of what God will make of it. As W. Pannenberg has put it, if God and his rule are inseparable, and if he is known as God only in his effective action, then we must say 'in a restricted and important sense that God does not yet exist', and that 'his being is still in the process of coming to be'.[6]

The gospel material, however, has come down to us, because it came down to the evangelists themselves, in such brief and compressed units that, for all its forcefulness, it often lacks the sharp contours which would enable us to see more clearly what the particular circumstances were which provided the background for this judgment of how things were, and to detect the now unspoken assumptions behind what is being said. To take an example. It is evident that for each of the evangelists in his own way, and probably for Jesus himself, his mission and message were related to the phenomenon of John the Baptist, who was already an eschatological figure with his radical preaching of an imminent judgment, his ascetic withdrawal from the world, and his unique baptism of preparation for the end (if this is a right interpretation of the evidence). But what was this relation? Was it one of association or of dissociation? The relevant material for answering this question belongs in different sources, and is for the most part brief and highly concentrated. It consists of such passages as the appeal to contemporary miracles characteristic of the time of salvation in answer to John's question whether Jesus was the coming one; the parable about children playing in the market place who petulantly object both to mourning and jollity; the statement, obscure in either of its variant forms, of John's position as a dividing line between the law and the prophets on the one hand and the violence associated with the kingdom on the other; the distinction between John's disciples who fast and Jesus' disciples who do not; the identification of John with Elijah the precursor of the new age; the parallel of his death with the coming suffering of the Son of man; and the question about the earthly or heavenly origin of John's baptism in counter to attacks upon Jesus for what he is doing (Matt. 11.2ff.; Luke 7.18ff.; Matt. 11.16ff.; Luke 7.31ff.; Matt. 11.11–13; Luke 16.16; Mark 2.18f.; 9.11–13; 11.27ff.). This material may be held to point in two different directions. Some of it points in the direction that the radical dissociation from a world under judgment had been initiated by John and had brought the divine rule near, and that Jesus' message was in continuation of that, and was uttered from substantially the same standpoint. Some of it, on the other hand, could point in the direction that his message, and the experience which it articulated, involved a radical discontinuity even from John, and required for its expression association with, and blessing on, the disinherited and the outsiders, whose enforced absence of status and satisfaction marked them out as the natural recipients of the divine rule as he saw it.

Consideration of the background and basis of Jesus' proclamation of the kingdom of God raises sooner or later the question of what is called his ethical teaching, which in its own way has proved as embarrassing as the eschatology. Eschatological urgency, which confronts the present moment with the possibilities it has for God's rule in it, may be primary, and may provide the framework of authentic existence, but it does not of itself suffice. For it says too little about the God whose rule it is. Others have thought themselves to be living in this situation, including as we now know the Qumran community, but they have not drawn identical conclusions from it. Here we come to the real problem of eschatology, which was the title of a striking lecture delivered as long ago as 1916 by Henry Scott Holland. He approached the matter as one who was at the same time a biblical

scholar and a protagonist of Christian socialism, and he was
writing at a time when the apocalyptic background of the ministry and teaching of Jesus had just been rediscovered. He began
from conclusions which were being drawn from this at the time,
notably those of the Roman Catholic modernist George Tyrrell.
Tyrrell had written,

> Pessimism is the verdict of experience . . . The verdict of the deeper
> spiritual intuition is always pessimistic . . . Righteousness was not the
> substance of the Kingdom; eternal life was not the moral life . . . Christ
> had not come to emphasize the religion and revelation implied in
> righteousness. His emphasis was on the other-worldly, supermoral
> life of the coming kingdom. What need of a new ethics for an expiring
> humanity?[7]

On this, and on similar judgments which Tyrrell and others who
shared his view had made, Scott Holland made the following
comments.

> We are in the presence of two antagonistic motives, two incompatible
> ideals: (1) The intense expectation of a sudden coming, and (2) A vivid
> interest in the present; or again (1) The motive of world-renunciation,
> and (2) The motive of world-redemption; or (1) The ideal of a catas-
> trophic arrival from without, and (2) Of grace instilled from within. . . .
> These pairs of conceptions are supposed to negative and cancel each
> the other. If men expect the future they cannot care for the present.

He then concludes, 'We should naturally suppose that a passionate expectation of a tremendous change should disturb and
destroy the interest of the present. But the real problem of Christian Eschatology is that it does not.'[8] And he devoted the rest
of his lecture to illustrating this conclusion from the New
Testament, and to exploring its implications.

On occasions in the teaching of Jesus the specific injunction is
grounded in the proclamation of the kingdom as the way things
are, as when anxiety over food and clothing is forbidden because
these things are addenda to the primary search for the kingdom
of God; or when renunciation of all possessions is required of a
man who desires to inherit eternal life, which is here a synonym
for the kingdom. This may have been the presupposition in all
cases, even if it was an unspoken presupposition. But as we now
have this teaching there is often some other starting-point to it,
either in the Old Testament law as the authoritative description of
what life is to be in Israel, or in some practice articulating this life
such as sabbath, ritual purity, or the religious duties of prayer,

fasting and almsgiving. And the procedure, which can still be detected underneath what in many cases look like later adaptations of his teaching to other circumstances, would seem to be always in the same style and to have the same drift. This was different from that of his contemporaries. The contemporary method, which is that of most ethical systems of a heteronomous kind, was the laudable one of casuistry, by which it was hoped that the commands uttered a long time ago with divine authority might be made alive in the present moment by being applied to the conditions of individual cases. The style of Jesus is different. It also starts from what had been anciently spoken with divine authority, but over against it he insists with his own authority that the commandments shall be restated in such a way that their full intention is made plain and is exhausted, and they cannot be pushed any further. In this way they are thrust into the marrow of human life, and there are no conditions of the present where their force is not inescapable. So the prohibition of murder is prohibition of anger, adultery takes place in the heart, standing by one's word is not to use an oath at all, recompence is the renunciation of it, love of the neighbour is love of the enemy in reproduction of the perfect love of God himself. And along with the commandments the religious practice which goes with them – cleanness is interior of the heart, the sabbath is for what is man's good, prayer, fasting and almsgiving are to be performed so that what the performance is good for defies human calculation, and is known only by the God whose relationship to life they presuppose.

Thus the same accent as governs his proclamation of the kingdom governs also his ethical teaching – if indeed words like 'ethics' and 'teaching' really apply any longer here – and with the same paradoxical result, that what appears to have a far away look about it bears immediately and directly on the present moment, and that what has a transcendent origin is not experienced as something arbitrarily imposed upon life, but as reaching to and exposing the human condition. It is this which, as John Knox has observed, intensifies the problem of what to do about the ethics of Jesus.

The problem, he writes,

> has a deeper, more existential ground than the reported sayings of Jesus and the exhortations of the apostles. We are not in the position of having to wait upon an interpretation of some ancient words to know

what kind of obligation we are under. I do actually find myself under an impossible demand. I know I am deceiving myself when I imagine I have reached, or can reach, the point where I can say: 'I have done all I ought to do. I am all I ought to be.' Thus, if Jesus had not, in his most characteristic teaching, defined God's will for us in terms of utterly unqualified and unrestricted good will, one can reverently say, 'He should have.' Nothing short of that would have been true to what, at our deepest and best, we know to be true about God and about ourselves. We would not have known this about God and about ourselves if Jesus had not made it known. But once he has made it known, we see for ourselves that it is true: that is, it finds us at our deepest and most real.[9]

But if the truth once stated is recognized as the truth, does it matter who stated it? How did Jesus arrive at what he said to be the condition of things, and wherein does his authority lie? The traditional answer to such questions, which is derived from the New Testament itself, has been in some kind of christology some doctrine of the person of Jesus. His authority lay in the fact that he was, or was conscious of himself as Messiah, or son of David, that is, the king in the kingdom of God. Or that he was the Son of man, and therefore privy to the divine secrets. Or that he was the unique Son of the Father who reproduces the intentions and acts of the Father. But this christology can bring about a serious shift in emphasis. 'The kingdom precedes every Christology and every new qualification of human existence.'[10] Even in the synoptic gospels, lying as they do under the influence of christological doctrine, the connection between Jesus' authoritative utterances and summons on the one hand, and who he is who utters them and on what grounds he utters them on the other hand, is seldom explicitly made. And it may be noted that one result of the Fourth Gospel's preoccupation with him as the Son of the Father is that in that gospel Jesus no longer proclaims the kingdom of God, and that he hardly teaches anything at all except the commandment of love, and then a commandment only to love of the brethren. The question here is whether Jesus was the the object as well as the subject of his own definition of human life as the contingent faced with the promise of God's future consummating power.

In the end, therefore, this question itself must converge, as it did for the first Christians, on Jesus' death and resurrection, and especially on the latter. For whatever else it may be, the resurrection belongs to the vocabulary of apocalyptic, and in speaking

of it, and of Jesus as the firstborn from the dead, the intention was
to speak of the beginning of God's rule and of the consummation
of all things. Hence the great difficulties in speaking about it
which are only too evident in the gospel narratives. But what God
consummates and draws into his rule so immediately through
the resurrection is the death of Jesus, upon which the light from
the ultimate then shines back. But what was this death in its
contingency? Here very much is in doubt, because the narratives,
which were predominantly shaped to answer a different kind of
question from this, are so compressed and impregnated with the
interpretation of hindsight. Why Jesus left Galilee for Jerusalem
at all; whether he went up, as depicted in the synoptic gospels but
not in John's gospel, with deliberation for a single decisive visit;
how far the issues which had emerged in his proclamation and
teaching were also the issues which occasioned the conflict in
Jerusalem; what led to what in the chain of events; whether the
chain was forged from one side or the other or both; whether it
was a chain of events or a concatenation of circumstances ; what
were the precise actions of the persons concerned and the
motives behind the actions, whether they were serious or frivol-
ous, well-intentioned or malevolent; how far martyrdom, mis-
carriage of justice, misunderstanding or misfortune contributed
to what took place – these and other possible factors related to the
contingency of events are bound from the nature of the material
to be matters of speculation. In all the uncertainties, however,
what may probably be said from the point of view of the resurrection, and from almost any point of view other than that the
event did not happen, is that the death of Jesus took place in the
context of, and was itself the occasion of, an extreme disjunction.

This, at any rate, is how our earliest witness, Paul, appears to
have seen it. When he writes to the Galatians, 'Christ became a
curse for us', and then goes on to explain what he means by
adding as scriptural justification a quotation from Deuteronomy,
'Cursed is he who hangs on a tree' he is making a judgment
which is as much historical as theological. For the words in
Deuteronomy pertained to the judicial sentence on certain classes
of criminals to the effect that after death they should be publicly
exposed by being hung on a tree and then cut down before
sundown because they defiled the sacred land of Israel. Applied
here to what had turned out contingently to be the non-Israelite
and Roman punishment of the cross, these words indicate that

for Paul the real issue was not the law of the Roman occupying power. The issue was that Israel, the church of God, executing God's law, was on one side, and Jesus alone, as the herald of the kingdom of God and as the spokesman of the will of God, was on the other. Where then was God to be found? Within the context of Judaism this was the maximum possible breach in the order of things. The author of Hebrews says the same in his milder fashion when he reminds his readers that Jesus suffered 'outside the camp' or consecrated ground of Israel, while Jesus himself may have been saying it even more violently than Paul with the words, 'My God, my God, why hast thou forsaken me?' It is this death which is affirmed by resurrection as capable of confronting every present moment.

To examine how this was felt to be so would be to begin to explore the tradition, beginning with Paul, its earliest and most extensive representative. In Paul the same elements are present as with Jesus, but in the reverse order. If Jesus' proclamation of the kingdom, his eschatological ethic and his death and resurrection unfold in the order a,b,c, in Paul they appear to have the order c,b,a. Permanently prior now is the death with its affirming resurrection. This is seen as the negation of those elements in human life which have already shown themselves to be negative in seeking to exist in their own right and to secure their own fulfilment. It is also the disclosure of the possibility of an existence of obedience and creatureliness which is authentically human. One mark of this is freedom, a freedom from what is itself stultifying and distorting, and a release into an engagement with things as they really are. With this death and resurrection the believer is united in such a way that they determine his thinking and willing. Paul can describe this as a continual 'bearing about in the body the putting to death of Jesus that the life of Jesus may also be manifested in the body', where the word 'body', here as elsewhere, denotes the human person not in the closed circle of his subjectivity but in his personal relationships. These relationships then stand under an eschatological ethic, which is given further form and content by this death and resurrection. This can come out in some such form as that since the fashion of this world is transient 'those who have wives may be as those who have none; and those that weep as though they did not weep; and those who rejoice as though they did not rejoice; and those who buy as though they did not possess; and those who

use the world as not abusing it' (I Cor. 7.29ff.). There is here a
freedom of manoeuvre which comes not from an isolation of the
self over against the discernible facts of life, but rather from a full
engagement in them in the present, because their ultimate fulfilment and satisfaction, though certain, are not expected from
the present itself. And for Paul the kingdom of God has now
become the furthest outreach of this, when the operation of
Christ's dominion is finished through the destruction of all
enemies, including death, when the human being puts on the
spiritual 'body' as the form corresponding to the person in his
maturity, and when Christ resigns his rule to the Father for God
to be all things to all. To explore the Christian tradition beyond
Paul up to the present time would be to explore how far and in
what ways this understanding of human existence has or has not
maintained itself in the course of that process of development
from which no living thing can escape.

11

The Christian Future – Eschatology

The ejaculation in the Epistle to the Hebrews from which we started has a curious order of words in the Greek which is sometimes obliterated in translation. If the purpose of the ejaculation was to affirm the essential identity of Jesus Christ in all possible circumstances, and especially if it was some kind of formula, one would have expected it to run either,' 'Jesus Christ the same yesterday, today and to the ages', or 'Jesus Christ yesterday, today and to the ages the same'. In fact it runs 'Jesus Christ yesterday and today the same', with the result that the concluding phrase 'and to the ages' has the appearance of an afterthought or perhaps a pious addition. And this impression is not entirely removed if 'and' is taken here in either an emphatic or resumptive sense – 'even to the ages' or 'yea to the ages'. Is then the truth which it intends to convey also an appendix? Is Christian faith for all practical purposes complete with the apprehension somehow of Jesus Christ as the same yesterday and today?

To judge from the New Testament writings themselves it was very far from being an appendix. It turns out to be an entirely proper question to put to any of these writings where it stands with respect to the consummation of all things and the connection of Christ with this consummation. And such an enquiry will be found not to be dealing with matters on the circumference, but to be directed towards the very heart of the creative life and thought of the early church to which these writings bear witness. In one way or another what had taken place within the context of Judaism in Jesus Christ, in his proclamation of the rule of God, in his physical actions and ethical demands, and especially in his death and resurrection, was apprehended already by faith as being of unique and ultimate significance, not only for men but for 'ta panta' or 'all things'. For that reason it was apprehended as a phenomenon of the past and of the present which by its very nature carried with it the necessity of some future manifestation of itself in a form which would make this significance palpable and incontestable.

What lay behind this was primarily the apocalyptic mode of thought within which the gospel was moulded. Characteristic of apocalyptic was totality. All was felt to be at stake. It saw human perplexities and evils in a universal perspective and on the background of a far reaching chaos. These perplexities were bound up with history as a whole in a kind of cosmic drama played out between the creation of all things and an ultimate end. Its vision was correspondingly of a transformation of all things by a transcendent God which would suffice in being immediate and total. In early Christian theology Christ, and especially his resurrection as belonging naturally within this mode of thinking, were conceived of and set forth in various ways as both the effective anticipation and the paradigm of this total transformation. It is important to stress that this was done in various ways if the depth and range of early Christian theology is not to be unduly stultified. Thus, for example, the mode of thinking denoted by the parousia or coming of Christ, thought of now as a second coming or coming again for the dissolution of the universe and the gathering of the elect, may have been the earliest form of this expectation, may have caused the most ferment, and brought most problems with it. But it was one mode amongst others. It was not, as it has been and still is often taken to be, the only or canonical mode; and despite its survival through repetition in creeds to the present day it turns out to be the most restricted and least repeatable. For when an early Christian said that he lived in expectation of Christ's coming again soon, he was not only saying something about the future as a residue still left over to be experienced. He was also saying something about how the past event looked to him, namely, that as he saw it it was the kind of revelatory event it was precisely in being a past event which required a speedy consummation of this kind. Subsequent generations were not able to see it in this way, not only because with the passage of time the parousia did not happen, but because the event as a whole, past, present and future, could no longer have this particular shape in their eyes. If they went on repeating the early Christian's words to express their own belief, they could only delude themselves if they thought that in so doing they were reproducing his belief or sharing in it.

There is not one eschatology in the New Testament but several. They draw on and refashion different aspects of a total picture in exploring the possible range of that transformation of life which had already been in part introduced and experienced through Christ, and in exploring the extent to which the action of Christ was united with that of the transcendent God. Thus in the Epistle to the Romans, chapters 9–11, Paul stated it in terms of the mission in which he was engaged. What lay behind his mission was his expectation that the whole of the Gentile world would be drawn to Christian faith in the persons of its main representatives, and that as a result the whole of Israel would be moved to come in also. This did not materialize any more than did the parousia, and subsequent generations were quite unable to think of the mission of the church in this way even if they made use of Paul's words. But in the previous chapter 8 of the same epistle Paul also, in a passage which on account of its creative possibilities deserves more consideration in the church than it generally gets, had expressed it in terms of the Spirit and divine sonship. A sonship of God has already been experienced in moral life and prayer through the possession of the Spirit; but it is also something which is still awaited in its completion in the form of adoption and of being conformed to the one who is Son by his resurrection. This completion will consist for the believer in the liberation of the body, and involves with it the whole created order, and this awaiting brings with it a fellow feeling with a creation which also still strives and groans. The author of the Epistle to the Ephesians expresses it in terms of fullness. The divine secret for the fullness of time is the unification of the multiplicities of the universe under one head, Christ. This is a secret about the universe already disclosed to the universal church as the present fullness of the Christ who is to fill all things completely, and it is so disclosed through his resurrection as an instance of unlimited power and authority. The author of Hebrews expresses it in terms of a perfection of Christ, in which temporal suffering and death are the means of his passing as the high priest of humanity into the invisible eternal sphere of the presence and worship of God, and so to what will remain intact when all that is collapsible has collapsed. The author of Revelation expresses it in apocalyptic imagery refashioned to depict a

heavenly political order, in which the world's kingdoms have
become the kingdom of Christ and God, and to Christ the titles of
God – first and last, beginning and end, alpha and omega – are
now properly applied.

This last instance is a reminder that while eschatology is a
doctrine of the end, we have surprisingly not yet reached the end
of the matter in these various visions of the consummation. So far
as the New Testament is concerned – and this is perhaps the most
remarkable thing in it – the last word has not been spoken until,
as it were, the first word has also been spoken; until, that is, the
Christ who is seen as the focus and instrument of this consummation, however it may be envisaged, has also been declared
to be the creator of the world he consummates, or the Father's
agent of its creation. It is remarkable in itself that the erstwhile
teacher of Nazareth and the one judged a pseudo-messiah by his
nation should in Christian faith have come to be assigned the
supreme status of responsibility for the world. It is further remarkable that this should have taken place in so many of the main
lines of Christian thinking that have come down to us, independently it would seem of one another, and as the furthest thrust
along each separate line. The chief passages concerned are as
follows. Along the Pauline line there is not only such a passing
remark as that in I Cor. 8.6, 'For us there is one God, the Father,
from whom are all things and for whom we exist, and one Lord,
Jesus Christ, through whom are all things and through whom we
exist.' There is also the extended exposition in Col. 1.15–17,
where it is said of Christ as the agent of deliverance that he is 'the
image of the invisible God, prior to and superior over all creation,
for within (or, by means of) him all things were created in heaven
and earth, not only visible things but the invisible thrones,
sovereignties, authorities and powers; (the) all things were
created through him and for him, and in (or, by) him (the) all
things cohere'. In the Epistle to the Hebrews the opening sentence – perhaps the most elaborately constructed sentence in the
New Testament – first contrasts the varied and fragmentary
speech of God through prophets with his utterance in the final
age through one who is a Son. It then continues of this Son that
he has been appointed the inheritor of all things, that through
him God created the worlds, that he reflects the glory of God and
bears the stamp of God's being, and that he upholds the universe
by his power. And we may mark the way we have come by taking

note of the fact that, by a shift of meaning from the temporal to the spatial, 'the worlds' here is the same Greek word as 'the ages' in the ejaculatory statement 'to the ages'. Moreover the author proceeds to apply to this Son the words of Psalm 102.26–28 which referred to God as the world's creator. In the Fourth Gospel it is a matter of the prologue, where this gospel's account of the life, death and resurrection of Jesus in the form of the inter-relation between the Father and the Son is presented as a reflection of the relation between God and his eternal Word, who was in the beginning with him, through whom all things without exception were created, and who enters a world of his own making. In Revelation it is, as already indicated, that amongst the riot of images expressive of the exalted Christ's control of the book of the destiny of the universe are images which unite him to God as first and last, beginning and end, and the author of creation.

As this last instance makes clear, what we see here, to put it in technical jargon, is an eschatology begetting a protology. Exploration to the furthest degree of who Christ is to be in the end turns round on itself and takes in the beginning. To ascribe to him ultimate authority, effective and controlling power, and wisdom involves the question of his authorship of, ownership of, and responsibility for the world. Common to both eschatology and protology is the constantly recurring phrase, *'ta panta'*, which is so difficult to translate – not 'the all', for that would be too abstract and would require the neuter singular, nor simply 'all things' indiscriminately, which would ignore the definite article, but literally 'the all things', the sum of contingents grasped as a unity. All this was not, however, theology in a vacuum. It was produced in face of concrete issues, even if we can only catch glimpses of what these issues actually were, and are unable to make much of them even when we can. In the case of the Epistle to the Colossians the issue appears to be that of the possible ultimate malignancy of the universe in, to quote a modern scholar, 'a cordon insanitaire' of cosmocrats, elements or elemental forces encircling the globe in the sublunary regions, and determining its life, perhaps outside Christ's control, or else disputing his power to restore the goodness of creation by reconciling men to God. In the case of the Epistle to the Hebrews the issue appears to be that of the faintheartedness and instability of his readers, who have failed to appreciate that in Christ it is human nature itself which has been elevated above any angelic nature, and has access to the very presence of God, and so to power over the world. In the case of the Fourth Gospel the issue appears to be that of the widely felt and deeply ingrained sense of a radical cleavage and incompatibility between the two elements of experience, namely the physical or what is gross, sensual, earthbound and self-centred, and the spiritual or what is light, heavenly and capable of divinity; and of the overcoming of this cleavage by the presence of the spiritual flesh of Christ, its creator, in his creation. In the case of Revelation the issue appears to be the ideology of an imperial power with universalist claims, which in offering salvation and playing at being God so perverts the created order as to let loose the powers of antichrist, death and Hades.

Various as were these expressions of the cosmic role of Christ, and various as would appear to have been the circumstances of their orgin, they seem to have two features in common. First, the forms of expression are in varying degrees visionary and poetic. This is strictly so in Revelation which is visionary throughout. The prologue to the Fourth Gospel has been labelled by one of its recent commentators as 'an early Christian hymn, probably stemming from Johannine circles, which has been adapted to serve as an overture to the Gospel narrative of the career of the incarnate Word'.[1] Several scholars have claimed to detect in Colossians 1.15–20 a hymn, possibly a baptismal hymn, already in use in some areas of the church and here appropriated to the argument. The opening sentence of the Epistle to the Hebrews has the elevated tone of high rhetoric, and something of the same may be said of Romans 8. Secondly, the main instrument of expression of the cosmic role of Christ appears to be the Jewish-hellenistic speculation concerning Sophia or Wisdom. 'The image of God', 'the beginning of creation', 'the reflection of God's glory', 'the stamp of God's substance', 'existence before all things', 'coherence', these are terms which belonged in the sphere of thought represented by such books as Proverbs, Ecclesiasticus and the Wisdom of Solomon, with their common concern for the human condition as such, and their hymns about Wisdom as the archetype or agent of God's creative activity and as the mediator between him and the world of men. They, or their like, are also to be found in the writings of the Jewish philosopher Philo, and in other examples of literature designed to introduce the Jewish faith to the hellenistic world. It is significant that almost all the statements about the Word in the Johannine prologue have parallels in what is said about the cosmic Wisdom. This is not as surprising as might be expected. The visionary fantasy of apocalyptic and the sober realism of Wisdom literature are not as far apart as might be supposed, and the possible connections between them have perhaps been insufficiently studied. Different as they may be, there is a kinship between them, and they approximate to each other in being cosmic in outlook. The connection between them is in '*ta panta*', 'the all things', and in the divine secrets for the consummation of a creation which is of divine origin. Precisely because apocalyptic envisaged a universal history, whose shape and purpose could only be known from its ultimate goal, it came to include within itself speculation concerning the origin and character of the whole, a kind of primitive science in poetic form.

The combination of these two features, poetic expression and Wisdom theology, in the various affirmations of the authorship of the world in the different streams of primitive Christianity, points to their being products of what one might call the visionary intelligence or inspired reason; and this constituted perhaps a good deal of what the early church meant by prophecy. The wider aspects of this are noted by Teilhard de Chardin when he observes that poets and philosophers have had in common a concern for the whole.

> There is no profound poetry, no true lyricism, no sublimity in words, in art or in music, that does not rest upon the evocation of the Whole, presentiment of, nostalgia for, the Whole. . . . Philosophers, too, of all times have tried to record the exact characteristics of, and to systematize, what poets of all times have experienced and celebrated when this universal vibration reverberated in their souls – either because the philosophers also had this world-feeling, or simply because they wanted to understand what the poets meant.[2]

He argues from this that concern for the whole is deeply rooted in the human being as human.

Is this in fact the case? Does any of this matter? We return to our opening question whether 'to the ages' is an appendix or afterthought, at best something marginal, the result of skirmishes conducted by theologians out of sight on the frontiers in a dated warfare, for which it is indeed theoretically possible that we might one day be grateful if the centre was ever felt to be threatened by the same kind of enemies, though that is hardly likely. For the situations have radically altered. We know of no modern equivalent to the sublunary elemental spirits of the universe. The dualism of matter and spirit is not easily entertained by our scientific and historical consciousness. Our political ideologies, however perverse, remain regional rather than global. Can it then be seriously suggested that the man in the pew ought to have a lively sense of the cosmic creator Christ? Can the initial statement of the creed, 'I believe in one God, the Father, Almighty, maker of heaven and earth and of all things visible and invisible' not look after itself on its own, and can it be in any meaningful way undergirded by the further statement of its second paragraph, 'through whom [sc. Christ] all things were made'? To judge from such sampling as one is able to conduct amongst men in the pew, or even amongst theologians, the answer would be pretty clearly 'No'. It was a professional theologian, Robert Mackintosh, writing on another professional theologian, Albrecht Ritschl, and castigating the Ritschlian system for claiming too much in the sphere of religion, who compared the doctrine of Christ as creator to those astronomical hypotheses regarding the back side of the moon (he was writing in 1915), and who concluded that it may be a Christian duty to be 'icily indifferent' to affirmations of this kind in that they have no discoverable bearing on the moral and spiritual life. 'What is the relation between Jesus Christ and the nebula in Orion? With the utmost reverence, speaking in God's presence, I answer that I neither know nor care.'[3]

Yet the question nags, perhaps, in the recesses of the mind of the simplest believer. Are we able permanently to acquiesce in such a divorce between Christian faith and the world of nature and its processes and development, of which we are a part, in any moral or spiritual life we may have? Feuerbach once complained that 'Nature, the world, has no value, no interest for Christians. The Christian thinks only of himself and of the salvation of his soul.'[4] This has never been strictly true, and would not even be true, if, in view of what has taken place since Feuerbach's time, we were to add 'and of the salvation of the church'. That Christ is to be taken as a principal clue to the structure of reality only as that reality is experienced within a private and personal world or at best in an ecclesiastically corporate world, with the rest of what exists as a dispensable backdrop, would at any time be an impoverished Christian faith. An icy indifference towards the question might serve to cover up how schizoid Christian faith has actually become, and how debilitated in fact is belief in the creator God of the first paragraph of the creed without some recourse to the gospel of Christ in its furthest outreach.

The problem is peculiarly modern. For the New Testament theologians, and for Christian believers after them until comparatively recently, it was possible to pass intellectually and imaginatively backwards and forwards between the gospel and creation, between the visible and the invisible, between man and the principalities and powers, with the one illuminating the other. This was because, so to speak, they all belonged on the same map. This was a mythological map, on which all things were connected in a continuum of divine action and purpose, and were to greater or less degree thought of as personal. The end was a counterpart to the beginning, from which it might be extrapolated in various ways. It could be that the end was already contained in the beginning, as when it was thought of in terms of entry into a sabbath which was already pre-existent with the creator. Or it could be arrived at by way of a return to the beginning, as to a paradise. Or it would somehow correspond to the beginning, as in the hope expressed of a new heavens and a new earth. Or it could be conceived of by means of a typology, whether of similarity or contrast or both, as with a first Adam and a second Adam, both of whom included in themselves the destiny of mankind, but the one a living being whose fall brought about a permanent state of death, and the other a transforming spirit by his exaltation. For some time now this way of thinking in any of its forms has been impossible for us. We have had to learn that the sphere of the scientist and that of the theologian have to be distinguished and kept apart, so that the attempt to bring them together again by such means would be to engage in pseudo-science and pseudo-theology. The visionary intelligence, the inspired reason, have been split, and we are at a loss to know how, if ever, they can be united again. Our intelligence is so predominantly a scientific and historical intelligence, and this does not provide the substance of the visionary faculty, which has to look around elsewhere for what assistance it can find.

Whatever may be thought of his suggested solutions to this problem, no one has felt it more acutely or stated it more forcibly than Teilhard de Chardin, as the following quotations show.

I wonder whether a single person today can *at the same time* focus his mind on the geological world presented by science, and on the world commonly described by sacred history. We cannot retain both pictures without moving alternately from one to the other. Their association clashes, it rings false. In combining them on one and the same plane we are certainly victims of an error in perspective.[5]

Human knowledge is developing exclusively under the aegis of evolution, recognized as a prime property of experiential reality. So true is this that *nothing can any longer find place in our constructions which does not first satisfy the conditions* of a universe in the process of transformation. A Christ whose features do not adapt themselves to the requirements of a world that is evolutive in structure will tend more and more to be eliminated out of hand – just as in learned societies today articles on perpetual motion or squaring the circle are consigned to the wastepaper basket, unread. And correspondingly, if a Christ is to be completely acceptable as an object of worship, he must be presented as the saviour of the idea and reality of evolution.[6]

Our Christology is still expressed in exactly the same terms as those which, three centuries ago, could satisfy men whose outlook on the cosmos it is now physically impossible for us to accept. Unless we admit that religious life and human life are independent of one another (which is a psychological impossibility) such a situation must *a priori* produce a feeling of dismay, a loss of balance . . . What we now have to do without delay is to modify the position occupied by the central core of Christianity – and this precisely in order that it may not lose its illuminative value.[7]

So long as the Church neglects, by means of a refashioned Christology (all the elements of which are available to us) to solve the apparent conflict that henceforth exists between the traditional God of revelation and the 'new' God of evolution, so long . . . will there be increasing distress not only on the fringe of the believing world, but at its very core; and, *pari passu*, Christianity's power to attract and convert will grow less.[8]

These passages voice some of the difficulties; and not everyone will share the author's confidence that they can be overcome, and that all the elements for refashioning christology are readily available. Evolution and process hardly provide a model for thinking about a recreation of a disordered creation, when this has hitherto been presented as, and it would seem cannot be presented otherwise than as, the striking into the process from outside by a Christ who, however deeply he may be thought to enter it, also in some way bestrides it. Nor does our awareness of the vast range of the impersonal elements in nature, or of the long history of biological development below the level of the rational creature, point towards a sphere of special grace, where men are dealt with on the basis of moral will and response to it, and are directed towards a fullness of personal life, which is how the gospel is experienced. The question, however, remains whether we have to be prepared to continue to live with these antinomies; or whether we may believe and hope that our greater awareness of the operation of natural causes and of the roots of our own life in them, may not leave us wholly destitute of ways of passing backwards and forwards between the gospel and the world, and of grasping a divine action in both, which in its different manifestations is yet a single action. Perhaps three very tentative observations may be made in this context.

First, we are told that the basis of all things is energy, and that what is primarily there to be observed is activity. It has, perhaps, been insufficiently noted that a doctrine of energy, of veiled energy indeed, belongs throughout to the biblical picture of God. Energy is itself without moral quality, and Christians have preferred to concentrate on the love of God almost to the exclusion of all else, and not without risk of sentimentality. But love itself, even when identified with the good, is also an energy, and it may not be allowed to exclude the concept of the power of God. This is enhanced rather than otherwise by the gospel. To develop this at any length would require amongst other things attention to be given to the remarkable place which physical action or works of power – so inadequately translated 'miracles' – play in the gospel narrative, and to the manner in which the evangelists can place the whole of that narrative under the heading of power. Are these actions an accidental adjunct to the ministry of Jesus, or – as they have so long been interpreted in the tradition– external guarantees of it, or are they integral to the proclamation of the liberating rule of God to men who are so physically conditioned? Attention might also be given to the fact that the so-called ethical teaching in the gospel is frequently delivered in the context of conflict and debate as the exercise of moral energy. Attention would certainly have to be given to the resurrection of Jesus, upon which the gospel converges, and which is inseparable from the idea of divine power, as notably in that remarkable sentence in Ephesians 1.19, which musters most of the available words for power in the Greek language to speak of 'the excessive greatness of his power towards us who believe according to the energy of the force of his strength with which he energized in raising Jesus from the dead'.

Secondly, the process of evolution is the action of energy by which more complex and organized systems emerge out of the simpler and more elementary. This also has no moral quality in itself. But it is a fact that the process is marked throughout by a certain upthrust, and the special position of man is that, while being himself a part of this process and a product of it, he is also unique in it by knowing this to be so, and this knowledge of the process is now bound up with his knowledge of himself. It is perhaps to be included from now on in what is to be meant by the biblical statement that he is made in the divine image. From this vantage point he is able to see what was past physical fact in the light of what it was to lead to, and he is aware of a process in which things have not remained static but have gone beyond themselves and transcended previous states. To that extent a closed account of reality as self-contained is forbidden. This upthrust is continued in man himself, who must now face both ways, towards the natural and the historical which has brought him where he is, and to the future and to what he may become. Nor is this brought to a halt in Christ, but rather continued. It is a mark of Christ's existence that all comes as grist to his mill, and is made to cohere through his freely willed subordination to God and to God's future activity. By reason of this he is potentially victorious over the recalcitrant forces in the world, and passes through death into an enhanced life which requires more than spatio-temporal terms to set it forth. But this is the verdict upon him only of those who participate in some measure in the effects he has produced, and who have some experience of themselves as persons in the process of being freshly created with freedom and responsibility towards both God and the world. They are then driven to see Jesus as something more than one who has already risen from the dead, and as himself the resurrecting power and the proximate cause of their divine sonship. It is this condition which Paul interprets in a passage of high visionary intelligence in Romans 8. The ecstatic cries of worship with which men as sons call on God as Father he construes as a species of groaning, through which the divine Spirit conveys a double affiliation, an affiliation with God and with the natural creation. They groan because they are frustrated, and the natural creation also groans. Frustration here means to have a form of existence which is inadequate for the life which is now known to be the full life of men and which has been in a measure anticipated. This is experienced by the believers as the desire for the liberation of the present body or form of existence into the spiritual body, which is Christ's form of existence. But this action of the Spirit, so far from segregating them in some spiritual realm, reminds them of their origins in and affinity with a natural creation, which itself knows in its own way something of what this frustration is.

Finally, the word 'creation', which the theologian has to use with reference to the evolutionary process. It has often been remarked that this is intended to denote primarily not beginning but absolute dependence, the fact that all things exist from a source other than themselves. Just as 'end' is more than 'finish', and means rather 'consummation', so 'beginning' is more than 'commencement', and denotes rather 'origin'. Dependence means to be not of, or from, myself. This is true as far as it goes, but so far the thought is a negative one, marking the fundamental distinction between creation and creator. The word 'creation' is, however, as much positive as negative in intention. For what is brought into being not of itself is by the same act related to the one who so creates it, and is related not simply with a backward reference to its origin, but with a forward reference to what it may become as the creature of this creator. This double reference is to be found in most of the New Testament statements about creation, whether with reference to God or Christ. Thus, in I Corinthians 8.5f. Paul states that in contrast to the many gods of the ancient world 'to us there is one God, the Father, from whom are all things and we unto him'. In Colossians 1.16 it is said of Christ that 'all things were created through him and unto him'. Creation is for participation in an activity of energy directed towards the one who has brought it about. If we get as far as saying with Paul something to the effect that 'God was in Christ reconciling the world to himself', we are saying that Christ participates so closely in the divine action towards the world that he makes it possible by his life in, and use of, the world to recognize it once more as divine creation, and to echo God's verdict on it that it is good. To say that Christ is the agent of creation is to say that he does this by a certain native intelligence, which is able to recognize how things are because he is from God's side responsible for them. His being the Christ of yesterday and today in the past and present experience of believing men has behind and within it his knowledge of the way things are. The fourth evangelist says the same in his own way when he presents Christ as the 'I am' or substantial reality of what is in the world, and the eternal Word as being in a world of his own making and as coming to those who belong by right to him.

Notes & Index

Notes

PART I THE PASSION OF CHRIST

1. The Tradition of the Passion

1. H. Frei, *The Eclipse of Biblical Narrative*, Yale University Press 1974.
2. Leonard Hodgson, *For Faith and Freedom*, SCM Press 1968, vol. I, p. 88.
3. In these three passages may be noted the unspecified and somewhat exaggerated use of 'all' which is typical of Luke.
4. Matthew replaces the aposiopesis by 'And this all took place in order that the writings of the prophets might be fulfilled' (Matt. 27.56). For a general reference to scripture in this connection Mark 9.12; 14.21.
5. Tertullian, *Adv. Marc.*, III. 19.
6. For the influence of Ps. 22, H. Kee, 'Scripture Quotations and Allusions in Mark 11–16', *The Society of Biblical Literature Seminar Papers*, 1971, vol. 2, pp. 475ff.
7. For the influence of Ps. 69.9 see John 2.17; Rom. 15.3.
8. Matthew of all people mistakes the Hebrew parallelism and supplies two beasts.
9. Cf. V. Taylor, *Jesus and his Sacrifice*, Macmillan 1957. For a critique of this position M. D. Hooker, *Jesus and the Servant*, SPCK 1959.
10. E.g., Matt. 8.17 applies Isa. 53.4 to the miracles of Jesus, and I Peter 2.22–25 applies phrases from Isa. 53.4–7 to depict both the effect of the death of Christ and its manner as an object of imitation. Matt. 12.18–21 applies a similar Servant passage, Isa. 42.1–4, to the hiddenness of the ministry of Jesus.
11. See C. K. Barrett, 'The Background of Mark 10.45', *New Testament Essays in Memory of T. W. Manson*, ed. A. J. B. Higgins, Manchester University Press 1959, pp. 1ff.
12. For more exhaustive analyses C. H. Dodd, *According to the Scriptures*, Nisbet 1952; B. Lindars, *New Testament Apologetic: The Doctrinal Significance of the Old Testament Quotations*, SCM Press 1961; on Matthew, R. H. Gundry, *The Use of the Old Testament in St Matthew's Gospel*, E. J. Brill 1967; on Mark, J. C. Fenton, *Preaching the Cross*, SPCK 1958; on John, J. C. Fenton, *The Passion according to John*, SPCK 1961; E. D. Freed, *Old Testament Quotations in the Gospel of John*, E. J. Brill 1965.

13. C. H. Dodd, op. cit., pp.126ff.

14. See E. Schweizer, *Lordship and Discipleship*, SCM Press 1960.

15. For the maximizing view C. H. Dodd, op. cit. passim, and for it in operation with respect to a passion narrative J. Pobee, 'The Cry of the Centurion – a Cry of Defeat', *The Trial of Jesus*, ed. Ernst Bammel, SCM Press 1970, pp.91ff., where the martyrological character of the Markan passion story is deduced from the use of psalms which had already been given martyrological associations. For the minimizing view H. J. Cadbury, *The Peril of Modernizing Jesus*, Macmillan, New York 1937, and SPCK 1962, pp. 47f.

2. The Event of the Passion

1. So Phil. 2.8, obedience consequent upon taking the form of a slave; Rom. 5.19, obedience contrasted with the disobedience of Adam. Paul nowhere further specifies in what this obedience consisted. It was, perhaps, for him a general concept deduced from the resurrection as divine approval of Jesus and as his constitution as the Son.

2. E. Käsemann. *The Testament of Jesus*, SCM Press 1968, p. 2.

3. F. C. Burkitt, *The Gospel History and its Transmission*, T. & T. Clark 1906, p. 79.

4. See R. Bultmann, *The History of the Synoptic Tradition*, Blackwell 1963, pp. 275ff.; M. Dibelius, *From Tradition to Gospel*, Ivor Nicholson and Watson 1934, reissued James Clarke 1971, ch. XII; V. Taylor, *The Formation of the Gospel Tradition*, Macmillan 1933, ch. III, and *The Gospel according to St Mark*, Macmillan 1952, Additional Note J.

5. C. H. Dodd, *The Founder of Christianity*, Collins 1971, pp. 78f., Fontana edition 1973, p. 90.

6. See C. H. Dodd, 'The Historical Problem of the Death of Jesus', *More New Testament Studies*, Manchester University Press 1968, ch. 7.

7. See J. Blinzler, *The Trial of Jesus*, Westminster Press 1959.

8. D. R. Catchpole, 'The Historicity of the Sanhedrin Trial', *The Trial of Jesus*, ed. Ernst Bammel, SCM Press 1970, p. 59.

9. P. Winter, *On the Trial of Jesus*, second edition revised, ed. T. A. Burkill and Geza Vermez, Walter de Gruyter 1974.

10. H. A. Rigg, 'Barabbas', *Journal of Biblical Literature*, vol. 64, 1945, p. 454.

11. S. Zeitlin, *Who Crucified Jesus?*, New York 1964, ch. V and p. 164.

12. As perhaps suggested by the Collect for Good Friday: 'Almighty God, we beseech thee graciously to behold this thy family, for whom our Lord Jesus Christ was contented to be betrayed, and given up into the hands of wicked men. . . '

13. See Ch. Guignebert, *Jesus*, Kegan Paul 1935, pp. 480ff.; M. Goguel, *The Life of Jesus*, George Allen & Unwin 1933, pp. 463ff. Much patient research on some aspects of the matter is to be found in the previously mentioned *The Trial of Jesus*, ed. Ernst Bammel.

14. O. Cullmann, *The State in the New Testament*, SCM Press 1957, pp. 15ff.

15. Zeitlin, op. cit., p. 162.

16. See especially S. G. F. Brandon, *Jesus and the Zealots: A Study of the Political Factor in Primitive Christianity*, Manchester University Press 1967.

17. See O. Cullmann, op. cit., pp. 14ff.

18. See O. Cullmann, *Jesus and the Revolutionaries*, Harper & Row 1970; M. Hengel, *Was Jesus a Revolutionist?*, Fortress Press 1971 (and the bibliography).

3. The Passion of Mark and the Passion of Luke

1. Matthew's Gospel has many glories, but its Passion is hardly one of them. A glance at a synopsis shows that it is simply a transcription of Mark's with a customary Matthaean strengthening of the fulfilment of scripture (e.g., the citation of Ps. 22.8 in 27.43), and with the following 'novelistic' additions which the tradition would surely have been better without – the suicide of Judas (27.3–10), Pilate's wife's dream (27.19), an earthquake at the time of the crucifixion which opens graves so that the bodies of dead saints emerge to appear to many after the resurrection (27.51b–53), and the guard at the tomb (27.62–66; 28.11–15). The only additional sayings are the reference to legions of angels (26.53) and to Jesus having called himself the Son of God (27.40, 43), and 'His blood be upon us and upon our children' (27.25), which has perhaps been responsible for more anti-semitism in connection with the crucifixion than any other single statement. Unfortunately the priority of this gospel since the second century has meant that by liturgical custom its Passion has been read first in Holy Week and so has been heard by the greatest number, and for the same reason it has established itself in the musical tradition, as in the 'Matthew Passion' of Bach and others.

2. It established itself in this form as the canonical gospel in Syria, and was ousted only in the fifth and sixth centuries by the gospels in their separate form.

3. Irenaeus, *Adv. Haer.*, III. 11.8.

4. For a description of the method see N. Perrin, *What is Redaction Criticism?*, SPCK 1970, and for a critique Morna Hooker, 'In his own Image?', *What about the New Testament?*, ed. Morna Hooker and Colin Hickling, SCM Press 1975, and C. J. A. Hickling, 'A Problem of Method in Gospel Research', *Religious Studies*, vol. 10, 1974, pp. 339ff.

5. T. S. Eliot, *Murder in the Cathedral*, Faber & Faber 1935, p. 21.

6. For a review of research on this subject see I. H. Marshall, 'The Son of Man Sayings in Recent Discussion', *New Testament Studies*, vol. 12, 1966, pp. 327ff.

7. See R. H. Lighfoot, *The Gospel Message of St Mark*, Oxford University Press 1950, ch. IV.

8. See R. J. McKelvey, *The New Temple*, Oxford University Press 1969, ch. V.

9. For the former view see J. M. Creed, *The Gospel according to St Luke*, Macmillan 1930, especially pp. l–lxiv, and S. Maclean Gilmour, 'A Critical Examination of Proto-Luke', *Journal of Biblical Literature*, vol. 67, 1948.

10. For a more sympathetic treatment of this incident, which Guignebert, op. cit., pp. 467f., deems 'impossible to imagine' and Goguel, op. cit., p. 515, says 'cannot be historical', see Harold W. Hoehner, 'Why did Pilate hand Jesus over to Antipas?', *The Trial of Jesus*, ed. Ernst Bammel, pp. 84ff.

11. So G. Kittel (ed.), *Theological Dictionary of the New Testament*, Eerdmans 1964, vol. II, p. 187, 'innocent and a saint', as in Matt. 27.19. The thesis of John Pobee, 'The Cry of the Centurion – a Cry of Defeat', *The Trial of Jesus*, pp. 91ff., that Ps. 22 was already martyrological and that Mark understood the last words of Jesus in this sense, I do not find convincing.

12. For a full discussion of this difficult textual problem, on which he himself changed his mind, see J. Jeremias, *The Eucharistic Words of Jesus*, new edition, SCM Press 1966, ch. IV.

4. The Passion of John

1. On this see B. Lindars, *The Gospel of John*, Oliphants 1972, passim; D. W. Wead, *The Literary Devices in John's Gospel*, Basel 1970; C. R. Bowen, 'The Fourth Gospel as Dramatic Material', *Journal of Biblical Literature*, vol. 49, 1930, pp. 293ff.; W. L. Knox, *Some Hellenistic Elements in Primitive Christianity*, Oxford University Press 1944, p. 46, n. 1; E. D. Freed, *Old Testament Quotations in the Gospel of John*, E. J. Brill 1965, p. 93. For this Passion as a whole see J. C. Fenton, *The Passion according to John*, SPCK 1961.

2. See C. K. Barrett, *The Gospel according to St John*, SPCK 1955, pp. 34ff. and comments ad loc. on chs 19–20.

3. R. Bultmann, *The Gospel of John*, Blackwell 1971, pp. 635f.

4. C. H. Dodd, *Historical Tradition in the Fourth Gospel*, Cambridge University Press 1963, Part I, A.

5. See Ernst Bammel, 'Ex illa itaque die consilium fecerunt . . .', *The Trial of Jesus*, ed. Ernst Bammel, pp. 11ff.

6. See R. H. Lightfoot, *St John's Gospel*, Oxford University Press 1956, pp. 233ff.

7. See C. H. Dodd, *The Interpretation of the Fourth Gospel*, Cambridge University Press 1960, pp. 390ff.

8. E. Käsimann, *The Testament of Jesus*, SCM Press 1968, p. 3.

9. See H. St J. Hart, 'The Crown of Thorns in John 19.2–5', *Journal of Theological Studies*, n.s., vol. iii, 1952, pp. 66ff.

10. Suetonius, *Lives of the Caesars*, VIII, ch. XIII, of Domitian, 'He issued a circular letter in the name of his procurators "Our Lord and God orders this to be done", and so the custom arose of addressing him in no other way even in writing or in conversation.'

11. A. E. Dyson, *The Crazy Fabric*, Macmillan 1965, p. x.

PART II THE USE OF THE NEW TESTAMENT

5. *Hermeneutics*

1. A. Richardson and W. Schweitzer (eds), *Biblical Authority for Today*, SCM Press 1951; see ch. 6, pp. 240ff.
2. See Ellen Flesseman-van-Leer, 'Biblical Interpretation in the World Council of Churches', *Study Encounter*, vol. viii, no. 2, 1972, p. 5.
3. James Barr, *The Bible in the Modern World*, SCM Press 1973, p. 59.
4. *The Interpreter's Bible*, 12 vols, Abingdon Press 1951ff.
5. H.-G. Gadamer, *Wahrheit und Methode*, Tübingen 1960, p. 162.
6. John Dillenberger, 'On Broadening the New Hermeneutic', in *The New Hermeneutic*, ed. James M. Robinson and John B. Cobb, Harper & Row 1964, p. 148.

6. *Queen or Cinderella*

1. Dean Church, the historian of the Oxford Movement, wrote of Rose that he 'was the most accomplished divine and teacher in the English Church. He was a really learned man.' *The Oxford Movement*, Macmillan 1891, p. 96.
2. H. J. Rose, *An Apology for the Study of Divinity*, Rivington 1834, pp. 2f.
3. Ibid., p. 24.
4. Hastings Rashdall, *Medieval Universities*, 3 vols, new edition, F. M. Powicke and E. B. Emden (eds), Oxford University Press 1936, vol. III, pp. 440f.
5. *An Apology for the Study of Divinity*, p. 48.
6. Ibid., p. 34.
7. Ibid., pp. 36ff.
8. Dean Burgon in his *Lives of Twelve Good Men*, 2 vols, John Murray 1889, gave to his study of Rose the sub-title 'The Restorer of the Old Paths'.
9. Albert Schweitzer, *The Quest of the Historical Jesus*, 1910, third edition with new introduction, A. & C. Black 1954, p. 6.
10. E. Bréhier, *Philosophy and History: Essays presented to Ernst Cassirer*, Oxford University Press 1936, p. 160.
11. Quoted in F. G. Kenyon, *Handbook to the Textual Criticism of the New Testament*, Macmillan 1901, p. 236, second edition 1912, p. 277.
12. So F. H. A. Scrivener, *A Plain Introduction to the Criticism of the New Testament*, George Bell 1894, vol. II, p. 209; cf. also Adam Fox, *John Mill and Richard Bently*, Blackwell 1954, pp. 124f.
13. Kenyon, op. cit., 1901 edition p. 244, 1912, p. 286.
14. Sir Richard Jebb, *Essays and Addresses*, Cambridge University Press 1907, p. 551.

15. See Duncan Forbes, *The Liberal Anglican Idea of History*, Cambridge University Press 1952.
16. See Mark Pattison, *Essays*, Clarendon Press, Oxford 1889, vol. I, pp. 386ff.
17. A. Keissling and U. v. Wilamowitz-Moellendorff, *Philologische Untersuchungen Siebentes Heft*, Berlin 1881; U. v. Wilamowitz-Moellendorff, *Homerische Untersuchungen*, Berlin 1884, Julius Wellhausen gewidmet. I was indebted for reference to this passage to a very 'esteemed friend', W. D. M. Fraenkel.
18. R. G. Collingwood, *The Idea of History*, Oxford University Press 1946, pp. 257ff.
19. See Rudolf Bultmann, *Theology of the New Testament*, ET, SCM Press 1952; and to some extent A. Richardson, *An Introduction to the Theology of the New Testament*, SCM Press 1958. E. Stauffer's *New Testament Theology*, ET, SCM Press 1955, is hardly a Theology of the New Testament, but a series of studies of New Testament concepts.
20. See W. Bousset, *Kyrois Christos*, Göttingen 1913, p. vii; ET, Abingdon Press 1970, p. 14.
21. E. Norden, *Agnostos Theos*, Leipzig 1929, p. v.
22. See W. G. Kümmel, *Das Neue Testament*, Freiburg/München 1958, p. 313 and n. 315; ET, SCM Press and Abingdon Press 1973, p. 249 and n. 331.
23. See W. F. Howard, *The Romance of New Testament Scholarship*, Epworth Press 1949, p. 79.
24. W. Telfer, 'When did the Arian Controversy begin?' *Journal of Theological Studies*, vol. xlvii, 1946, pp. 135ff.
25. W. K. Lowther Clarke, *Concise Bible Commentary*, SPCK 1952, p. 261.
26. See C. King, 'The Outlines of New Testament Chronology', *Church Quarterly Review*, vol. cxxxix, 1945, pp. 129ff.
27. C. H. W. Johns, *The Relation between the Laws of Babylonia and the Laws of the Hebrew Peoples*, The Schweich Lectures 1912, The British Academy, London 1914, p. 20.
28. W. O. E. Oesterley, in R. H. Charles, *Apocrypha and Pseudepigrapha of the Old Testament*, Oxford University Press 1913, vol. I, pp. 60f.
29. Origen, *Comm. im Johannem*, X.4.
30. Collingwood, op. cit., pp. 282ff.
31. Kümmel, op. cit., p. 456, quoting Karl Holl; ET, p. 355.

7. Christology and Theology

1. A. Harnack, *What is Christianity?*, Williams & Norgate 1901.
2. P. T. Forsyth, *The Person and Place of Jesus Christ*, Hodder & Stoughton 1909, p. 101.
3. G. K. A. Bell and A. Deissmann (eds), *Mysterium Christi*, Longmans Green 1930.
4. A. Harnack, *The Mission and Expansion of Christianity in the First*

Three Centuries, 2 vols, 1904–5, second enlarged edition, Williams & Norgate 1908, vol. I, p. 312.

5. The reference is probably to II Sam. 22.51 in the LXX version: 'magnifying the salvations of his king, and performing mercy to his anointed, David, and to his seed for ever'. See F. J. Foakes Jackson and Kirsopp Lake (eds), *The Beginnings of Christianity*, New York and London 1920–33, reissued Eerdmans 1966, vol. IV, p. 152.

6. Acts 10.42; 17.31; 3.22ff., 7.37ff.; 17.7; 1.6 (cf. Luke 1.32); 5.31; 4.12; 15.11; 16.31.

7. 'According to promise has God brought to Israel a saviour' (13.23); 'we bring you good tidings of the promise made to the fathers' (13.32).

8. E. Lohmeyer, *Gottesknecht und Davidssohn*, W. Bousset and H. Gunkel (eds), Forschungen zur Religion und Literatur des Alten und Neuen Testaments, no. 61, Göttingen 1945, second edition 1953, p. 76.

9. Ibid., p. 66.

10. R. Bultmann, *Theology of the New Testament*, SCM Press 1952, vol. I, p. 65.

11. The situation is hardly less puzzling if the majority were from 'the devout Greeks' (Acts 17.4), since these were in intention monotheists. Martin Dibelius (*Handbuch zum Neuen Testament*, Tübingen 1925, ad loc.) explains the language as due to the use by Paul of commonplace missionary terminology, but this throws us back on the question of what the missionary preaching actually was.

12. See B. Rigaux, *Les Épîtres aux Thessaloniciens*, Paris 1956, p. 392.

13. Bultmann, op. cit., vol. I, p. 78. 'I Thess. 1.9f. attests the interrelatedness of monotheistic and eschatological preaching', p. 74.

14. Ibid., p. 78.

15. Cf. Romans 4.24; 8.11; I Cor. 15.14; II Cor. 1.9; 4.14; Gal. 1.1; Col. 2.12; I Peter 1.21; Ignatius, *Trallians* 9.2; Polycarp, *Philippians* 12.2. Note the piling up of words expressing energy and power in Eph. 1.18ff., where God, who is called 'the God of our Lord Jesus Christ', displays towards believers 'the superabundant size of his power by reason of the energy of the effective power of his strength which he made operative in Christ in that he raised him from the dead'.

16. E. G. Selwyn, *The First Epistle of Peter*, Macmillan 1946, pp. 1ff.

17. F. W. Beare, *The First Epistle of Peter*, Blackwell 1958, p. 33; third edition, revised and enlarged 1970, p. 52.

18. Cf. Pliny's impression of the worship of the Christians that they 'sang Christ as to a god', *Epp.*, X.96.

19. Harnack, *The Mission and Expansion of Christianity*, vol. I, p. 382.

20. Rengstorf, article on 'ἀπόστολος', G. Kittel (ed.), *Theological Dictionary of the New Testament*, Eerdmans 1964f., vol. I, p. 437.

21. Ibid., p. 438.

22. H. L. Goudge, *The Second Epistle to the Corinthians*, Westminster Commentaries 1927, p. 2.

23. Cf. the analysis of 'aretalogy' by R. Reitzenstein, *Hellenistiche Wundererzählungen*, Leipzig 1906. Ἀρετή only occurs four times in the

New Testament, and only once in the plural, I Peter 2.9, where it means 'the wonderful works' or 'miracles' of God – see F. W. Beare's note, op. cit., third edition, p. 131.

24. R. Bultmann, *Das Evangelium des Johannes*, Göttingen 1941, pp. 167f.; ET, Blackwell 1971, p. 226, n. 3.

25. Professor D. M. Mackinnon takes them as the starting point of an essay on 'Philosophy and Christology', which is his contribution to T. H. L. Parker (ed.), *Essays in Christology for Karl Barth*, Lutterworth 1956.

26. *Mysterium Christi*, p. 89.

27. See the statements in D. M. Baillie, *God was in Christ*, Faber & Faber 1956, pp. 71ff.

8. Parable and Dogma

1. Notable protests were made by Luther, though they were not sustained subsequently by Lutheranism. This type of exegesis could continue into this century – see, for example, Cosmo Gordon Lang's book, *Thoughts on Some of the Parables of Jesus*, Pitman & Sons 1906.

2. Augustine, *Quaestiones Evangeliorum*, II. 19.

3. Cf. Origen, *De Principiis*, IV.1.7, as the doctrine of providence is not weakened by human inability to understand all visible events, 'so neither is the divinity of scripture, which extends to the whole, lost on account of the inability of our weakness to discover in every expression the hidden splendour of the doctrines veiled in common and unattractive phraseology'. IV.1.15, of the impossibilities included in scripture 'for the sake of the more skilful and inquisitive, in order that they may give themselves to the toil of what is written, and thus attain to a becoming conviction of the manner in which a meaning worthy of God must be sought out in such subjects'.

4. Adolf Jülicher, *Die Gleichnisreden Jesu*, Marburg, vol. 1, 1888, vol. 2, 1898.

5. Ecclus. 24.23.

6. See P. Fiebig, *Die Gleichnisreden Jesu im Lichte der rabbinischen Gleichnisse des neutestamentlichen Zeitalters*, Tübingen 1912; I. Abrahams, *Studies in Pharisaism and the Gospels*, Cambridge University Press 1917, ch. xii.

7. See especially C. H. Dodd, 'Jesus as Teacher and Prophet' in G. K. A. Bell and A. Deissmann (eds), *Mysterium Christi*, Longmans Green 1930, pp. 53ff.; F. Gils, *Jesus prophète, d'après les Évangiles synoptiques*, Louvain 1957; F. Schnider, *Jesus der Prophet*, Freiburg 1973.

8. Rudolf Bultmann, *Theology of the New Testament*, SCM Press 1952, vol. I, ch. 1; *The History of the Synoptic Tradition*, Blackwell 1963, passim.

9. See M. Hengel, *Nachfolge und Charisma*, Berlin 1968, pp. 46ff. E. Lohse, article on 'ραββί, ραββουνί', in G. Kittel (ed.), *Theological Dictionary of the New Testament*, ET, Eerdmans 1964f., vol. VI, pp. 961ff.

10. See C. H. Cave, 'The Parables and the Scriptures', *New Testament Studies*, vol. 11, no. 4, July 1965, pp. 374ff.

11. See M. D. Goulder, 'Characteristics of the Parables in the Several Gospels', *Journal of Theological Studies*, n.s., vol. xix, part 1, April 1968, pp. 51ff.

12 . R. W. Funk, 'The Parables: A Fragmentary Agenda', in D. G. Miller and D. Y. Hadidian, *Jesus and Man's Hope*, Pittsburgh 1971, p. 295.

13. C. H. Dodd, *The Parables of the Kingdom*, Nisbet 1935.

14. J. Jeremias, *The Parables of Jesus*, ET SCM Press 1954, revised edition 1963.

15. Ibid., part III.

16. See J. J. Vincent, 'The Parables of Jesus as Self-Revelation', in *Studia Evangelica*, Texte und Untersuchungen 73, Berlin 1959, pp. 79ff.

17. Jeremias, op. cit., pp. 38ff., 132ff. How curiously reduced and forced Jeremias' interpretation thus becomes may be seen in his comment: 'The *tertium comparationis* in Luke 15.4–7 is not the intimate bond between the shepherd and the flock (as in John 10, but this does not suit Luke 15.8–10), nor is it the unwearied search (as in Matt. 18.12–14, in the present context), but simply and solely the joy. . . . As the shepherd rejoices over the lamb [sic] brought home, and the poor woman over her recovered drachma, so will God rejoice. The future tense in Luke 15.7 is to be understood in an eschatological sense: at the final judgment God will rejoice when among the many righteous he finds a despised sinner upon whom he may pronounce absolution, nay more, it will give him even greater joy. Such is the character of God; it is his good pleasure that the lost should be redeemed, because they are his; their wanderings have caused him pain, and he rejoices over their return home' (pp. 135f.). This amounts to saying that the figures in these parables contribute virtually nothing to their meaning, which is deduced rather from the setting provided for them in the gospel.

18. Mark 2.17; Matt. 12.28f.

19. Middleton Murry, *Countries of the Mind: Essays in Literary Criticism*, 2nd series, Oxford University Press 1931, p. 1, quoted in Sallie TeSelle, *Speaking in Parables*, SCM Press and Fortress Press 1975, p. 46.

20. P. Ricoeur, 'On Listening to the Parables of Jesus', *Criterion*, vol. 13, 1974, pp. 18ff.

21. Dan Otto Via, *The Parables*, Fortress Press 1967.

22. TeSelle, op. cit., especially chs 2 and 3.

23. Funk, in *Jesus and Man's Hope*, p. 300. 'In earlier periods, the church did not hesitate to extract theology from the parables via the allegorical method, but there the parables were being taken up, naively, into a faith already well articulated. Where the parable is respected as parable, the tendency was to and is to let them speak for themselves. That intuition is no doubt correct. I have endeavoured to suggest in another place that parable and discursive theology lie on opposite ends of the language spectrum. The parable funds faith with foundational language at the threshold of faith – gives faith permission, grants the rights and the rites of passage, "celebrates". Theology, on the other hand, is faith reflecting upon itself in discursive mode.'

24. Apart from books on the parables, see Amos N. Wilder, *Early Christian Rhetoric*, SCM Press 1964, pp. 82ff.

25. Boris Pasternak, *Dr Zhivago*, Collins 1958, pp. 45f.

26. See J. Drury, 'The Sower, the Vineyard, and the Place of Allegory in the Interpretation of Mark's Parables', *Journal of Theological Studies*, n.s., vol. xxiv, part 2, October 1973, pp. 367ff.

27. See J. Schniewind, *Das Evangelium nach Markus*, Göttingen 1949, p. 77.

28. Dodd, op. cit., p. 21.

29. G. Eichholz, *Tradition und Interpretation: Studien Zum Neuen Testament und zur Hermeneutik*, Munich 1965, pp. 57ff.

30. See D. W. Wead, *The Literary Devices in John's Gospel*, Basel 1970.

PART III THE CHRISTIAN

9. The Christian Past – Tradition

1. G. Kittel, 'The Jesus of History', *Mysterium Christi*, ed. G. K. A. Bell and Adolf Deissmann, Longmans 1930, pp. 31f.

2. Gunther Bornkamm, *Paul*, Hodder & Stoughton 1971, p. 111.

3. Karl Barth, *Church Dogmatics*, T. & T. Clark 1960, III/2, pp. 437ff.

4. Edwyn Bevan, *Symbolism and Belief*, George Allen & Unwin 1934, p. 274.

5. J. R. Geiselmann, *The Meaning of Tradition*, Burns & Oates 1966, p. 102.

6. T. S. Eliot, *What is a Classic?*, Faber & Faber 1944, p. 14.

7. Georges Tavard, *La Tradition au XVIIe Siècle en France et en Angleterre*, Editions du Cerf 1969, p. 503.

10. The Christian Present – Existentialism

1. See F. Temple Kingston, *French Existentialism*, University of Toronto Press 1961, pp. 39f.

2. E. R. Dodds, *Pagans and Christian in an Age of Anxiety*, Cambridge University Press 1965.

3. W. B. Yeats, 'The Second Coming', *Collected Poems*, Variorum Edition, Macmillan 1957, pp. 401f.

4. ' . . . anything but a legitimate form of reflection, because of its over-indulgent attitude towards the illusions of subjectivity. The raising of personal preoccupations to the dignity of philosophical problems is far too likely to lead to a sort of shop-girl metaphysics.' Claude Levi-Strauss, *Tristes Tropiques*, Penguin Books 1976, p. 71.

5. See the extended discussion of the two views in O. Cullmann, *Salvation in History*, SCM Press 1967, IV. I, pp. 186ff.

6. W. Pannenberg, *Theology and the Kingdom of God*, Westminster Press 1975, p. 56.

7. George Tyrrell, *Christianity at the Cross Roads*, Longmans 1909, pp. 117f.

8. H. Scott Holland, *The Real Problem of Eschatology*, Longmans 1916, pp. 15f.

9. John Knox, *The Ethic of Jesus in the Teaching of the Church*, Epworth Press 1962, pp. 50f.

10. W. Pannenberg, op. cit., pp. 52f.

11. The Christian Future – Eschatology

1. Raymond E. Brown, *The Gospel according to John*, Doubleday 1966, Geoffrey Chapman 1971, vol. 1, p. 1.

2. Pierre Teilhard de Chardin, 'Pantheism and Christianity', *Christianity and Evolution*, Collins 1971, p. 59.

3. Robert Mackintosh, *Albert Ritschl*, Chapman & Hall 1915, pp. 256f.

4. Ludwig Feuerbach, *The Essence of Christianity* (1843), trs George Eliot 1853, Harper & Row 1957 edition, Appendix §5, p. 287.

5. Teilhard de Chardin, 'Historical Representations of Original Sin', *Christianity and Evolution*, p.47.

6. 'Christology and Evolution', ibid., p. 78.

7. Ibid., p. 77.

8. 'What the World is looking for from the Church of God at this moment', ibid., p. 212.

Index of Authors and Works